Confederate Colonel and Cherokee Chief

Confederate Colonel and Cherokee Chief

THE LIFE OF
WILLIAM HOLLAND THOMAS

E. Stanly Godbold, Jr.
AND
Mattie U. Russell

The University of Tennessee Press
KNOXVILLE

Copyright © 1990 by The University of Tennessee Press / Knoxville.
All Rights Reserved. Manufactured in the United States of America.
Cloth: 1st printing, 1990.
Paper: 1st printing, 2001.

Frontispiece: William Holland Thomas in 1858.
North Carolina Division of Archives and History.

The paper used in this book meets the minimum
requirements of ANSI/NISO Z39.48-1992 (R 1997)
(Permanence of Paper). The binding materials
have been chosen for strength and durability.

Library of Congress Cataloging in Publication Data

Godbold, E. Stanly.
    Confederate colonel and Cherokee chief : the life
of William Holland Thomas / E. Stanly Godbold, Jr.,
and Mattie U. Russell. — 1st ed.
      p.   cm.
    Includes bibliographical references.
    ISBN 0-87049-664-6 (cl.: alk. paper)
    ISBN 1-57233-161-5 (pbk.: alk. paper)
    1. Thomas, William Holland, 1805–1893. 2. Soldiers—
Confederate States of America—Biography. 3. Confederate
States of American. Army—Biography. 4. Cherokee Indians—
Biography.   I. Russell, Mattie U.   II. Title.
E467.1.T48G63   1990
973.7'092—dc20
[B]   90-32971

To
Robert Hilliard Woody,
our own man of the mountains

Contents

	Preface	xi
1	Little Will and Chief Yonaguska	1
2	Businessman in Indian Country	17
3	Let My People Stay	36
4	Both White and Cherokee	56
5	The Chief in Love	78
6	Secession and War	90
7	Colonel Thomas	110
8	In a Mad Man's Cell	129
	Notes	151
	Selected Bibliography	183
	Index	197

Illustrations

FIGURES

Oconaluftee River, 1888	4
Cherokee County, North Carolina, 1888	6
Site of Stekoa Fields, 1989	14
James W. Terrell, 1874	61
The Wolftown Ballplayers, 1888	62
Women Making Pottery, 1888	66
Typical Cherokee Cabin in 1880s	68
Sarah Love Thomas, Wife of William Holland Thomas, 1867	81
Officers in Thomas's Legion	108
Railroad Bridge at Strawberry Plains, 1864	112
Confederate Veterans of Thomas's Legion, 1901	126
North Carolina Hospital for the Insane, Raleigh, 1857	134

Sarah Love Thomas, Daughter of
Sarah Jane Burney Love Thomas
and William Holland Thomas   143

Western Hospital for the Insane,
Morganton, ca. 1900   148

MAPS

Western North Carolina in 1833   15

Western North Carolina Counties in 1872   70

Western North Carolina and East Tennessee
in the Nineteenth Century   106

Preface

FOR SHEER HUMAN DRAMA, the story of William Holland Thomas rivals fiction. Born fatherless on the rugged, mountainous North Carolina frontier in 1805, he was reared by his widowed mother and the native Cherokee Indians. When Thomas was twelve, the local Cherokee chief, Yonaguska, adopted the youngster into his band. Thomas learned the languages and customs of both the whites and the Cherokees. During the upheavals of Indian Removal and the Civil War, he was an unusual transcultural figure. Named chief in 1839 of a small group of North Carolina Cherokees, he won for them the right to remain in North Carolina and to receive payments that the federal government had promised them. He was also a state senator, an ambitious and energetic businessman, the builder of railroads and turnpikes, a staunch advocate of internal improvements, and a controversial colonel in the Confederate Army.

Thomas' life divides into three major stages: his work to protect the Eastern Cherokees from being removed west against their will, his service as colonel in the Confederate Army, and his career as developer and capitalist on the Southern frontier. The tragedies of his bankruptcy after the Civil War and long hospitalization for mental illness did not deprive either the white or Cherokee societies of the services he had already rendered them. Encompassed by his life, too, is a tender story of the unconditional love between a man and a woman that triumphed over adversity.

The coauthorship that produced this book springs from a professional association and warm friendship that lasted for almost a score of years. I met Mattie Russell when I was completing my graduate studies at Duke University in 1970. We shared a common mentor and close friend in the person of Robert H. Woody. By 1956, when Mattie had completed her dissertation on the life and times of William Holland Thomas, she was already immovably set on the path that led to her long, busy, and distinguished career as Curator of Manuscripts in the library at Duke. In 1981, as she approached retirement, she invited me to become her coauthor for a biography of Thomas. She contributed her dated dissertation and the notes and materials she had collected; my task was to expand and bring the research up to date and to write the manuscript. Before her death on May 4, 1988, Mattie discussed all of the new research that I had completed and the outline for the entire book. She read the first three chapters. Much of her work, and some of her words, remain.

The authors are indebted to many individuals for their help. The following descendants of William Holland Thomas shared with Mattie Russell family papers and records in their possession and offered her other kindnesses: Mr. and Mrs. James R. Thomas, Jr., Mrs. Sarah Thomas Campbell, and Mrs. James R. Thomas, Sr., all of Waynesville, North Carolina; Mr. William Holland Thomas III of Asheville, North Carolina; and Mrs. Gladys Avery Tillett and Mrs. Dorothy Thomas Hodges of Charlotte, North Carolina.

Others who granted Mattie Russell interviews and access to papers include Hiram C. Wilburn, Felix E. Alley, and Margaret Stringfield of Waynesville; Joel K. Terrell and William E. Bird of Cullowhee, North Carolina; George M. Stephens, Samuel E. Beck, and J. Scroop Styles of Asheville; and Adelaide Taylor Matthews of Claremore, Oklahoma. Robert Varner of Bryson City, North Carolina, gave me a fine tour of the house currently on the site of Stekoa Fields. Robert H. Woody, a native of the Smoky Mountains, knew more about growing ginseng and other fine points of mountain life than I could find in any book.

The staffs of the following libraries and institutions extended many courtesies and sometimes help beyond the call of duty: the Southern Historical Collection in the Louis Round Wilson Library of the University of North Carolina at Chapel Hill; Special Collections in the Hunter Memorial Library at Western Carolina University, Cullowhee, North Carolina; the William R. Perkins and Medical Center libraries at Duke University, Durham, North Carolina; the Federal Records Center, East Point, Georgia; the State Historical Society of Wisconsin, Madison; the North Carolina Division of Archives and

History, Raleigh; the National Anthropological Archives of the Smithsonian Institution and the National Archives and Records Administration, Washington, D.C.; the South Caroliniana Library at the University of South Carolina, Columbia; and Mitchell Memorial Library at Mississippi State University, near Starkville. Lynne Mueller and Anne Wells of Special Collections in Mitchell Memorial Library deserve special thanks. To the professionals at the University of Tennessee Press, we offer admiration and gratitude.

I gratefully acknowledge financial assistance from the American Philosophical Society and the National Endowment for the Humanities. The Department of History, the College of Arts and Sciences, and the Office of Graduate Studies and Research in Mississippi State University gave me generous support in the form of research assistants, a sabbatical leave, and several travel grants.

The following students, while pursuing their own graduate work in history at Mississippi State University, served as able research assistants: Michael B. Ballard, Connie L. Cartledge, Thomas D. Cockrell, Mark H. Langford, and Clifford E. Mullen. Working with extraordinary dedication for two years on this project, Connie L. Cartledge combined her impressive skills as both librarian and historian to produce an abundance of useful information. Several years later, she went the second mile: she took time from her busy career as an archivist in the Library of Congress to read and comment upon the entire manuscript.

For their meticulous reading of the manuscript and well-informed suggestions for improvement, we thank the following professional scholars: John R. Finger, George E. Frizzell, Pepper Holland, Gordon B. McKinney, Richard M. McMurry, William E. Parrish, Theda Perdue, and Roy V. Scott. Any errors of research, fact, and interpretation that remain are the sole responsibility of the authors.

Thanks, last, to the two who come first: Jeannie and Heidi. Their unwavering faith that anything is possible somehow seems to make it so.

E. STANLY GODBOLD, JR.
Starkville, Mississippi
March 15, 1989

Confederate Colonel and Cherokee Chief

CHAPTER I

Little Will and Chief Yonaguska

THROUGH THE STILLNESS of the majestic mountains of western North Carolina, a small white boy rode on horseback to a trading post on Soco Creek. An exotic and tragic destiny awaited him. He was not yet twelve, and his father had died before his birth. Sometimes as he rode through the captivating wilderness he was on an errand for his widowed mother, but he seemed always eager to see the native Cherokee Indians who traded at the post. Born in 1805, he was named William Holland Thomas, but the Indians, impressed by his small, tight stature, called him "Wil-Usdi," which meant "Little Will." Their aging chief, Yonaguska, or Drowning Bear, quietly noted the boy's fascination with the Cherokees, his gestures of kindness and friendship, and his yearning to make them his people. Yonaguska, the father of seven Indian children, began to think of Little Will as a member of his clan.

Little Will learned Indian games and customs and thought of the Cherokees as his family. Yet he never removed himself from the white world of his mother. He was straddling two civilizations on the brink of their "clash" with each other. Twice in the mid-nineteenth century would his Indian friends need his help to survive the greed and turbulence of the advancing whites. In their struggle to escape removal west along the Trail of Tears and to survive the Civil War, one small group of Cherokees came to depend more and more upon the affection and ingenuity of Little Will.

The attraction of land in the West had brought Little Will's parents to the Allegheny Mountains early in the summer of 1804. Both were English by birth, but they had grown up in Virginia. Richard Thomas was born in Dover, England, after the middle of the eighteenth century. His ancestors were Welsh. Little Will's mother was a member of the respected Strother family of Virginia; her mother was a sister to the mother of Zachary Taylor. Exactly when Richard came to Culpeper County, Virginia, is unknown, but his name appears on the sketchy pay and muster rolls of the American Revolution. He enlisted for three years in the 11th Virginia Regiment. From August 1, 1776, until September 1, 1777, he was held prisoner by the enemy; on December 16 of the latter year, he disappeared. He later rejoined his regiment, for on October 7, 1780, he was fighting with it under Colonel William Campbell at King's Mountain.[1]

Richard was about twenty-five years older than his bride, Temperance Calvert Thomas. They were married in Richmond on May 6, 1804. She had been born in Newcastle on Tyne, England, in 1775, the daughter of William and Mercy Holland Calvert. How and when she came to America are not known, but her progeny believed that she descended from a brother of Cecilius Calvert, the founder of Maryland.[2]

Soon after their marriage, Richard and Temperance, accompanied by his cousins, John and George Strother, set out for the West. They planned to settle on 228 acres of land that had been given to Richard twenty years earlier for his service in North Carolina during the Revolutionary War.[3] Richard was a civil engineer and a horse trader, ambitious to make his way in the untamed and sparsely populated mountain wilderness. He and his young wife, who had become pregnant shortly after their marriage, settled in a log house on Raccoon Creek, a wilderness area two miles east of Mount Prospect, later Waynesville, North Carolina.

The father did not share in the joy of the birth of his child, because in the fall of 1804 Richard drowned. According to one account, his death occurred in northern Georgia where he had gone on a business trip. A family tradition maintains that he was swept away by a flash flood while he and one of his Strother cousins were attempting to cross the Big Pigeon River in North Carolina. Still another version suggests that he was trying to make his way back to Virginia. His body was not recovered. His pregnant, twenty-nine-year-old widow probably never knew the details of his death. A few months later, on February 5, 1805, she gave birth to their child, naming him William Holland Thomas, after her ancestors.[4]

Temperance Thomas was equal to the task of rearing her son alone on the frontier. If she needed help she could call upon the Strother brothers or David Nelson, an in-law who lived on Jonathan's Creek a few miles northwest of Mount Prospect. In addition there were a number of Colvard families living in the area. "Colvard" was a common misspelling of the name "Calvert," and these families were probably related to her. In fact, her son William wrote his mother's maiden name as "Colvard," although his daughter said that it should be "Calvert."[5] How Temperance Thomas herself spelled her maiden name is unrecorded, but she was intelligent, capable, and sensible. She managed her small farm, tended to her domestic chores, and taught her son reading, writing, arithmetic, and Christianity.

From the homestead of Little Will and his mother, mountains rose in every direction. To the northeast were the Newfound Mountains, to the southeast Pisgah Ridge, on the west the regal Balsams, and far to the north the towering Great Smokies. These mountain chains stretched out in varying shades of blue to the horizon, and occasionally in winter they took on a purplish hue. During rainy weather, clouds hid the higher peaks, and wisps of vapor floated like transparent ghosts among the valleys. Several of these peaks rose to more than six thousand feet. The principal outlets from the Thomas farm were eastward along Hominy Creek, northward through Pigeon Valley, and westward across the Balsams to Soco and Balsam gaps.

Growing up on such a mountainous frontier was not a bad fate for Little Will. There were other boys for him to play with after his chores had been completed; he could hunt, fish, attend church, and participate in social gatherings. The climate was healthy. There were towering waterfalls and swift, clear streams; hundreds of flowering flame azaleas, mountain laurels, and rhododendrons in the spring and summer; and virgin forests of pine, hemlock, spruce, and balsam fir. The bright colors of spring flowers merged into the lush green vegetation of summer. The dazzling spectacle of the brilliant leaves of hardwood trees in fall yielded to the cold, bleak, gray and white days of winter.

In that ruggedly beautiful world Little Will grew up. He added to his love of nature the urge to create order in his mountains and to free himself from their isolation. Introspective, inquisitive, long of memory, wise, wary, and aware, he developed characteristics prized by mountain people.[6] In addition to his mother and her friends, his teachers were the hills themselves and the Cherokee Indians, who for almost half a century before his birth had become hospitable to the white settlers.

Oconaluftee River, 1888. Photograph by James Mooney. National Anthropological Archives of the Smithsonian Institution.

Under the terms of treaties with the United States government in 1817 and 1819, the Cherokee Nation reduced its land in the Southeast in return for land in the West. The ceded property went to the respective eastern states, which could sell it as they saw fit. Article 2 of the Treaty of 1819 gave any Indian head of a household the option to claim 640 acres apart from the tribe if he would agree to become a citizen of the United States. Exercising that option, sixty Cherokee families staked their claims to live in western North Carolina.

Yonaguska, Euchella, and fifty-eight others settled with their families east of the Nation, along the Little Tennessee, Tuckasegee, and Oconaluftee rivers. White settlers moved in, claiming some of the same territory. Rather than protecting the rights of the Indians, North Carolina sold some of their lands to the whites. The confusion was ended by a state supreme court decision in the 1824 case of *Euchella vs. Welsh*. The state admitted its error and upheld the rights of the Cherokees. In cases where the Indians had already been deprived of their property, the state compensated them with land elsewhere in the area. The aggrieved Euchella moved back onto tribal land, but Yonaguska and the others remained outside the Nation.[7] Yonaguska brought a companion case, *Yonaguska vs. Coleman*, but the court disposed of it because it was so similar to *Euchella* and was not accompanied by adequate documentary evidence.[8]

Yonaguska sold his original reservation and soon settled near the confluence of Soco Creek and the Oconaluftee River. He and his followers formed the beginning of the group of Cherokees who later became known as the Eastern Band. They were the adoptive people of Little Will's childhood and the welcomed burden of his manhood. As an adult, he worked hard to define an acceptable legal sphere for them.

To young Will Thomas, however, the lore of the Cherokees was more important than their legal status. They had created a world view that fascinated the lively, imaginative, growing boy. In their Upper World lived deities who controlled the natural phenomena of their mountain home. The Sun was female and divided the day from the night, life from death. The Moon was her brother; he controlled rain, menstruation, and fertility. Fire was sacred. Thunder, or "the Red Man," was a friend; he sometimes killed white men with lightning, but never Indians unless they had treated him disrespectfully. Since the Red Man became angry if men took his name in vain, the Cherokees

Cherokee County, North Carolina, 1888. Photograph by James Mooney. National Anthropological Archives of the Smithsonian Institution.

called him "white," using his real name only on ceremonial occasions. Creatures of the Upper World were capable of assuming varied shapes and doing marvelous things. A river was a deity, a giant with its head in the mountains who spoke in a murmur that only a priest could interpret.[9]

The Cherokees thought the forces of good were pitted against those of evil. They believed in a personal devil whose footprints were the bald spots on the slopes and whose bedchamber was in Old Field Mountain in the Balsams.[10] The most horrible monster of the Under World was the terrible Uktena. He had the large scaly body of a serpent, the horns of a deer, the wings of a bird, and a brilliantly flashing, diamond-shaped crest on his forehead. He lived in the deep pools and could bring instant death to any who looked upon him. The Indians had a friendly spirit in Nunnehi, who had once helped repel an enemy. The bear, who had once been human, was regarded as a special friend.[11]

In Cherokee mythology, the Great Buzzard was sent from the Upper World to prepare a place for others. When he reached the Cherokee country, "his wings began to flap and strike the ground, and whenever they struck the earth there was a valley, and where they turned up again there was a mountain." The trees that stayed awake for the entire seven days were the cedar, the pine, the spruce, the holly, and the laurel; hence, they became evergreens and the best sources of medicine. Men were created after the animals. At first there was only a brother and a sister. He struck her with a fish and told her to multiply. She produced offspring so rapidly that a modification was needed to restrict the birth of human babies to one per year. Thus the Cherokees created a belief system, rife with stories of adventure and logic, that gave them a universe of order in their striking mountain home.[12]

Essential to the Cherokees' search for natural order was their belief that to be a member of a clan was more important than to be an individual. A person without a people had no identity; a boy without a father needed an older male of the same clan. In the matrilineal Cherokee society, Yonaguska assumed the role of Little Will's maternal uncle.

Little Will absorbed the world view of the Cherokees as readily as he did that of the Virginia aristocracy. The unquestioning young mind may have found as much truth in the drama of the Great Buzzard as it did in the story of Adam and Eve. His biological inheritance, the persistent teachings of his mother, and the steady tug of the mountainous environment blended so smoothly that he was at home in both the white and Cherokee cultures.

Little Will grew up quickly. He was a small boy with close-set blue eyes, a high forehead, and long, wavy brown hair. He was boyishly cute but not handsome. He was a "little man" who unconsciously elicited sympathy from whites and Indians alike. Early he assumed an air of responsibility toward his mother, seeing himself as an orphan who must take a job as soon as possible. His demeanor was determined rather than relaxed or jovial. The absence of a father made an indelible impression upon him. One emotion that seemed to drive him as a child and later as a man was the yearning for an always-absent father.

The society of William's childhood was peaceful and serene. Meeting no resistance from the Cherokees, whites moved into the region between the French Broad River and the western boundary of the Cherokee Cession of 1789, which ran west of the Balsam range about one and one-half miles east of the spot later called Quallatown. Colonel Robert Love and his brother, General Thomas Love, both veterans of the Continental Army and natives of Augusta County, Virginia, acquired large grants of land along Richland Creek and built their homes on the ridge between it and Raccoon Creek. Soon, others began to settle on the ridge, and by 1800 the village of Mount Prospect had been formed.[13]

General Thomas Love took a leading role in developing the area. As a member of the North Carolina General Assembly, he introduced a bill to carve a new county out of the western part of Buncombe County. The bill passed on December 23, 1808, creating Haywood County, which stretched from the present eastern boundary of Haywood southward to the Cherokee Nation and northward to the Tennessee line. By 1811 the name of the town had been changed from Mount Prospect to Waynesville. According to tradition, Colonel Robert Love suggested that it be changed to honor the memory of General Anthony Wayne, under whom he had served during the American Revolution. Half a century later Waynesville was still a small, dirty village.[14]

There is no record of the establishment of a school in Haywood County during William's youth, nor did he receive any formal education. He later said that his mother was his only teacher, but a family tradition maintains that she sometimes asked an educated German neighbor to help teach him. There were few books in his boyhood home, but what he learned, he learned well. He was a thorough student of the Bible. He was so good at arithmetic that even in old age his ability to solve complex mathematical problems in his head excited comment.[15] His correspondence, speeches, and other writings are marked by logic and clarity of expression. His spelling, vocabulary, and syntax improved through the years. He was an effective public speaker.

Besides being taught by his mother, young William was influenced by George Strother and Felix Walker. Strother was a civil engineer who in 1799 had helped to survey the first boundary line between North Carolina and Tennessee. A cousin of William's deceased father, perhaps he felt some responsibility for helping to rear the boy. Felix Walker had fought in the American Revolution, served as clerk of the court in three western North Carolina counties, and had represented Rutherford County in the General Assembly. In 1807 he moved to Jonathan's Creek in what became Haywood County. He acquired large tracts of land in several counties and practiced law. In 1817 voters from the Twelfth Congressional District, which included Buncombe and Haywood counties, elected him to the Congress of the United States, where he served until 1823. He was such a persuasive speaker and smooth politician that he was nicknamed "Old Oil Jug." Walker's eldest son, Felix Hampton, became Little Will's first employer and his closest white friend.[16]

William was a lad of thirteen when he went to work as manager of Felix Hampton Walker's trading post in 1818. Located on the south side of Soco Creek, the post was a branch of Walker's store in Waynesville. Mature for his young age, Thomas signed a contract promising to operate the post for three years in return for one hundred dollars, board, and clothing.[17] Separated from his mother by a short distance for the first time, young William's companions were Felix and the people who came to the post.

The majority of the customers at the trading post were Indians who bartered furs, hides, herbs, and other items for general merchandise. The most highly prized of the herbs was ginseng, or "sang." The wild plant was preferred, although it could be raised in gardens. After about seven years of growing, the root was ready for barter. Some people thought ginseng had marvelous medicinal values. William Byrd II had believed that it could prolong life, warm the blood, frisk the spirit, and cheer the heart even of a man with "a bad wife." Walker instructed his young clerk to pay only ten cents per pound in goods for ginseng when it was green. William did as he was told, but the magic herb did not prove to be a financial panacea for Felix Hampton Walker. He made no money from it, and three years later he closed the post.[18]

The three years that William passed managing the trading post at Soco Creek sealed his friendship with the Cherokees. Working with him at the store was an Indian boy who taught William to speak their language. Later, Little Will also learned to read and write it. He spoke and wrote Cherokee as fluently as he did English.[19]

The white teenager who spoke Cherokee to his Indian customers captured the attention of Chief Yonaguska. Born in 1759, Yonaguska was past fifty when he met William Thomas. A family man with two wives and seven children, the chief felt a peculiar sympathy for the young white boy who had no father or brother and who lived separated from his mother. Yonaguska noticed, too, the boy's fascination with the Cherokees and his unusual benevolence toward them. Wishing both to protect him and to repay him, Yonaguska adopted William into his clan. Apparently there was no ceremony, nor was either William or his mother consulted in advance. Henceforward the Cherokees regarded him as a brother and called him "Wil-Usdi."[20] Yonaguska must have thought of Wil-Usdi as his nephew. William, chafing from the thought of being an orphan, and thinking in white rather than Cherokee terms, accepted Yonaguska as a surrogate father. They developed a close personal relationship with each other.

Yonaguska was a man of considerable physical and intellectual stature. A vital figure in the Eastern Band, he set examples, instilled in other Cherokees the need to retain those aspects of their culture that he thought were valuable, and had faith in his people's ability to survive. Relatively unknown to the whites, he was the most prominent chief among the Eastern Cherokees. He was reputed to have been an eloquent orator. Thomas, who recorded most of what is known of the chief, thought that Yonaguska's mind was superior to those of most Indians and whites of his time. Yonaguska had been chief of his band since the turn of the century. Strong and handsome at six feet three inches tall, he was brown with a tinge of red and had a white grandfather on his father's side. Bold, serene, and benevolent, he advocated peace and controlled the warriors of his band.[21]

A man of devout religious faith who believed in a heaven to which he would someday go, Yonaguska never accepted the white man's Christianity. After the Bible had been translated into Cherokee, someone sent a copy of the Gospel according to Matthew to the North Carolina Indians. Yonaguska insisted that it be read to him before it was read to his people. After listening carefully to a few chapters, he commented: "Well, it seems to be a good book—strange that the white people are not better, after having had it so long."[22]

Yet, Yonaguska possessed many of the ethics of a Christian. His outstanding characteristic was such fatherly concern for his people that he thought no sacrifice for them too great.[23] His religion was anthropomorphic and monistic. His belief in a god and angels who could intervene personally in human affairs was similar to the belief of many evangelical Christians. Since his views were atypical of most Cherokees, he may have been influenced by Evan Jones's mission at Valley Town, by itinerant Christian missionaries, or even by Little Will.

Yonaguska occasionally had visions. At the age of twelve he saw a middle-aged man with a staff in his hand, walking on a cloud, with "great drops of sweat" falling from him. The man was wearing a hat "with a long sharp spear attached in front having a beautiful appearance." None of Yonaguska's playmates could see it, and they thought he was a liar.[24] Nevertheless Yonaguska in his later years sometimes had other visions, related to his own death, that he interpreted in religious terms. He also succumbed to the temptation of whiskey, and although in 1830 he reformed, at the time he adopted Wil-Usdi he was leading a dissipated life.

The vices of Yonaguska held no attraction for Wil-Usdi. Perhaps William was too young, too strongly influenced by the teachings of his mother, or too intelligent to waste time in drunken revelry. He already knew that whites were not supposed to practice polygamy, and as a teenager he was committed to remaining celibate until he married. Although he later broke that commitment as casually as the United States government broke some of its Indian treaties, he struggled to become a man more in the style of the Calverts than the Cherokees. The strict Protestant morality of his mother, the more natural approach to sex that he saw among the Cherokees, his fatherless childhood, and the tensions of adolescence created inner conflicts, but reason and the instructions of his mother were force enough to keep the young man's surging passions in check.

In 1820, when William was fifteen, he moved back to his mother's house because Walker's store went bankrupt. Unable to pay Thomas the one hundred dollars he owed him, Felix gave the precocious youth a set of law books. William studied them with enough diligence to become a frontier attorney. Since there was no state bar association before 1899, anyone who read law could practice. William took extensive depositions in a case involving the contested ownership of a slave girl. The case, according to William, was settled in December 1828 by compromise.[25] Ten years after William acquired the law books, Yonaguska asked him to become the attorney for the Cherokees, and they became his most important clients.

When he had abandoned the Soco Creek store, Felix Hampton migrated to Hinds County, Mississippi, where he hoped to practice law. He missed William and perhaps felt guilty about not having been able to pay him. In a long letter in 1821, referring to William as "near to me as a Brother," he said he appreciated William's "honesty of heart and sprightly genius." Reinforcing the teachings of Temperance Thomas, Felix advised her teenaged son William not to "take up with the bad habits of the vulgar class of mankind" who lived in western North Carolina and to read good books — "history particularly." Felix said he hoped eventually to be able to repay young William by helping him acquire an education. He also hoped that someday William would join him in Mississippi.[26]

William did not go to Mississippi; he remained with this mother and his adopted people. From Felix Hampton he had learned about the law and business, and he was smart enough to turn these things to practical advantage. Exercising the "sprightly genius" that his friend saw in him, he had already acquired more education than his older friend would have dreamed.

Unruffled by the loss of his job, young William opened his own store in 1822 at Indiantown, about four miles from his home. He got the money for it from his mother, who sold enough of her real estate to set him up in business.[27] In 1839, when a post office was established at Indiantown, the village was renamed Quallatown in honor of an old Indian woman named Qualla, or Polly. The store was located at a crossroads in trade. It was about sixty miles west of Asheville near the confluence of Soco Creek and the Oconaluftee River. One road led eastward through Soco Gap to Waynesville; it crossed another running southward from Sevierville, Tennessee.[28] From every direction

Indians and white settlers could get to the store along established paths. William could use those same paths to import the goods they wanted.

By the time the post office had been built at Quallatown, Yonaguska had moved there. He sold his reservation on the Tuckasegee River for $1,300.[29] He and the other Cherokee families who followed him became known variously as the Qualla or Lufty Indians.

By 1839, too, William and his mother had established their permanent home. They moved a dozen or more times during the 1820s and 1830s. As William made the transition from an orphan clerk into an independent attorney, store owner, and creditor, his increasing prosperity was reflected in a search for a better farm and house. They finally settled on a farm on the south side of the Tuckasegee River just above the present town of Whittier.[30]

William and his mother named the farm Stekoa Fields, or Stekoa Old Fields, because it included the site of the Indian village of Stekoa that had been destroyed during the American Revolution. Stekoa Fields lay in the region the Cherokees had surrendered in 1819. Sometime in the 1820s the state had granted it to Abraham, Wesley, and Scroop Enloe. By the mid-1830s, they owed Thomas $3,400, which they could not pay. To settle the debt, he took the farm, which then comprised one thousand acres. Thomas eventually expanded the farm to both sides of the Tuckasegee River. Instead of constructing a bridge, he kept a dugout to use when the water was too deep to ford.[31]

William and his mother built their house on a ridge high enough above the Tuckasegee valley to be safe from floods. It was a modest five-room log structure that they did not enlarge as his wealth and reputation grew. They built a cold cellar into a hillside behind the house. Water was supplied by a clear creek that descended from a nearby ridge; eventually, hollowed-out logs soaked in a salt solution were used as pipes to bring the water to the house.[32] From their yard the Thomases could see spurs of the Cowee Range rising directly behind the house and stretching to the west, offshoots of the Smokies looming a short distance to the north, and the Tuckasegee valley running far to the south. Below the house flowed the clear, boulder-strewn river along which lay the paths in and out of that peaceful valley.

In that rich, scenic valley the formative influences of Little Will's youth came together. The unpretentious house at Stekoa Fields and the presence of his mother forever anchored him in the ways of her

Site of Stekoa Fields, 1989, with Tuckasegee River in foreground.

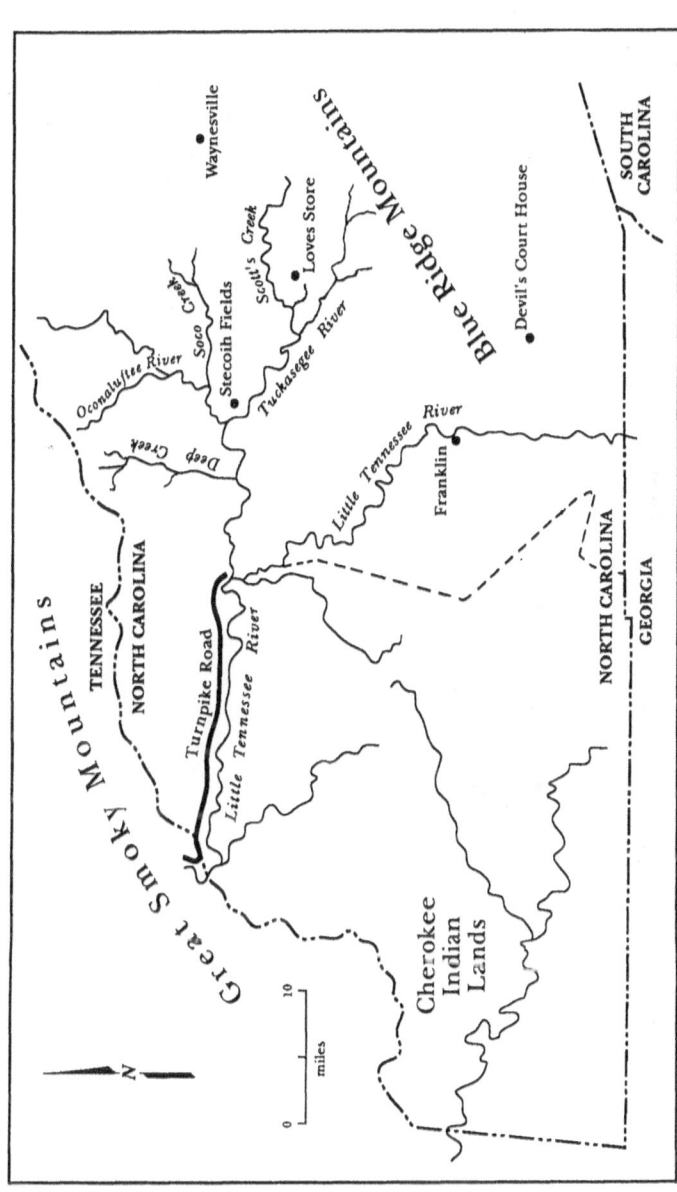

Western North Carolina in 1833. Based on "A New Map of the State of North Carolina," constructed from actual surveys and published for the state legislature by John MacRae in 1833, North Carolina Division of Archives and History Map Collection. Map by The University of Tennessee Cartographic Services Laboratory.

world. A few miles away lived Chief Yonaguska, an adopted father, a man of deep compassion and native virtue who provided Wil-Usdi with the people he needed and who needed him. The Quallatown store not only offered the hope of livelihood, but it placed him at a strategic mountain crossroads. To an ambitious young man with an inquisitive mind those roads beckoned to a broader world.

CHAPTER 2

Businessman in Indian Country

AT SEVENTEEN, WILLIAM THOMAS launched an independent business career that was compatible with the dual cultures in which he lived. His store at Quallatown served both Indians and whites. The need for merchandise to stock his shelves whetted his interests in trade, transportation, politics, and the law. He became a typical frontier American businessman. A versatile jack of many trades, he boosted the economic potential of his region and was willing to take risks. He seized whatever opportunities he found in his mountain environment, and he dealt effectively with competitors who followed his example. He did not need any specialized skills that he could not readily acquire from reading, observing, and experience.[1]

Thomas was more like the Western businessman and the Northern entrepreneur than the Southern planter. Because he did not live in plantation country, he was in the mainstream of the early development of American business. He wanted to earn commissions from the transactions he later conducted for the Indians with the United States government just as surely as he wanted profits from his stores and other enterprises. He bought and sold on credit, often keeping records so poorly that the size of his indebtedness sometimes took him by surprise. He was constantly expanding.

Thomas began as a merchant. The store that he, as a young man, opened in Quallatown in 1822 was the first of seven that he came to own within the next fifteen years. Sometime before 1832 he contracted with William Welch and James R. Love I to operate his second store on Scott's Creek, near modern Dillsboro. He also operated a tannery that was connected with it. In 1833 he bought Welch's share for an unknown amount, and in 1834 he purchased Love's part. He paid Love

$2,300, $1,400 of which was in the form of three slaves.² The remaining five stores he operated in the late 1830s.

An ambitious and intelligent youth, living in a vast wilderness ripe for development and sparsely populated by people of two distinct cultures, Thomas was motivated by both the desire to serve people in his area and to get ahead. At first, though his own boss, he was basically a shopkeeper. He often lived at his store, bartered for supplies, and kept his own ledgers. Occasionally he accepted payment for his goods in gold nuggets or gold dust, 3.5 grains of gold being judged as equivalent to a pint of whiskey.³ His limited inventory included gunpowder, pocket handkerchiefs, butcher knives, checked cloth, striped cloth, beads, whiskey, snake root, deer skins, and ginseng. The customers to whom he extended credit included Big Buck, Standing Wolf, Dick Nanlahaly, Eyetoogah, Yonaguska, and others of the Oconaluftee Cherokees.⁴

Very early, Thomas learned that the job of shopkeeper did not satisfy him, and he began to hire helpers to operate his stores. He was thus free to make buying trips to towns and port cities in Georgia and South Carolina. Since he sometimes had stiff competition from other merchants, such as Nimrod Jarrett, he was constantly attempting to expand his business.⁵

Young Will Thomas also began to pursue other entrepreneurial interests. On September 14, 1824, when he was nineteen, he paid forty dollars for 79.5 acres of land located between the Oconaluftee and Tuckasegee rivers.⁶ With that modest start he began a forty-year career of buying land. By the end of the Civil War he owned thousands of acres himself and held thousands more for the Indians. He owned and traded a few slaves, but neither slaves nor the slave trade were significant factors in his increasing wealth.⁷

Thomas did not escape the gold mania that swept through western North Carolina and north Georgia in the 1820s. In October 1829 he departed Quallatown planning to investigate sites that might be rich in gold ore and to travel to New Echota, Georgia, to examine the laws of the Cherokee Nation relative to mineral rights. There is no evidence that he planned to intrude illegally upon the rights of Indians, as so many whites were doing, but it seems equally certain that he would have welcomed the legal opportunity for prospecting and mining on Indian lands.

Thomas's trip from Quallatown to New Echota took six days and gave him his first experience in prospecting. Along the way he visited with Indians and whites and occasionally conducted experiments to determine if gold were present. Chief Junaluska and Willnotah joined him. On October 15, 1829, Thomas attended the Council at New Echota and read the 1827 Constitution for the Cherokee Nation, finding it "framed pretty much on the same principles of the laws of the United States." Thomas was also "astonished" to learn that "all mines were considered as the property of the nation & no individuals had any right to work at any of them." Unless the law were changed, he said, neither he nor anyone "could hunt mines in the limits of the Cherokee Nation." After meeting with several committeemen and councillors, he believed that he had persuaded them to change the law.[8] The Nation did not have a chance to act upon his recommendations, however, because the Georgia legislature passed a law forbidding Indians to dig gold on their own land.[9]

After his trip to New Echota, Thomas decided to help his Indian friends by encouraging temperance. By the late 1820s some members of the Cherokee Nation had begun to work for temperance.[10] Perhaps both Thomas and Yonaguska had been influenced by them. More than a dozen years had passed since Yonaguska had adopted him; the old chief was now past sixty and an alcoholic. Little Will set about sobering him up. The influence of Wil-Usdi reinforced a series of bizarre supernatural events that both Yonaguska and Little Will believed had changed the old chief's life.

Sometime before 1830, Yonaguska fell into a trance, or coma, which according to Thomas lasted for twenty-four hours. Yonaguska's brother, Willnotah, said it lasted for two months and that during much of that time "'he neither moved hand nor foot." Other sources say the Indians thought he was dead, and for fifteen days twelve hundred of them marched and counter-marched around his prostrate body. Just as they were about to bury him, Yonaguska sat up on his bier and told them that he had been on a visit to the land of the Great Spirit. According to Willnotah, he "appeared to be in his natural and right Senses." Claiming that he had seen heaven, Yonaguska said it was a pretty place, many of his friends were there, and that "the angels" promised him that he, his children, and their horses and cattle would go there. After that event, some of the Lufty Indians believed that Yonaguska was himself like an angel and perhaps even a supernatural being. Little Will accepted the old chief's story, later recorded it as told to him by Willnotah, and eventually passed it on to James Mooney, the ethnologist for the Smithsonian Institution who worked to understand and preserve Cherokee culture.[11]

After that experience, Yonaguska became a teetotaler. Deciding that teaching temperance to his people was the mission for which the Great Spirit had prolonged his days, he organized a temperance society. Little Will attended the first meeting and listened attentively as his surrogate father delivered an eloquent speech about the evils of drink. Liquor, Yonaguska said, could destroy individuals, families, and whole tribes. At the end of his address, he asked his listeners to sign a pledge that they would no longer use spirituous liquors. Thomas said that the whole town signed, and for the remainder of his life, Yonaguska refused to touch liquor. The chief decreed that any person who broke the pledge would be fined two shillings for each offense, and that the money thus collected would be spent to purchase additional land for the tribe.[12]

Yonaguska's temperance society was quite effective. In 1838 Thomas said that it was responsible for teaching the Lufty Indians not to waste time. Some whites even claimed that the Indians had become more temperate than the whites in the area. In 1845, citing evidence that there had been no murder or case of assault in the area for several years, Thomas boasted that there was no drunkard in the group and that no more than eight of the Lufty Indians drank liquor even in moderation. James Terrell, who lived among them, said the Lufty Indians were still keeping their pledge in 1873.[13]

Although Thomas attended temperance meetings regularly, he did not demand total abstinence. He continued to drink in moderation, to treat Indians to a little brandy at their dances, and to sell them liquor in his stores. Thomas's ledgers from the early 1840s show that he sold whiskey and wine to Indians, sometimes as much as half a gallon to a single customer. After that, his sales of liquor dropped off sharply, perhaps because he decided to make it less available to the Indians and because they were less eager to buy it. Thus, the sales record supports his claim of their sobriety by 1845, but that claim was also exaggerated in order to make the Indians appear stable and worthy citizens to the whites who desired their removal.

Both Thomas and Yonaguska knew that drunkenness and dissipation among Indians would be used as arguments by white Georgians and other Americans who wanted to remove them. The same day that

Yonaguska made his speech against liquor, he reminded the Lufty Indians that he had served them for forty years without pay and was solely concerned with their welfare. He advised them to remain in North Carolina. Although some Cherokee Indians were already yielding to pressures to go west, Yonaguska said that if they did they would soon be surrounded by white settlements and incorporated into a state that would oppress them.[14]

Thomas was of like mind, for in 1830 the memory of what he had seen in Georgia the previous year was still fresh. With the discovery of gold in north Georgia in 1828 and the election of Andrew Jackson as president of the United States that year, the troubles of the eastern Cherokees began in earnest. Thousands of white prospectors poured into Cherokee lands hoping to get rich quickly, and Jackson was ready to yield to pressure to have the Cherokees removed.

When white prospectors also poured into Indian territory in western North Carolina in the 1830s, the Cherokees were at their mercy. Since the laws of Thomas's native state did not apply to the Cherokee Nation's lands within its boundaries, Governor Montford Stokes appealed to Secretary of War Lewis Cass. With the approval of President Andrew Jackson in May 1832, Cass sent General Walker K. Armstead and sufficient troops to remove the intruders. Completing his work in July, Armstead left two companies of federal troops in the area to guard against further intrusions.[15] The troops officially protected only the lands within the Cherokee Nation. The Lufty Indians, who were not a part of the Nation, resided on lands clearly within boundaries over which North Carolina had authority. Since North Carolina had only 711,680 acres of Cherokee lands compared to 4.6 million in Georgia, it had low priority during debates over Indian policy in the nation's captial.[16]

Both Thomas and Yonaguska realized that the security of the Lufty Indians was in jeopardy and that they would need an agent to represent them in Washington. In 1831, Yonaguska, his brother Willnotah, Long Blanket, and fifty-seven other Cherokees asked Little Will to take that job.[17]

Will Thomas was uniquely qualified to serve as the Cherokees' agent. At age twenty-six Thomas was versed in the white man's law, and he knew the affairs of the Cherokee tribe intimately. His love for the Indians, his willingness to earn commissions on their business transactions with the government, and his desire to get to Washington made him willing to embark upon eight years of work as special agent for the Lufty Cherokees. He assumed the role of mediator between the Lufty Indians and the United States government at a fluid and complex time. The lack of unity among the Appalachian Cherokees, the pressures upon them to emigrate west, the insulated status of the Lufty Indians, and the conflicting demands upon all Cherokees to demonstrate that they were as civilized as their white neighbors — while at the same time struggling to maintain their traditional identity — were challenges that would test the skill and commitment of their young white agent.

Thomas was unconcerned about the majority of the eastern Cherokees, but he was devoted to the small group in North Carolina with whom he had contracted. The Lufty Cherokees were usually full-blooded. They raised cattle and sheep, farmed, traded, and lived in a society that was as complex, varied, and stable as that within the Nation.[18] They were very poor. Methodist and Baptist missionaries, particularly the Baptist Evan Jones, had introduced them to Christianity, but most of them did not abandon their tribal customs and beliefs. Although Thomas favored their conversion to Christianity, he also respected their traditions. His job was to prove that they were law-abiding residents of North Carolina, peaceful, and legally outside the boundaries of the Cherokee Nation.

Thomas drafted for the Lufty Indians a simple form of government, which remained in operation until after the Civil War. He laid off their lands into five additional towns, which after 1838 became known as Bird Town, Wolf Town, Yellow Hill, Big Cove, and Pretty Woman Town. Each town had its own chief and tribal council. Although all of the Lufty Indians recognized Yonaguska as their chief and Thomas as their agent, their government was decentralized, informal, and bound largely by traditional Cherokee customs.[19] The independence from the Nation that the Lufty Cherokees enjoyed, however, could not be secured by isolation; it could be preserved only by the legal arguments set forth by their white agent and by their own determination.

The number of Cherokees who moved west in the 1820s and early 1830s was not sufficient to satisfy the whites in the East and in Washington. In 1835, in preparation for a general removal, the federal government ordered a census of the Cherokees to be taken. That census, which included the Lufty Indians, showed 3,644 Cherokees in North

Carolina. The total number of Cherokees counted was 16,542, and of these almost 10,000 were in Georgia.[20]

The Cherokees divided on the issue of whether to accept the government's offer of land in the West and other perquisites for surrendering their homes in the Southeast. A minority of them, led by Elias Boudinot, Major Ridge, John Ridge, and Stand Watie, feared the consequences of further resistance to President Jackson so much that they signed the infamous Treaty of New Echota on December 29, 1835. Known as the treaty party, they were also ambitious to collect federal money and to control tribal politics. The majority followed the fiery Chief John Ross, son of a Scotsman and only one-eighth Cherokee by virtue of his mother's ancestry. Ross did not want this faction, known as the national party, to move, but if they were forced to do so, he wanted it to be under terms favorable to them. Only a few hundred Cherokees, all representing the treaty party, out of a total population of over 16,000, were present on that fateful day at New Echota to witness their disgruntled leaders sign the treaty. By a single vote, the treaty was approved by the United States Senate on May 23, 1836. The Removal was to take place within two years. Indians who would not emigrate peacefully could now be forcibly removed by federal troops. The treaty bound the Cherokee Nation to cede to the United States all of its lands east of the Mississippi River in return for five million dollars and joint interest in seven million acres already given to the western Cherokees. The government would pay the Cherokees for improvements that they had made on their lands and provide them with removal and subsistence allowances.[21]

President Jackson's desire to remove all of the Indians had resulted in a treaty so loosely constructed that bitter dissent and heated wrangling over the extent of its application were certain. In the first place, those Cherokees living outside the Nation who agreed to move would be entitled to the same conditions as the others. In the second place, the treaty did not take into account what would happen if a majority of the Cherokees within and outside the Nation, and many of their leaders, did not approve the treaty. Perhaps the most confusing clause was Article 12, which wary Indians had managed to have inserted as a loophole to help those who could meet certain conditions escape removal. This section provided the basis for many of Thomas's future defenses of the Lufty Indians. Under its provision, individuals and families who did not want to move, who agreed to become citizens of the states in which they resided, and who could care for themselves were "entitled to receive their due portion of . . . benefits accruing under this treaty . . . as soon as an appropriation is made." Certain Cherokees could thus remain and receive the same per capita payment as those who moved.[22]

In the interim between the signing of the treaty on December 29, 1835, and its ratification on May 23, 1836, Chief Yonaguska and Agent Thomas went to work to determine how the treaty would affect the North Carolina Cherokees. Not a single North Carolina Cherokee had attended the Council at New Echota or had signed the treaty. John F. Schermerhorn, a clergyman from New York and the principal representative of the federal government at New Echota, visited the Valley Towns and attempted to get the Cherokees there to sign, but he met with failure. "I visited the North Carolina Indians," he later wrote Thomas, but "I did not succeed in getting any of them to sign the said Treaty."[23] To the contrary, 3,250 North Carolina Indians within the Cherokee Nation, which included all of them except those in Haywood and Macon counties, signed a protest against ratification and sent it to Washington; more than 12,000 others in Georgia, Alabama, and Tennessee did likewise in a separate document.[24]

The Treaty of New Echota afforded Thomas his first opportunity to travel to Washington on behalf of his Indian clients. On January 31, 1836, he signed a contract with Yonaguska and fifty-three other Indians binding him to go to the national capital, examine the treaty, and to sign it for them if he found that it provided for them "equal and unconditional rights." This contract further stipulated that, if Thomas signed the treaty and it were ratified, he was to collect any money due the Lufty Indians from the government. He was to spend it for land and improvements for the Indians. He agreed to purchase a thousand additional acres for them and to build a sawmill on it. He also was bound to buy them a set of blacksmith tools, a "sufficient quantity" of books, and two hundred bushels of corn. Finally, he was to pay for printing in their own language part of the laws of North Carolina. The balance Thomas could have as payment for his service. If he were to collect the annuity that they also claimed, he was to retain half of it for himself and spend the other half on land for them.[25] Thomas worked for his clients on a contingency basis, but if he collected money he thought they were due under the terms of Article 12, his job might become lucrative.

Before leaving for Washington in March 1836, Thomas traveled, in his own words, "through a considerable part of the Cherokee nation." He determined to learn what the Cherokees themselves thought. He found very little excitement among them. They understood that their land had been sold, but they did not understand any of the details about how the treaty must be ratified. Some whites and Cherokees of mixed ancestry living among them, who used the Indians for cheap labor and cultivated the best land without paying rent or taxes, opposed the treaty. Thomas found the Cherokees in the upper part of the Nation to be "wretched in the extreme." A frost had destroyed their crops, and they were "complete objects of pity." "Should the treaty be ratified," Thomas continued, "which is the only prospect of relief, the assistance is requested to be afforded as soon as the nature of the case will permit."[26]

Thomas favored ratification of the treaty. He saw it as the only way to gain government assistance for the Lufty Indians while at the same time preventing their removal. The Senate was already deliberating the matter when Thomas arrived in Washington. He had no time to examine the treaty or to propose amendments. Thomas wanted the treaty ratified as soon as possible, but he also wanted assurance from Major Ridge, the leader of the treaty party of Cherokees, that he and his party would not claim for themselves the government benefits that had been promised to those Indians who chose to become state citizens and stay behind.[27]

Thomas passed much of his time in Washington in discussion with Major Ridge. Thomas understood that if the Haywood and Macon County Cherokees were to receive their rights and remunerations under Article 12, they must have a commitment from Major Ridge as well as from the government. In order to get the agreement he wanted from Ridge, Thomas promised to support the treaty, but only after he had persuaded eleven members of the Ridge party to sign the agreement he wanted from them. These eleven treaty party men guaranteed certain things to the Cherokees who then belonged or might later belong to the towns of Qualla, Alarka, Aquone, Cheoah, and Stekoa. The first three of these settlements were in Haywood and Macon counties, but the last two were in the Cherokee Nation. That Thomas included all five suggests he was determined to protect the rights of the Cherokees in the general vicinity of his home regardless of whether they were legally outside the Cherokee Nation.

The agreement between Thomas and the Ridge party consisted of seven articles. First, the treaty party agreed that the Cherokees in the five named towns would be entitled to such land and annuities that the federal government owed them under the terms of earlier treaties and Article 12 of the Treaty of New Echota. Second, two acting justices of the peace were to take a census of the population in the five towns for the purpose of determining their fair apportionments. Third, Thomas's clients would be bound by any additions to and interpretations of the New Echota Treaty. Fourth, the $53.33⅓ per capita removal payment, if collected, was to be deposited in a bank where it would draw interest and be available to pay the expenses of those who chose to emigrate in the allotted two-year time limit. Fifth, the Cherokees belonging to the five towns were to use the hunting grounds adjoining their settlements and preserved for the Cherokee Nation by Article 7 of the Treaty of Philadelphia made in 1791. Sixth, the Cherokees in the five towns agreed to pay a translator $500 to render the Bible into their language and another $500 to have copies distributed. Finally, if a division or sale of the land west of the Mississippi River belonging to the Cherokee Nation should ever take place, Thomas's Cherokees would be entitled to their share.[28]

Thomas was as successful in dealing with the federal government as he was with the treaty party of Cherokees. He won a promise from the secretary of war that the Cherokees not only at Quallatown but at Cheoah, or Buffalo, which was in the Nation, would not be disturbed.[29] That agreement was not in the form of a binding treaty, nor, as Thomas would later learn, was it intended to be permanent. Before the United States government would grant permission for the sixty Qualla heads of families, representing 333 Indians, to remain in North Carolina, however, Thomas would have to prove that they were citizens of that state. Acquiring that proof would demand time and considerable politicking back home. Nevertheless, Thomas returned from his first errand in Washington as agent for the Oconaluftee Indians with a double victory: a promise from the secretary of war that they would not be removed, and a contract with Major Ridge promising that the Indians who moved would not deprive those who stayed of their rights under the treaty.

Despite his political success in Washington, Thomas also knew that the Lufty Indians were safer because they lived on land that the whites did not want. One major reason the people in his area might escape removal was because they inhabited marginal lands. Located on mountainous, rocky soil far to the north of the more progressive Cherokees in Georgia, the impoverished Qualla Indians had very little that white men wanted.[30]

Thomas, and those whose writings he influenced, recalled the episode with a more romantic than realistic flair. In 1848, when Charles Lanman, a journalist whose work became a major source of information about the Lufty Indians, recorded Thomas's account, he did so with a literary flourish that omitted the hard realities. Thomas, according to his own report to Governor Edward B. Dudley, assembled the Lufty Indians at Quallatown in the fall of 1836 and asked them to make their choice between moving to Indian territory and remaining in North Carolina. He asked two Indians to stand. Then he asked for those who wished to remain in North Carolina to walk between them. The whole group arose and did so.[31]

Yonaguska, some months later, made an eloquent speech reminding his friends of "the white man's nature and the Indian's fate":

> I am an old man, and have counted the snows of almost eighty winters. My Hair, which is now very white, was once like the raven's wing. I can remember when the white man had not seen the smoke of our cabins westward of the Blue Ridge, and I have watched the establishment of all his settlements, even to the Father of Waters. The march of the white is still toward the setting sun, and I know that he will never be satisfied until he reaches the shore of the great water. It is foolish in you to tell me that the whites will not trouble the poor Cherokee in the Western country. The white man's nature and the Indian's fate tell a different story. Sooner or later one Government must cover the whole continent, and the red people, if not scattered among the autumn leaves, will become a part of the American nation. As to the white man's promises of protection, they have been too often broken; they are like the reeds in yonder river—they are all lies. North Carolina had acknowledged our title to these lands, and the United States had guaranteed that title; but all this did not prevent the Government from taking away our lands by force; and, not only that, but sold the very cow of the poor Indians and his gun, so as to compel him to leave his country. Is this what the white man calls justice and protection? No, we will not go to the West. We wanted to become the children of North Carolina, and she has received us as such, and passed a law for our protection, and we will continue to raise our corn in this very land.[32]

Yonaguska's contention that his Indians were protected by the state was based upon the 1824 state supreme court decision in *Euchella vs.*

Welsh and upon an act of the North Carolina legislature in January 1837. Thomas understood that if he were to collect the per capita payment due his Indians under Article 12 of the New Echota Treaty and at the same time prevent their removal, he must persuade North Carolina to guarantee their continued residency. Thomas got the Haywood County Court to send a petition to Governor Edward B. Dudley explaining that the Qualla Indians were peaceful, industrious citizens. The Cherokees themselves petitioned the state to protect them. The General Assembly responded with a vague act on January 21, 1837, promising to protect the Indians from fraudulent contracts only after the removal of the majority of the Indians had taken place. As additional proof that the Qualla Indians were worthy of North Carolina citizenship, in April 1837 Thomas had twenty-four white citizens of Haywood County send a memorial to Governor Dudley. It explained that their Cherokee neighbors were "fast improving in Civilization, knowledge of the arts and agriculture," were more sober than the whites, and were "qualified to make useful citizens," and "have heretofore lived in peace and friendship with the whites."[33] Sixty heads of Qualla families asked the federal commissioners to permit them to remain as North Carolina citizens. The commissioners gave them preliminary approval in September 1837, but their legal status remained tenuous and a continuing dilemma for their white agent.[34]

Six years into his eight-year tenure as agent for the Lufty Indians, Thomas had not received any payment for that work and thus had to depend upon other ventures for his livelihood. Now past thirty and still a bachelor living with his mother, Thomas was also developing his own mercantile and business interests. He was acquiring land and expanding his chain of stores. While his stores at Quallatown and Scott's Creek served the Indians who were to remain, his other five enterprises, located in the Nation, were more likely to serve the Indian emigrants and the troops who were sent to remove them. The stores were located at Nottely in southern Cherokee County; Valleytown or Jamesville, near modern Andrews, the site of Fort Delaney; Fort Butler, or Murphy; Fort Montgomery, or Cheoah, near modern Robbinsville; and Fort Cass at Calhoun, Tennessee.[35] All stores were patronized by the increasing number of white settlers moving into the western mountains. Although Thomas protected and even funded the Qualla Indians, he also sought his own financial advantage from the Removal.

Supplying seven stores on a rugged frontier while hiring clerks who were honest and selling to an odd assortment of native Indians, white settlers, and United States troops required time, luck, and skill. Since Thomas bought and sold on credit, he tried to collect debts owed him and to satisfy his own creditors. He entrusted the clerking in the stores to hired helpers while he traveled to the markets where he purchased the wide variety of goods that he offered for sale. Often he took goods with him, ranging from live cattle to bacon, lard, and ginseng, to sell or barter.

Thomas's first trip to market had been in 1833 when he drove a herd of cattle to Charleston, South Carolina. Driving cattle to market required patience and courage. Some animals became sick along the way and either died or were destroyed; others became too lame to travel and were sold for whatever they could bring. Others sometimes strayed and had to be retrieved. At night the men could not stop just anywhere but had to reach a "stand" where they could pen up the cattle. Since the driving of cattle to market was common before the availability of railroads, rental stands were constructed at regular intervals along the main roads. Adjacent to the stands were either taverns or private residences where the drovers could take their meals and find lodging. One day during that trip in 1833, Thomas and his men traveled nineteen miles, a substantial distance for a herd driven by men on horseback.[36]

When Thomas went to market in Georgia or South Carolina, he was accompanied by drovers and wagoners. He sometimes rode horseback all the way, but he preferred to travel by stagecoach or train whenever possible. Occasionally he overtook his helpers and camped with them at night, but he preferred to sleep in a tavern or private residence. During his trip to Charleston in 1833 he spent a night in Coosawhatchie, a small village in the Carolina low country, in the home of a Frenchman named Murat. Once he arrived in a city, Thomas savored the comforts of civilization, often choosing to mingle in groups where he might meet single young women.[37]

How often Thomas had cattle driven to market is not known. He mentions doing so only occasionally, and since his records are so sparse and his diary so incomplete, no accurate conclusion can be reached. An account of a comparable trip by H. P. King in 1844 shows that King sold twenty-one head of cattle in Augusta for $265.82 and that the expense of the trip was $64.51.[38] How Thomas acquired the cattle is also unknown. He may have raised some of them himself, or he may have purchased them for resale. Since he was a trader rather than a producer, the latter is more likely.

Thomas employed overseers for his farms, mills, and shops, and managers for his stores. Often the managers became partners. Several of them later became prominent and prosperous citizens. Thomas began in a modest way on January 9, 1833, when he contracted with Johnson W. King to manage his store at Quallatown for three years at an annual salary of $100. King had been working for him as a clerk for $8 a month. King was honest and efficient, and soon Thomas took him in as a partner. In 1839 King transferred to the new and larger store at Murphy. At that store, which was near Fort Butler, King remained as manager and equal partner until his death in 1845. The initial investment of each man was $3,000. King did the work, hired an assistant when needed, and tended to any other aspects of Thomas's business in the vicinity. Both men made money.[39]

On March 7, 1834, Thomas contracted with Allen Fisher to manage his store at Scott's Creek. The pay was $100 per year, one-third to be paid in goods at retail prices, and two-thirds in "notes on Solvent men . . . with the exception of what may be necessary to discharge the Cost &c. of an assault and Battery case now pending against him." Fisher promised to keep accurate records, stay sober, take in no strangers, drive wagons and cattle, butcher cattle, collect debts, and "use his best skill and ability to Honestly promote the Interest of Said Thomas."[40]

Thomas's business expanded rapidly in the 1830s. On May 28, 1834, he contracted with Joseph Keener to clerk at another store for two years at an annual salary of $100, plus an equal amount of stock in the store. Keener's salary, except for the income from the stock, was to be paid in notes on customers. Keener later rose to sufficient prominence to be elected to the North Carolina legislature. In 1839, after briefly employing J. W. King's brother, H. P., Thomas contracted with George W. Hayes to manage the Quallatown store.[41]

The only factories in North Carolina that were accessible to Thomas's stores were located near Lincolnton. From them Thomas bought cotton and woolen cloth and yarn, "sawmill irons," nails, bar iron, and lead. Sometimes he purchased as much as five thousand yards of cloth from John Hoke, a Lincolnton merchant. Once he asked Hoke to manufacture a stout, coarse cotton cloth called "osnaburg." Thomas stocked large quantities of it for the Indian trade. He paid for the manufactured goods with such commodities as deer skins and pork, but Hoke also gave him liberal credit.[42]

Thomas had by this time become a general merchant who stocked a much wider variety of goods than he had in 1822 at Quallatown. He tried to keep on hand such essentials as groceries, hardware, cotton and wool cloth, books, almanacs, yarn, shoes, liquor, and drugs. For the more discriminating of his female customers, he purchased silk bonnets, other silk goods, and leghorn hats. He also—in a limited sense—served as an agent of culture. He brought back news and information from the national and state capitals and other places. The books he sold included textbooks for the most elementary instruction, biographies, histories, Bibles, New Testaments, works on philosophy and etiquette, dictionaries, and current almanacs. Among the titles were Edward Gibbon's *Decline and Fall of the Roman Empire*, the *Encyclopedia Americana*, William Blackstone's *Commentaries*, *The History, Laws, and Religion of Greece*, and *The English at Home*. The principal markets and shopping centers for Thomas before 1836 were Athens, Augusta, and Savannah, Georgia; and Charleston, South Carolina. After he started going to Washington on behalf of the Indians, he added Philadelphia, New York City, and Baltimore, but he traded most extensively with Georgia and South Carolina merchants.[43]

The rules Thomas wrote for his clerk at the Quallatown store in 1838 are typical of the way he operated. Credit was to be given wisely and cautiously; the same price was to be charged to every customer. Clerks were to begin work early, cultivate no bad habits, and record in a ledger every article removed from the store. No trading was to take place on Sunday except in an emergency, the Lord's name was not to be taken in vain, and the Ten Commandments were to be "recollected."[44] In the era before the cash register, the detailed handwritten record of goods sold was posted in a ledger or daybook. This practice kept the clerk honest as well as made a complete record.

Thomas attempted to deal as strictly with himself as he did with his clerks. He vowed to be sober, honest, clean, Christian, and frugal. He insisted that items he, his mother, or others from his household or in his employ took from the stores were to be recorded as accurately as those purchased by other customers.

Because Thomas traveled extensively in the course of developing his stores and working for the Indians, he developed an interest in building turnpikes and railroads. In the 1830s Thomas became acquainted with Senator John C. Calhoun of South Carolina. Thomas first met him in Washington when Thomas was there on Indian business. Apparently they were not intimate although both wanted internal improvements in their respective states. In 1836 Thomas traveled with Calhoun and other South Carolinians searching for a railroad route across the Blue Ridge Mountains.[45] The time for the railroad had not yet come, however, and Thomas turned his attention to the more pressing matter of the removal of the Cherokees.

In the late summer of 1836, acting on a promise from Schermerhorn that he would be repaid by the government, Thomas bought and distributed provisions to hungry Indians. He purchased all of the corn available around Quallatown. Then he gave Ute Hyatt money to go to Tennessee for more. A considerable number of Cherokees with backpacks went along to transport it. Thomas also supplied the Cherokees with other provisions and clothing. Dispensed from his Quallatown store, these goods were distributed among the needy Indians in Alarka, Nantahala, Acquone, Stekoa, and Cheoah; a few Indian families on Valley River; and the destitute Indians of Quallatown. The Nation's council had decided that three dollars worth of provisions to each of about 250 Cherokees would keep them from starving until their new corn crop was ready.[46]

Many whites who lived in Haywood, Macon, and Cherokee counties were not as sympathetic with the Indians as was their white agent. They were fearful that the Cherokees who hated the Treaty of New Echota would rise up in rebellion against the whites. Speaking for many whites in the western part of Haywood County, Michael Francis, a three-hundred pound Scottish lawyer, reported to Governor Edward B. Dudley that the Indians along Soco Creek thought they would be permitted to remain and were persuading members of the Nation to settle among them. Forty or fifty Cherokees had moved from the Nation to the Quallatown community in three weeks, Francis continued, and Indians who had lived within that vicinity for years were becoming sullen, ceasing to deal with the whites, and threatening vengeance against them if the government attempted to remove them.[47]

Thomas called the Qualla Indians together at their townhouse on Soco Creek to ask them about the rumors. They reassured him that there was no foundation for such stories, that no more Indians were passing to and from the Nation than had previously been the case, and that there had been no threats against the whites. Thomas drew up a memorial to reinforce his argument, asked eleven white men who were present to sign it, and sent it to the governor. In an accompanying letter, Thomas explained that the rumors of possible rebellion among the Qualla Indians were false. "Those unfortunate people," he wrote, "became citizens of the State under the provisions of the Treaty concluded in 1819," obeyed the law, paid their taxes, and "lived in peace and friendship with the whites."[48] Thomas did tell the Qualla Indians, however, that no Cherokee could come from the Nation to settle among them without a certificate of citizenship in accord with the provisions of the New Echota Treaty.[49]

Governor Dudley was satisfied with Thomas's explanation. He replied that the reports against the Indians were not strong or numerous, but without being corrected they might have injured the Cherokees.[50] Nevertheless, as Thomas undoubtedly knew, Dudley would likely get other complaints from mountain whites, and he might be forced to act upon them.

Although Thomas did not want the Lufty Indians themselves to be cheated, he did plan to take honest economic advantage of the Indian Removal. In January 1837 he went to New Echota to confer with Brevet Brigadier General John Ellis Wool, who had been sent with a small contingent of regular troops to prepare for the Removal. Thomas requested permission to build a store near Fort Butler at Murphy, North Carolina. Four hundred troops stationed there were expected to remain for about eighteen months. General Wool gave his consent, stipulating that Thomas sell no liquor and recommending that he also get permission from the Nation. No mention was made of how close to the fort the store could be built. Thomas asked a committee of the Nation for permission to sell goods within its boundaries and for a guarantee that he and his clerks could live there without being molested. The Nation granted both requests. Since Fort Butler was under the jurisdiction of North Carolina as well as the United States government, Thomas sent the six-dollar fee and an application to the state comptroller for a license to operate the store. The comptroller granted the license for one year to commence on April 1, 1837.[51]

Thomas began construction of his store on February 20, 1837, on the Hiwassee River within one mile of Fort Butler. Soon he ran into trouble. Three weeks after the work began, Captain Moses Cunningham, commander of the troops there and under the orders of Major N. N. Payne, told the workers to cease building. Thomas sent his carpenters back to work and joined them, but on March 19 Cunningham commanded his troops to tear down the building. Cunningham said that he acted upon orders from General Wool prohibiting the construction of a store within one mile of the fort. Thomas did not resist. Instead, he purchased a cabin from an Indian, stored his goods in it, and headed for New Echota to see Wool.[52]

At New Echota, Thomas learned that Wool had voluntarily withdrawn from the command of the Cherokee Army and had been replaced by Colonel William Lindsay. Major Payne was present at the meeting. Thomas discovered that two of his competitors, Colonel Archibald R. S. Hunter and one Holt, had a store even closer to Fort Butler than Thomas's; they wanted no competition and had ingratiated themselves with Wool and Payne.[53]

Thomas left New Echota understanding that he would get no help from Lindsay, but he was determined to rebuild his store. He attempted to prove to the visiting military men that he was an honest person. In April 1837 a group of thirty-five Haywood County men signed a petition that Thomas was an honest merchant. Wool returned in June, changed his mind, and allowed Thomas to complete and stock his store. Lindsay, however, did not agree with Wool and sent armed guards to frighten away customers and force Thomas to close the business. In the meantime, Thomas had appealed to Governor Dudley for help. Thomas warned Dudley that "a high state of excited feelings" existed in that section between the citizens and the soldiers. He mentioned that Hunter and Holt sold liquor to both groups. Dudley, who had received other communications indicating that Hunter and Holt were disreputable characters, advised Thomas to ask Lindsay to investigate his own character. Thomas followed the governor's suggestion, and Lindsay was soon convinced that he had been deceived about Thomas. Lindsay therefore gave Thomas permission to reopen his store and to sell corn, forage, bacon, and other commodities at four other stores within the Nation.[54]

Thomas, now a successful young merchant, skillfully played his dual and sometimes contradictory roles of adopted Cherokee Indian and ambitious white entrepreneur. Not without his enemies and critics, he nimbly maneuvered among the worlds of the Lufty Cherokees and those Indians within the Nation, the white settlers and the United States troops, and the governments of his state and the nation. As agent for the Lufty Cherokees, Thomas had won for his clients a commitment from North Carolina, the United States, and the Cherokee Nation that they would not be removed or molested. He was demanding furthermore that the same payment be made to them as to those who emigrated. At the same time he had expanded his holdings of land, tanneries, grist mills, and sawmills — but especially stores — until he had become one of the more prosperous merchants on that mountainous frontier.

CHAPTER 3

Let My People Stay

AS THE DESOLATE WINTER OF 1838 changed into a lush spring, the stillness of William Thomas's mountains and valleys belied the tumultuous upheaval of the people that was about to take place. By May 23 about 7,000 troops under the command of General Winfield Scott were stationed in Georgia, Tennessee, Alabama, and North Carolina, ready to evict 16,542 Cherokees from their homes. The security the Oconaluftee Indians may have felt under the terms of Article 12 of the Treaty of New Echota, and the promises their white agent had won from the state and nation, were not guaranteed. Of the thirteen forts and stockades the army had constructed to accomplish the Removal, six were located in North Carolina.[1] There was no way to know whether the army would distinguish between the Indians of the Cherokee Nation in that state and those who claimed to be citizens of North Carolina.

Thomas's agile defense of the Lufty Cherokees, together with the success with which he carved his financial empire in part out of the Removal of the other Cherokees, elicited heated complaints from some of his white neighbors. Evan Jones, a prominent missionary to the Cherokees, thought Thomas "a very busy little man" who had collected $50,000 for the Qualla Indians but was using it for himself. Furthermore, he thought Thomas was enticing Cherokee families over to the Qualla settlement.[2]

Jones knew little about Thomas's character or his relationship with the Indians. When Thomas had defended himself the previous year before Colonel Lindsay with regard to his store near Fort Butler, he had refuted such charges as those made by Jones. When another complainant, a surgeon named M. Killion, warned Governor Edward B. Dudley that the aggrieved North Carolina Cherokees might savagely murder many whites, Thomas for a second time reassured the governor that the Indians were peaceful and loyal to the state and that they deserved to remain and to be helped.[3] The whites who condemned Thomas did so out of ignorance, bitterness, envy of his success in business, or out of dislike for all Indians; they were unacquainted with the truth about Little Will and his unique bond to Yonaguska's band of Cherokees.

If General Winfield Scott had listened to his predecessor, General John E. Wool, he would have known that the Quallatown Indians would be difficult to evict. Wool had written a year earlier that the "Indians residing in North Carolina . . . have no idea of removing to the west." He predicted bloodshed at the time of the Removal and warned that the government had "not a single Agent, high or low, that has the slightest . . . control over the Indians."[4] Because the Quallatown Indians had a legal basis to remain, the removal instructions said that they were not to be disturbed. The North Carolina Cherokees within the Nation, however, were subject to the treaty and thus to forced removal. Thomas's Indian people stood firm. With the military force used to corral thousands of Cherokees in the Nation and transport them to what later became Oklahoma, Thomas did not interfere. When General Scott came to capture those who had sought refuge in the Smoky Mountains, however, he discovered that Thomas was a person with whom he must reckon.

Hundreds of Indians fled from General Scott's troops, and others escaped from the poorly-constructed stockades. They took cover north of Quallatown in the most isolated and rugged areas of the Smoky Mountains, on land that no one wanted. Among them was Euchella, a subchief who had once lived near Yonaguska on Soco Creek but who had sold his land and moved back into the Nation. He was the same man who in the 1824 case of *Euchella vs. Welsh* had won the North Carolina Supreme Court's endorsement of the Cherokees' right to their lands.

The legendary Cherokee hero Tsali, whom the whites called Charley, was another of the fugitives. Scott's determination to capture Tsali and his followers, and Thomas's equal determination to protect his Quallatown friends from removal, cast Thomas as a principal actor in the saga of Tsali.

Because Thomas believed that the surest way to save his Quallatown friends would be to cooperate with Scott in capturing fugitives from the Nation, he agreed to help the general locate the wanted Indians. On October 30, 1838, Thomas accompanied Second Lieutenant Andrew Jackson Smith of the First United States Dragoons and three enlisted men to Tsali's camp. The camp was on a steep cliff near the confluence of the Tuckasegee and Little Tennessee rivers. The eight people there surrendered without incident. Since Smith had been informed that there were twenty, he and his party waited overnight for the others to arrive. Only four did so, bringing the total number of captives to twelve. They included Tsali, now an old man, four younger men, and seven women and children. The next morning, November 1, Smith set out with the three enlisted men and the twelve Indian prisoners, but not Thomas. For some unexplained reason, which Thomas later described vaguely as an "accident," Thomas remained behind at the camp.

Toward evening on November 1, Smith suspected trouble and warned his men to be on guard. When the Indians began to walk more slowly, Smith attempted to speed them up by having some of the children placed on horses. After sunset he confiscated a concealed knife from one Indian. He spied a hidden axe on the person of another, but before he could order it taken, its owner sank it into the forehead of one of his soldiers. The Cherokees then killed a second soldier, wounded the third, and would have murdered Smith himself had his frightened horse not run away. Tsali and his men took caps and other articles from the bodies of the two dead soldiers, then fled with the women and children back into the mountains.

Thomas caught up with Smith shortly after the murder. Smith welcomed him for the remainder of the trip to Fort Cass, near Calhoun, Tennessee, where Thomas had a store. Smith reported the episode to his superior, Lieutenant C. H. Larned, who in turn reported it to General Scott at Athens, Tennessee. Scott summoned Thomas and Colonel William S. Foster, commander of the Fourth Infantry Regiment, to a conference. On November 7 he ordered Foster, his infantrymen, and some volunteers to find and shoot the Indian murderers, to protect white families living in the Smokies, and to collect "as many as practicable" of the Cherokee fugitives for emigration. Scott asked Thomas if he would go too, offering to pay him liberally for his services. Thomas declined the pay but agreed to help. Scott thought Thomas had "a lively interest in the success of the expedition," and for the first time in a report to the Department of War he distinguished "Mr. Thomas's Oconeelufty Indians" from the "outlaws" he was now about to pursue.

Thomas moved out ahead of Foster and his men. At Quallatown he sent Cherokee warriors to search for Euchella. Euchella was in hiding to escape removal; he was the chief of the town to which Tsali and his band belonged. Euchella's wife and son had died of hunger, and he was an old man who wanted to stay in North Carolina. He trusted Thomas and promised to help locate Tsali in return for his own protection. Commanding his own men, Euchella joined Flying Squirrel, who was in charge of the Cherokees. Sixty Indians thus joined Foster and his soldiers. After listening to Yonaguska advise his warriors always to obey and support the United States, they set forth on November 12 to find Tsali. Traveling through rough terrain, on November 19 they captured Big George and Tsali's oldest son, Nantayalee Jake. A few days later they took Tsali's wife and the wife and young daughter of Big George. One by one, they found others of the twelve fugitives, and finally on November 24 they caught Tsali himself. Several of the Indian men still had the items they had taken from the bodies of the dead soldiers.

Prior to the capture, Thomas, Foster, and their Indian allies had agreed that the five males in Tsali's group must be executed. They were Tsali himself, Jake, George, Lowen, and Washington. Since Washington, Tsali's youngest son, was only sixteen, they reconsidered his case and decided to spare him. Foster escorted Washington and the seven females to a fort in Tennessee where they were held for emigration. After the women and Washington had been taken away, on November 23, Euchella's warriors blindfolded and shot Jake, George, and Lowen. On November 25, the day after taking Tsali prisoner, they executed him. Thomas witnessed the executions and supervised the burial of their bodies near the graves of the two soldiers the Indians had killed.

In his final report on the death of Tsali, Colonel Foster commended Yonaguska and asked that Euchella and his band be allowed to join the Quallatown Indians. The next month, January 1839, the Commissioners of the Cherokee Removal officially permitted him and his followers a safe haven among the Qualla group. The persons who benefitted directly from the death of Tsali were Euchella and his band. Thomas and his Lufty Indians, however, gained indirectly. Their participation in the Tsali affair proved that they were as peaceful and loyal as Thomas claimed. Federal authorities recognized their right to remain in North Carolina.[5]

After the Removal, about 1,100 Cherokees remained in North Carolina. Seven hundred of those belonged to Quallatown. Of the North Carolina Cherokees, 1,046 gave Thomas their power of attorney to represent them in Washington and to collect any money due them.[6] The harsh winter of 1838-1839 left Thomas's Indians destitute. Many of them scavenged for food, and in some cases whether they lived or died depended upon what Thomas could provide. Their only hope, he thought, was to be paid the per capita owed them under Article 12 of the Treaty of New Echota.

Under the presidency of Martin Van Buren the officials in Washington to whom Thomas must present the case of the Lufty Indians were Secretary of War Joel Poinsett and Commissioner of Indian Affairs T. Hartley Crawford. Both men were reasonable, but Thomas had to defend his reputation and his credentials. Thomas suspected that General Wool had maligned him to the secretary of war. He therefore in January 1839 sent Poinsett a long letter with attached depositions from prominent Haywood County citizens attesting that he was an honest merchant, the legal agent to make claims for the Cherokees, and "a free American citizen." A few weeks later, Thomas went to Washington where he spent many months trying to get the money his Indians had been promised.[7]

In the late winter of 1839, while Thomas was in Washington, Yonaguska died. Thomas learned about it in April. Before his death, the old chief had summoned the men in his band to form a circle around his pallet in the Soco council house. They accepted his recommendation that Little Will be allowed to succeed him. Yonaguska then advised them to abstain from drinking liquor and never to move west. He wrapped his blanket about him, lay back on his pallet, and died. After burying him near Soco Creek, his men marked his grave with a pile of stones.[8]

William Holland Thomas became chief of the Oconaluftee Indians. He was the only white man to hold that office.

As chief, Thomas did not exercise dictatorial powers, nor did he abandon his life in the white world. Flying Squirrel, a son-in-law to Yonaguska, later claimed to be principal chief of the Lufty Indians, but neither they nor Thomas recognized that claim. Thomas appointed subchiefs of the various towns, and the loyalty he enjoyed from them and the rest of the Indians was voluntary. Thomas recommended temperance and the Christian religion, but he also respected native traditions.[9] His work as chief became a continuation of what he had done as agent. He acquired land for them, which became known as the Qualla Boundary. He argued their case in the nation's capital and devoted much of his time to their general well-being.

During 1839, both before and after he became chief in April, Thomas stayed in Washington to work for his people. Many of them had given him their power of attorney to collect and invest their money.[10] Since John Ross and other chiefs were also there attempting to claim all of the $200,000 that had been appropriated for the Cherokees, Thomas felt that he must keep in close communication with Commissioner T. Hartley Crawford and other federal officials. If he failed to collect the claims immediately, Thomas hoped at least to persuade the Board of Cherokee Commissioners to hold the money in Washington for future release to his clients.[11] Thomas assured Secretary of War Poinsett that the Indians could remain in North Carolina on lands that he had bought for them. When the news reached Washington of the deaths in Indian territory of the Cherokees who had signed the removal treaty, Thomas advised his people to have no more communications with the western Indians.[12] Those men in the West were executed under Cherokee law by followers of John Ross, who despised the treaty.

During the summer and early fall of 1839, Thomas completed his fifty-page report to Commissioner Crawford. He went to the War Office at nine o'clock each morning, researched and wrote there until five in the afternoon, and then worked in his room until ten or eleven at night. He believed that all Cherokees would move west within a few years, but he did not want them forced to do so, and he did not want them to be deprived of their money.[13]

In the meantime Crawford had made a decision on Thomas's claims. By mid-September 1839 the commissioner had reviewed three thousand claims and decided that the Indians should have the per capita allowance but not payment for removal and subsistence. Thomas asked him to reconsider and to pay for removal and subsistence, which he said amounted to $55,000 for the eastern Cherokees. Crawford, however, held firm and was supported by the secretary of war. Both the secretary and the commissioner were so upset by the violence among the western Cherokees that had resulted in the execution of the Ridges and Boudinot that they decided to suspend payments to all Indians on November 12, 1839.[14]

Crawford did, however, promise Thomas that he would pay about $150,000 on claims under the Treaty of 1835 for "improvements, spoliations per capita &c." This promise, like many others, did not come to fruition, for the first payment was only a fraction of the amount guaranteed. The claims of the Western Cherokees, continuing doubts about Thomas's motives, and pressure from whites in the Southeast to remove all Indians caused the federal officials to study and debate the plight of the Lufty Indians for almost another decade. The Lufty claims were not resolved until July 29, 1848, when an act of Congress allowed the eastern Cherokees to receive the benefits of the Treaty of New Echota.[15]

A disillusioned and tired Thomas yearned to go home that fall of 1839. His private affairs in North Carolina were suffering from his long absence. Since he could find no attorney in Washington to take charge of the Indian claims for him, however, he stayed. He wrote his creditors in Charleston and Augusta that he could not pay his debts until the government paid the Indians and he collected a commission from them. In addition to their claims, Thomas had filed a claim of his own to be reimbursed for $1,200 worth of food and provisions he had given the Indians three years earlier to prevent their starving. The best he could do, he told his creditors, was to pay 10 percent interest on what he owed and wait for the government money.[16]

While researching in the Indian Office, Thomas found a letter that General Wool had written about him two years earlier. Addressed to Commissioner of Indian Affairs C. A. Harris, Wool's letter stated that in his opinion Thomas had no legitimate claim to be reimbursed for personal money he had given the Indians. Upon discovering the letter, Thomas asked Wool for an audience. When they met, Wool confessed that he knew nothing about Thomas except what he had been told. Wool went with Thomas to the Indian Commissioner, repeated what he had told Thomas, and agreed to write others admitting his error. Whatever Wool did to make amends was not sufficient to convince either the commissioner or the secretary of war to change his mind. Both continued to refuse to reimburse Thomas, and his personal claim finally died in Congress in 1846.[17]

As Christmas 1839 approached, the empty-handed chief of the Oconaluftees urged his people not to be discouraged. He assured them that "the Being who ruled the destinies of Nations, the friend of the oppressed and distressed of every people will turn all things for good to those who act worthy of his favor and put their trust in him."[18]

Thomas had sufficient faith and diligence to keep after Crawford. The Indians desperately needed their money, he argued. He said it should be paid to him as their attorney. The Board of Cherokee Commissioners, the United States representatives from his district, and the two senators from North Carolina recommended that Thomas be appointed disbursing agent for the Cherokees remaining east of the Mississippi River. Finally, in July 1840, Thomas won a partial but significant victory: Crawford appointed him to take a census of all Cherokees remaining east of the Mississippi River and to serve as disbursing agent for them. The amount they were due, according to the Indian Office, was $24,013.51.[19] Of that total Thomas collected $17,797.50 for the Indians and $401 for his service.[20]

For the next five years Thomas's work to get the government to pay the eastern Cherokees became complicated by a second attempt at their removal. From 1841 through 1844 the pressure for this second removal was relatively minor, official efforts to bring it about inept, and the resistance by Chief Thomas and others stubborn and determined. This second removal failed. Nevertheless, some whites favored it because they genuinely believed the Indians would be better off in the West; they also hoped to find a practical solution to the problem of how to make a final settlement with the Cherokees. Both the Indian Office and the Cherokee Nation thought it would be more sensible to negotiate a new treaty to settle all claims, but they could not do so unless those Cherokees scattered from the Nation and claiming citizenship in various states would rejoin the larger group. Otherwise, claims would have to be settled by the commissioner of Indian affairs, boards that he appointed, and disbursing agents—a process that could drag on interminably.[21]

Thomas had a better chance to achieve his goals through working under the Treaty of 1835 than under a new treaty. He did not object to the removal of any individual Indian who wanted to go west, but he was adamant that those who wished to remain in North Carolina be allowed to do so. If he could have his way, neither the Indian Office nor the Cherokee Nation would get the chance to deprive the Lufty Indians of what was already due them under the Treaty of New Echota.

He accepted pay of five dollars per day in order to compile a new census and serve as disbursing agent for Crawford, but at the end of the summer of 1841 he left Washington fearful that in his absence the wily Chief John Ross would succeed in winning all government funds for the western Cherokees.[22]

Scarcely had Thomas returned home before he learned that his distrust of both Ross and the Indian Office was solidly grounded. Thomas C. Hindman, a man from Alabama who was closely connected with Ross, approached Acting Secretary of War Albert M. Lea. Hindman, who favored a new treaty and the removal of the remaining eastern Cherokees, argued that the Cherokees in North Carolina were at the mercy of designing whites, especially their white chief, who wanted only to enrich themselves. He recommended that Thomas be investigated and removed as disbursing agent.

On September 29, 1841, Crawford dismissed Thomas and appointed Hindman in his place. He also appointed John Timson, a Cherokee who could be counted upon to support government policy, as Hindman's assistant. The Indian Office gave Hindman the responsibility of disbursing funds and encouraging the eastern Cherokees to move west. The aggrieved white chief protested that as a Democrat he had become the victim of dirty Whig politics. He would welcome any investigation of his handling of Indian affairs, he said. He accused Hindman of being in conspiracy with Ross and bitterly hinted that Ross and his men were responsible for the deaths of Elias Boudinot and the Ridges. Thomas wondered if Hindman and Ross would have him murdered next.[23]

On December 5 Hindman arrived at Murphy, North Carolina, in a cavalier mood. He reported that he had not yet been able to see Thomas, because Thomas, "having no family nor settled home," was reported to be sixty miles away tending to his stores. Hindman promised to persuade the Cherokees to emigrate. Although Thomas had been encouraging the Indians to stay, Hindman naively predicted that he would be able to change their minds.[24]

When Thomas and Hindman met on December 17, 1841, they instantly disliked each other. Yet each man decided to tolerate and accompany the other for the next six weeks as they visited the Cherokee settlements. Hindman realized that he needed Thomas's assistance to locate and assemble the Indians. Why Thomas agreed to travel with Hindman, he did not say. Perhaps it was to prove his credibility to the Indian Office and to reassure his Indians with his presence. Hindman complained that Thomas used his influence indirectly, encouraging the Indians to stay, because they owed him a large amount of money.[25]

Hindman's efforts to persuade the Cherokees to move west failed. At Quallatown, 150 subchiefs and warriors refused to budge. Elsewhere the resistance was the same. Crawford finally gave up, dismissed Hindman, and attempted a new approach in the summer of 1842. He appointed a new board of Cherokee commissioners and a new agent, James Robinson, a merchant from Franklin, North Carolina. Timson remained as Robinson's assistant. They received unofficial help from William Rogers, a Cherokee in Forsyth, Georgia, who argued that William Thomas was a good man but that there would be no one left to protect the eastern Cherokees after his death.

This new effort at removal failed by the end of 1844. It fell victim to the counteroffensive of William Holland Thomas; the support he received from other western North Carolinians such as Felix Axley, an attorney from Cherokee County; the penurious tendency of President John Tyler's administration to spend no more than $2,500 on removal; the dogged resistance of the Cherokees; and the willingness of North Carolina and North Carolinians to let them stay. "The Indians would have removed long since," wrote one disappointed North Carolinian, "but for the improper interference of that cunning little Rascal, Billy Thomas."[26]

The role of Chief Thomas in the failure of the second removal and its aftermath displayed his self-interest, his love for his people, and his sound understanding of the labyrinth of national politics. In July 1842, as Commissioner Crawford revamped his plan for removal, Thomas sent him a letter asking to be paid his commission for working on Cherokee claims and to be reimbursed for the land and supplies he had given them. Thomas contended that he had spent more than $7,500 of his own money to purchase 50,000 acres of land around Quallatown. Thomas said he did not intend to take any more of the Cherokee's money other than what he had given them, plus interest, and that he intended for them to keep the land even if he did not get reimbursed. If anyone accused him of seeking personal gain, he implied, it must be some disgruntled Whig who wanted to slander a loyal Democrat.[27]

Much of the time Thomas spent in Washington in 1843 and 1844 he was busy explaining and attempting to collect the Cherokee claims. To assist him, in 1842 he hired Duff Green, a highly respected North Carolina attorney who was also in the nation's capital and who had many friends in powerful places in the national government. On August 28, 1843, Thomas petitioned Cherokee Commissioners John H. Eaton and Edward B. Hubley for more than $31,000 worth of claims for Indians. That effort was thwarted when Crawford replaced Eaton and Hubley with new commissioners.[28]

Through many more months of work in Washington, Thomas made no progress. After the election of James K. Polk to the presidency in November 1844, Duff Green wrote that he thought Polk would be more sympathetic to Thomas. In January 1845, Thomas returned to North Carolina, leaving Duff Green and his son Benjamin in Washington to lobby Congress for help with the claims of his Indian clients. By mid-February Thomas was back in Washington, paying all of his own expenses, again ready to work for the Indians.[29]

Through occasional long letters, Thomas informed the Lufty Indians, sometimes in minute detail, about the political maneuvering in Washington. On February 15, 1845, he wrote his "dear friends" at Quallatown that he had presented a memorial to the United States Senate representing "all the injustice which was done to you during emigration." He reassured them that the right of the Cherokees at Qualla, Cheoah, and Buffalo to "remain unmolested" had been "written and placed on the Big book in the War Department where it will remain while this government lasts." Thomas did not expect, he said, to get any of their financial claims through that session of Congress, but they must remain the "temperate, industrious, honest, truthful, peaceable, and good citizens" that he had portrayed them to be. He thought they could trust the new president, James K. Polk.

Chief Thomas always included in his letters to his people a plethora of warm and personal comments. In that same letter of mid-February, he said he hoped to see every family have enough land for themselves and their heirs, plenty of spinning wheels and looms, horses, and other livestock. Thomas hoped to complete their business and start home in March, "when I can retire and spend my days at Qualla Town—among you and all my friends."[30]

No matter how much Thomas may have desired it, it would be many more years before he could complete and retire from the Indians' business. On June 25, 1845, he again sent them a long progress report. President Polk, who had granted him an audience, seemed sympathetic, he said, but the situation was complicated by the difficulty in maintaining a responsible board of Cherokee commissioners, conflicting information that was funneled to the federal authorities, and the demands from the Ross party that they alone deserved payment. It was urgent for the Qualla Cherokees to continue to be model citizens, Thomas wrote. He had informed the president of their progress in temperance, mechanical arts, agriculture, spinning and weaving, and Sunday School attendance. The president had had an account of their Sunday Schools published in a paper that was distributed to all twenty-eight states, "which has raised you high in the estimation of the American people." The Cherokees in the West, he said, were "slaves to king whiskey," disorderly, unproductive, and held in poor esteem by the American people. "Your *Great Father*, the *President*," Thomas said, would look kindly upon temperate, industrious, and peaceable citizens. Thomas said he hoped to be home in time to attend their Green Corn dances and wished to be remembered "to your wives and children." He hoped they would soon have enough land to support themselves comfortably.[31]

Buying land for himself and for the Cherokees was one of Thomas's major endeavors. The amount of land he finally came to own personally is not known, but it was in excess of 150,000 acres. In 1840 he paid the heirs of William Cathcart $1,200 for 33,000 acres, and in 1841 he paid $7,500 for 55,000 acres adjoining Quallatown. He bought 35,000 acres in Tennessee and 25,000 more in Jackson County, North Carolina, both at low cost. He added more and more acres until the beginning of the Civil War. The land adjacent to Quallatown, known as the Qualla Boundary, he gave to the Indians, although he held the title in his own name. Much of the property was rough, isolated, or unusable, but Thomas became one of the largest landowners in western North Carolina.[32]

Thomas continued to enlarge his diverse business empire. His principal investment was in his seven stores. While federal troops were stationed near Quallatown and Scott's Creek, Thomas purchased all of the denim trousers and socks that he could find. Money was plentiful and prices soared as long as the troops were in the area.[33] He accepted Georgia money at a discount of 6 percent, but he refused worthless inflated Tennessee money on his contracts with the soldiers. He preferred "sound Van Buren" United States money and would offer better deals to those who paid him with it. Once in 1838 he bought a large quanitity of corn and used it in profitable barter. He stocked his store at Calhoun, Tennessee, with brandy and wine from Charleston, South Carolina, and paid his clerk there $15 per month. In August 1838 he reported that he had cleared $20,000 from all his stores by selling goods to the army and the Indians during Removal.[34]

Thomas's store at Scott's Creek, its contents, a tannery, and a turnpike road were worth $19,000 in 1839; that year he was paying eight cents per pound for ginseng and twelve and a half cents for pinkroot, both good prices. Not all of his stores were so successful. The one he opened at Fort Cass to serve the Removal closed in February 1839, showing a profit of only $130. The food and supplies he gave to his favored Indians were a financial loss. The considerable prosperity Thomas enjoyed from the Removal lasted but one year, for in 1839 Thomas was again earning his living by regular, hard work.[35]

Johnson W. King, Thomas's partner in the store at Murphy, became his principal helper and confidant in the early 1840s. King was entrusted with making decisions and keeping Thomas abreast of general events during the long months he was away on buying trips or in Washington. It was King who moved Thomas's mother to Stekoa Fields in May 1839, who reminded him that the Indians would never go west, who informed him when the cattle were fattened enough to send to market, and who rejoiced with him upon the election of James K. Polk. King was a friend whose death in 1845 left a void in Thomas's life.[36]

Upon learning of King's death in December 1845, Thomas hired Samuel R. Mount to replace him at the Murphy store. Mount was the son of the widow who owned the rooming house where Thomas sometimes stayed in Washington. Thomas promised to pay Mount one hundred dollars, plus board and laundry, for the first year and to give him a fifty-dollar pay raise the next year. At the end of four years, if both were satisfied, Thomas would take him in as a partner. Mount, who had business experience and was a slaveowner, set out for North Carolina immediately. He lived up to Thomas's expectations and became a prominent citizen and an active member of the temperance society. Thomas did make him a partner as promised, and that partnership lasted until Thomas lost his interest in that store during the Civil War.[37]

When away from North Carolina, Thomas sent advice, both business and philosophical, to his clerks. When the clerk at Scott's Creek notified him that a drought was hampering the operation of the tannery and that a horse had died, Thomas replied that man must trust Providence to send rain and that those who have must sometimes lose.[38] He advised his manager at Quallatown to increase business by paying one cent more, but in merchandise only, for ginseng than his competitor Nimrod S. Jarrett was paying.[39] He often wrote to John Schermerhorn trying to collect the money he had loaned him in 1836.[40] Thomas put H. P. King in charge of building the Oconaluftee road, a turnpike constructed of wooden planks intended to connect Webster, North Carolina, with Sevierville, Tennessee. He advised Allen Fisher that he complained too much and worked too little, suggested that J. W. King be gentle but firm with credit customers, and ordered Cudjo, a free black male who had once been a slave of Yonaguska's, to stay with Temperance Thomas to build the winter fires.[41]

Cudjo was a much trusted servant. He enjoyed a close relationship with Thomas. Thomas once allowed him to deliver $350 to a creditor in Tennessee. He had his own account at the Quallatown store, and later he accompanied Thomas throughout the Civil War.[42] Thomas may have been closer to him than he was to his clerks and partners.

When Thomas had the time, he attended to his own business. He attempted without luck in 1839 to locate a shipment of goods that had been lost four years earlier. For $1,000, late in 1841, he bought his third tannery and located it at Quallatown. In 1842 he took in 3,400 pounds of ginseng at Scott's Creek. He advertised in the Asheville newspaper that he had beef cattle, hides, corn, and iron for sale. He collected money on 5 percent commission for others, and in 1844 he employed a New Orleans attorney, Robert Rose, to buy land for him in Louisiana. When Rose lost his note, Thomas gave him another contract and $250 with the stipulation that if Rose failed he would repay the money with interest. Thomas solicited subscriptions to start a Cherokee County newspaper and sold bacon on commission of 8 percent.[43]

When Thomas was not in Washington, he traveled from store to store, frequently making buying trips out of the state. One of his more exciting adventures took place on March 22, 1839, when he was riding on an open railroad car bound for Charleston, South Carolina. The train jumped the tracks twenty-two miles short of its destination, tossing its passengers to the ground. The open car and slow speed made it easy for Thomas to leap clear of the wreck, but he dryly noted that there "certainly is a great Danger in riding on the Rail Road." Fortunately, there were no injuries, and the crew and passengers righted the train. It arrived in Charleston at four o'clock in the afternoon.[44]

After registering at the Norris Hotel in Charleston, Thomas passed an enjoyable evening in that sparkling, cosmopolitan city. He tended to the business of buying goods for his stores before turning to relaxation. In the evening he went down to the Bay and "viewed with wonder & amazement the Broad Atlantic Ocean, the fine and Beautiful Ships lying in the Harbour," the arrival and departure of steamboats, good-humored seamen at work, and colorful flags flying on ships from England, France, Spain, and Russia. "But above them all," he told his diary, "I looked and Beheld the American Eagle with extended wings as if conscious of the greatness of the nation that it is a sign of." A "charming sea breeze" made the scene "truly sublime," he said. After supper he went to a Protestant church, heard a "very good discourse," and listened to "truly charming music" that wafted from an organ that cost $3,000. The next morning he "Bid Adieu to the City with all its pleasing charms" and took a train for Augusta, Georgia.[45]

Thomas arrived in Augusta on the weekend and used Sunday to indulge his interest in religion. Although he was a Methodist, he liked to attend whatever church was nearby. He had a great curiosity about the varieties of churches and doctrines. On that Sunday in Augusta, in the morning he went to a Protestant service and in the evening to a Roman Catholic one. He thought that the Catholic "worship books" and their burning of "incense before the images" was "too much like Idolatry." The next day, when his wagons arrived, he loaded them with the goods he had bought and "started for home."[46]

The following year, 1840, he headed for Athens, Georgia, taking several days and spending the nights with acquaintances along the way. After putting up at the Athens Hotel, he set upon his routine of buying goods for his stores, learning all that he could, and enjoying himself. He found Athens to be "a most Beautiful City" that had "been laid out for pleasure" where it was "situated on the Oconee River." There he met Thomas Baxter, an agent for the Athens Manufacturing Company. On Monday he saw the factory in operation. It employed eighty-five workers and had "70 spindles & 24 Looms." The building was a spacious three-story brick structure. Thomas bought spun yarn and cloth, loaded his wagons on the afternoon of July 1, and departed for home.[47]

Apart from his peculiar role as chief of a small, isolated group of Cherokees, Thomas was becoming a man of considerable means and a well-known and prominent citizen of western North Carolina. A career in politics was inevitable. A lawyer and entrepreneur, he was keenly interested in and experienced with both local and national politics. In June 1840 the Democratic Party wished to nominate him for the state senate. He was thirty-five and had never sought elective office. Because a train accident prevented his return from Washington in time to accept the nomination, however, he did not become a candidate.[48] Thomas continued his life as white chief of the Oconaluftee Indians and frontier entrepreneur.

As landowner and businessman, Thomas bought and sold slaves. In a rugged Southern mountainous area where slavery was not as important as it was in the tidewater South, Thomas became one of the largest slaveowners in his region. He owned fifty at the time of Emancipation in 1865. In March 1841 he bought seven slaves from Andrew Colvard for $1,700. Later that year he sold an unknown number of slaves to Mark Colvard for $1,800. In 1843, for $2,400 he bought "eight slaves for life." They were Dick, Dinah, Tamar, Adaline, and four children named Allen, Louisa, Emaline, and Sarah. They came from Paulding County, Georgia.[49]

Thomas had some feeling for his slaves as human beings. Once he bought seven slaves, accepting the condition that their family would stay together. There are very few records of his selling slaves, and apparently he did not seek to make a profit in the slave trade. Once he stayed up all night to care for a sick black girl who belonged to Samuel Sherrill. He allowed his slaves to attend Indian religious camp meetings, and he provided a burial ground near Stekoa Fields for those who died. When Dave, an unruly slave at Stekoa Fields, refused to obey Thomas's mother and sometimes quarreled with other slaves, Thomas still declined to have him sent away. On another occasion he allowed his slave Wagoner Dick to travel to South Carolina and Georgia to purchase goods for him.[50]

The majority of Thomas's workers were hired helpers rather than slaves. In addition to his clerks, he hired wagon drivers and agricultural and mechanical workers of all kinds. In August 1840 he paid a group of Indians $358.95 to repair a turnpike, and in December he paid another Cherokee four dollars to shuck corn at Stekoa Fields.[51]

On one occasion in July 1835, he had hired a slave blacksmith to work for him for nine months.[52]

The hectic pace of maintaining a scattered business in North Carolina and defending Indians in Washington took its toll on Thomas's personal life. Preserving good health was a supreme challenge. Living at hotels, cattle shelters, store attics, open encampments, and assorted homes precluded the development of a healthy routine. Exposure to inclement weather, uncertain diet, innumerable diseases, and inadequate sanitation and bathing facilities sometimes made him sick. In his diaries and letters he frequently mentions health problems. In the summer of 1838 he complained that an attack of measles "has reduced me very much." In 1841, while en route to Augusta, he paid fifty cents to have himself bled and another twelve and a half cents for medicine. In 1843 he noted his recurrence of "bilious colic," characterized by diarrhea, vomiting, and abdominal pain. Attempting a cure, he doctored himself with Indian remedies, although he noted that the *Boston Guide to Health* recommended hot red pepper tea, sweating, castor oil, molasses, and a few drops of laudanum. When those remedies were not handy in 1844, he took rhubarb and wine for diarrhea. He frequently had colds, and he seemed forever struggling to keep himself and his clothes clean.[53]

Although his living with his mother suggests that she was important in his life, the details of that relationship are difficult to determine because there is no extant correspondence between them and only casual references in other sources. Still vigorous at age seventy, she operated the home at Stekoa Fields. In a handwritten note asking the storekeeper to send her "some coffee some salts one sack nothing more at present," Temperance Thomas reveals herself to be a woman of health, thrift, and command. On occasion Thomas would instruct a clerk to "furnish Mother what she wants."[54] Thomas's interest in religion may have been at least in part influenced by his mother.

Devoutly Christian, Thomas from time to time took a vow to live by the Ten Commandments. His faith in the omnipotence and benevolence of God he often revealed in his correspondence, diary, and even account books. In 1841 he built an Indian meeting house suitable for religious services.[55] On August 17, 1843, he sat for an hour and a half listening to Rachel Barker of the Society of Friends address a large crowd assembled in the chamber of the United States House of Representatives. Despite his dislike for Roman Catholicism, he sometimes attended mass. In November 1844 he attended a high mass at St. Matthew's Catholic Church in Washington. He did not care for the vestments the priests wore, nor did he like the way the church raised money by selling chances on articles.[56] His own faith was simple and rather unquestioning for such an inquisitive mind but sufficient to help him cope with the storms of his life.

A bachelor who loved children, Thomas adopted a white daughter named Angelina. Her age and the date of her adoption are not known. He took in other children who needed a home. Since he considered himself an orphan because his father had died before he was born, Thomas was especially sympathetic with orphans and illegitimate children. Perhaps the influence of Yonaguska also determined his attitude. In 1840 his household consisted of himself, his mother, a free black man, a young white man in his twenties, and a white girl between fifteen and twenty. The black man was Cudjo, the girl was Angelina, and the unidentified boy was perhaps a servant. Later he took in young Andrew Patton and reared him to maturity.[57]

Thomas also had an adopted Indian son, William Pendleton Hyde. Born on February 1, 1843, Hyde claimed that the Cherokee woman Catherine Hyde (Kanaka) was his mother and that "W. H. Thomas who . . . was Indian agent for years By whom I was adopted" was his father.[58] Although Hyde apparently did not live in the house with Thomas or know much about his life as a white man, the young Cherokee did always live near him, fought with him in the Civil War, and was buried near Stekoa Fields after his death in 1887. Hyde's descendants, hoping to collect money from the federal government under an act of Congress in 1906 that guaranteed them payment if they could prove that they had a Cherokee ancestor alive in North Carolina in 1835, simply listed Catherine Hyde as his mother and William Holland Thomas as his father with no reference to an adoption.[59] If such an adoption took place, it was probably like Yonaguska's adoption of Thomas: informal without recognition under the white man's law.

In his search for a wife, Thomas suffered numerous frustrating disappointments. The ideal of a loving wife, legitimate children, and a comfortable home was not to be his until he was well past fifty. In the meantime, he looked and dreamed. In 1841, he apparently anticipated a marriage that did not take place, for in a contract he made with

J. W. King he stipulated that if he, Thomas, should marry, his wife could share the room he reserved for himself in the house occupied by his partner.[60]

At what point Thomas abandoned his youthful vow to remain chaste before marriage cannot be known, but as he passed throught his twenties, thirties, and forties yet unmarried, he apparently surrendered to the demands of his sexual nature. Neither religion and conscience nor prevalence of venereal disease and chance of unwanted pregnancy could keep him absolutely celibate. If he fathered illegitimate children by both Indian and white women, their identities rest behind the veils of time, gossip, and legend.

The details of his dealings with women Thomas himself often told in his diary and letters. He found the women he met in Washington in 1839 to be frivolous, too concerned about money and fashion, and generally inferior to those of Buncombe County. He thought his inability to strike up a good courtship was caused by his fear that young girls would not return the love of an "old man" of thirty-four and his belief that "old maids scold" and "widows recollect the virtues of their first husbands & none of the vices."[61] Soon, however, the young white chief conquered his fears, for a succession of women, both in Washington and North Carolina, passed through his life.

Thomas's favorite Buncombe County lady in 1842 was an unnamed woman of undetermined age in Asheville. In the spring he called upon her, requested "liberties" which she refused, and, the next year, dropped her because of her bad disposition.[62] In 1844 he escorted two young Washington women to a Fourth of July fireworks display on the grounds of the President's House, where they witnessed a misdirected rocket fall into the crowd, killing one man instantly and injuring several more. On other occasions he escorted females to the National Observatory, to church, and to the theatre where he once saw the great tragedian Junius Brutus Booth star in Shakespeare's *Richard III*. For one young woman he wrote a love poem after attending church services with her.[63]

During 1845, his fortieth year, Thomas spent much time in the company of women. After ending a fascination with a Miss Barrett in North Carolina in March, he resolved to spend less time with females. That resolution lasted three days. He and Benjamin Green, sixteen years his junior, often matched wits in their search for women in Washington. In April, Thomas called upon a young lady in Asheville, took her fishing, and demanded sexual favors. When she refused, he left in a huff, reconsidered, returned, found her in a more agreeable humor, and stayed for three days. Once he decided that he was spending too much time "indulging in light chitchat conversation" and declared that he would spend less time with women. Once more his good intentions went awry. He indulged himself with the intimate company of an exciting variety of women until, a dozen years later, he found the lady of his dreams.[64]

As a bachelor in Washington, Thomas lived comfortably. In January 1844, for seven dollars per week, he stayed in a boarding house operated by one Mrs. Mount, a widow whose son Samuel he employed. For most of his stays in Washington, however, he preferred hotels. He found time for recreation. In 1844 he took a boat trip with Duff Green, Secretary of War William Wilkins, and two other men. They sailed down the Potomac River to the Chesapeake Bay on July 21, anchoring overnight and bathing in the bay early the next morning before making the return trip. In the summer of 1845 he joined Benjamin Green for a trip to New York and New England. They visited Niagara Falls and Saratoga Springs. At the springs, Thomas escorted a Miss Moran, "the great belle of Providence," to a ball that was also attended by former North Carolina Governor Edward B. Dudley and his daughter.[65]

A prolonged bachelorhood gave Chief Thomas more freedom to live easily in both the world of the Cherokees and that of his white family and friends. As agent and chief he had helped to persuade the United States government to let his people stay in North Carolina. He had acquired modest financial settlements for them, had added fifty thousand acres to their land holdings, and had nudged them toward a life of sobriety and industry. They owed more to him, and to Yonaguska, than they did to the heroic Tsali. Thomas had also managed to become very successful in business and moderately so in politics. He was both white and Cherokee.

CHAPTER 4

Both White and Cherokee

BY THE TIME THOMAS WAS FORTY, the lives of William Holland Thomas and Wil-Usdi were integrated into a single personality. Among the Indians he was a short white man, their chief and friend, their liaison with and defender against the white world. In return they gave him a surrogate father, a people, a mission, and an economic opportunity. Among the whites he was a fatherless boy who had risen to become a great landowner and entrepreneur, a budding politician, a ladies' man, and something of a character because of his intimate association with the Cherokees. In Washington he was a cultured, well-dressed, learned white man who was also, most peculiarly, an Indian chief with a passion to bring justice to a small group of Cherokees whom few others knew or understood.

Armed with powers of attorney from his Indians, and hopeful that the administration of James K. Polk would render them justice, Thomas passed all of 1846 in Washington. Progress was slow. The president, the attorney general, the Congress, and the Board of Cherokee Commissioners had to study the treaty of 1835 and weigh thousands of claims from Cherokees in Indian territory and in North Carolina. In February, Thomas attempted to explain the tedious negotiations to his people in Quallatown. He included copies of letters that had passed between President Polk and Attorney General John Y. Mason. Mason had advised Polk that an agreement between Thomas and those Cherokees in Quallatown and Buffalo Town permitted those Cherokees to remain in North Carolina. It was Mason's opinion, too, that they were entitled to the $53.33 per capita payment under Article 12 of the Treaty of New Echota, but Mason maintained that Congress should pass a new law authorizing the president to make the payment. In an interview with Polk, Thomas learned that the president concurred with the attorney general. Both the secretary of war and the commissioner of Indian affairs, Thomas reassured his friends, wanted the matter settled. Thus he advised the Indians to remain patient, temperate, honest, and industrious.[1]

Thomas's dream of returning to his native land of "high topped mountains and clear streams" was many months short of reality. The machinery of government worked slowly. The Cherokees were not its major concern on the eve of war with Mexico. Thomas continued to rely upon the help and companionship of Democrats Duff and Benjamin Green. Other white attorneys such as Felix Axley and Preston Starrett and the mixed-blood Johnson K. Rogers, with powers of attorney from other eastern Cherokees, were making similar demands. These men, along with agents from the western Cherokees, were such irritants that the government finally decided to make a new treaty with the Cherokee Nation.[2]

In the treaty of August 1846, Thomas won a major victory. He had worked hard with the congressmen from his state, the Indian Commissioner, and the president. The treaty of 1846 was in part the result of his influence. Under its terms, Thomas's clients were assured that they could remain in North Carolina and be paid the $53.33 per capita fee, with interest, which he had been attempting to collect.[3]

The way was cleared for actual payments after July 29, 1848, when both houses of Congress passed the Indian Appropriation Act. It guaranteed the per capita payment to eastern Cherokees who wished to emigrate, plus 6 percent interest until they did so. John C. Mullay, a clerk in the Indian Office, was appointed to make a census of eligible Indians, and the Treasury Department was instructed to make the interest payments annually. Although Thomas insisted that his Indians were entitled to the entire per capita and the interest without being required to move, he seemed pleased at least to have won the interest payment.[4]

Having returned to North Carolina in late spring, Thomas assisted John Mullay in drawing up his roll. When completed in the summer of 1850, Mullay's roll contained the names of 1,517 Cherokees. Thomas, however, had not waited for the completion of this roll—under which most of the Indian payments were finally made—before he began to file hundreds of claims for individuals who had given him their powers of attorney. By May 1848, the commissioner of Indian affairs had paid a total of $31,578.50, including commission, on 1,229 individual claims. Thomas, who had spent almost five years in Washington at his own expense, felt that justice was finally being done for the eastern Cherokees.[5]

Under the terms of the Indian Appropriation Act of July 29, 1848, Thomas could draw from the Indians' settlement the money due him for fees and owed him as their creditor. Some Indians had revoked his power of attorney; it was about to expire with others; and other attorneys were eager to get the Indian business. Thomas therefore renewed the powers of attorney the Indians had given him. The new documents stated that all powers of attorney to Thomas were irrevocable until all business with the government was completed and Thomas had been compensated for his labor and reimbursed for his credit. Three-fourths of the North Carolina Cherokees gave Thomas their powers of attorney; in most cases the commission to be paid Thomas and the Greens was set at 18 percent of the interest due the Indians, which was 2 percent less than typical. Although Thomas wanted his commissions, he also wanted the Indians to be treated well and fairly. In 1850 Thomas gave a bond to his Quallatown friends for $20,000 to guarantee that they would not be cheated. In 1851 he and the Greens collected $6,910 in fees under the 1848 law. Some of Thomas's Indian clients, however, swindled him out of commissions and debts they owed him.[6]

When the money began to flow, more Indians were eager to get on the roll, and more whites were anxious to become disbursing agents. Accepting powers of attorney from additional Cherokees in 1849 and 1850, Thomas won more and more claims. In 1851, the Indian Office, which had been transferred to the Department of the Interior in 1849, decided to take another census. This one was done by David W. Siler of Macon County, North Carolina. The total number of Indians enrolled was 2,133. The assistant disbursing agent was the wily Johnson K. Rogers, a mixed-blood individual who disliked Thomas and took advantage of his position to denigrate the white chief. Rogers persuaded fifty-five Quallatown Indians to pay him, rather than Thomas, a commission of more than $1,000. Despite complaints and investigations, Rogers's swindle of Thomas went unpunished.[7]

Although Thomas spent less time in Washington after 1848 when he was elected to the North Carolina Senate, he did in the early 1850s make several trips there to file his people's claims. Writing from Washington to his friends at Buffalo Town in March 1851, he reported that

Congress had appropriated the per capita due them under the treaty of 1846 and no doubt would soon pay them, as well, for the property they had lost in 1838. The Valley Indians who squandered their money would be encouraged to emigrate west, he said. Only the Cherokees at Buffalo Town and Quallatown would remain, he predicted, and only if they did not scatter among the white settlements. He advised them "as friends to live in peace with your white neighbors and each other, avoid all kinds of intoxicating drinks, be industrious, and you may ere long be a prosperous and contented people."[8]

In Washington, Thomas wrote a pamphlet addressed to the attorney general, giving a complete history of the rights of the eastern Cherokees who had escaped removal in 1838.[9] He continued to collect and disperse individual claims, the average amount for an individual being $38.28. The total amount Thomas was given to disperse to the Indians in 1850 was $12,122.78; in 1851 it was $26,160.18.[10] In a long letter to the commissioner of Indian affairs, published as a pamphlet in 1853, Thomas again reviewed the history of the eastern Cherokees and his relationship to them, and he reminded the commissioner that the Indians should not be swindled by corrupt government agents such as Johnson K. Rogers. The Indians must have their lands, their money, and honest legal counsel, he said.[11]

Thomas argued that it would be simpler for the Treasury Department to pay the claimants their $53.33 per capita, plus interest, in a lump sum rather than have an agent traipse along difficult mountain paths annually to hand out small interest payments. In January 1855 the federal government finally agreed to make such a payment to all persons listed on the Mullay roll, but only on condition that North Carolina would give them citizenship. Governor Thomas Bragg would recognize the right of the Cherokees to stay, but the legislature, although sympathetic with the Indians, would not grant them citizenship or, on the eve of civil war, yield what it considered a state privilege to the national government. Thus the matter went unresolved until after the Civil War, and Thomas was left with little choice but to accept the cumbersome system already in place. He continued to file individual claims or to get agents working for him, such as James W. Terrell and James Taylor, to do so.[12]

James W. Terrell became Thomas's friend, confidant, business manager, unofficial subchief of the Cherokees, and later principal defender of the integrity of their white chief. A young native North Carolinian with talent, ambition, scruples, and attachment to Thomas, Terrell in 1851 accepted an appointment by the secretary of the treasury, who was yielding to Thomas's influence, as disbursing agent for the Indians. Terrell collected a 5 percent commission for himself, but contrary to instructions from the secretary, he also paid Thomas the commission which Terrel thought the Indians owed him.[13]

In 1852 Terrell, still in his teens, entered into a partnership with Thomas that lasted for Thomas's lifetime. That year, Terrell contracted to operate a tannery at Quallatown. Thomas was to furnish the materials; Terrell was to do the work and market the leather goods. Terrell's initial salary was board, laundry, two hundred dollars annually, and unspecified credit at the store. When Terrell married in 1854 and needed more pay, Thomas raised his salary to three hundred dollars, provided a house for him and his bride, a garden, a pasture, and ten cords of firewood. In addition to the tannery, Terrell assumed responsibility for the store; a small post office in the store; and boot and shoe, blacksmith, and wagon-making shops. When money was too tight for Thomas to pay Terrell as agreed, Terrell continued his duties without complaint. In 1853 Thomas again got him appointed disbursing agent for the Cherokees, a position that was beneficial to both. The Indians came to regard Terrell with much the same affection that they had for Thomas. They called him *Dala:la*, "redheaded woodpecker." Terrell took complete charge of the Lufty Indians during Thomas's frequent absences.[14]

Although James Taylor held an affection for Thomas similar to that of Terrell, Taylor did not enjoy the close business association with the older man. A young mixed-blood friend, Taylor respected Thomas and was particularly attracted to his work for the Indians. He felt close enough to the white chief to name his son, born in 1857, Thomas. Taylor was also someone Thomas could trust. Therefore in the 1850s Thomas often used Taylor as his substitute in Washington.[15]

Thus it was Taylor, not Thomas, who dealt with a new feeble effort at removal in 1856. Believing that the eastern Cherokees would benefit by joining a consolidated tribe in the West and that many of them wanted to go, Taylor supported the idea. Thomas, as he had done in the mid-1840s, also approved the plan, provided that the Indians would volunteer to go. Thomas got Terrell appointed to enroll those who wished to remove. The effort fizzled in 1857 for lack of Indians who wanted to move and for lack of government money to support a new

James W. Terrell in 1874. Courtesy of William E. Bird.

The Wolftown ballplayers, 1888. Photograph by James Mooney. National Anthropological Archives of the Smithsonian Institution.

removal. Thomas, Taylor, and Terrell fell back into their customary roles of petitioning, often successfully, for interest payments due their clients and their descendants under the treaties of 1835 and 1846 and the act of 1848.[16]

Thomas complemented his work as agent and chief of the Oconalufty Indians with an intimate involvement in their culture. Caught between two societies, the Cherokees struggled to maintain their own traditions and to adapt for their own use those ways of the whites that they found beneficial. Thomas often exaggerated their progress in order to impress federal and state officials, but he sincerely steered them toward economic improvement, sobriety, honesty, education, and the Christian religion. Their family and social structures, games, and festivals, however, he left alone. Sometimes he used Indians to entertain visitors to the mountains, and at other times he immersed himself totally in the Cherokee world.

The activity to which Thomas escorted spectators and in which he sometimes participated was the Indians' vigorous and exotic ballplay. Similar to lacrosse, but without clear rules, the game was played by two teams, each of about thirty agile young men. The men went through an elaborate preparation consisting of ritual bathing and allowing bloodletting scratches to be made on their upper arms and chests. Unencumbered by clothing of any kind except waistbands worn occasionally by one team to distinguish themselves from their opponents, the athletic young men were as eager to impress the young women as they were to win the game. The female spectators often gave a piece of cloth or some other memento to a favorite player. A game master made sure that the field was a level plain, free of sticks and stones, and that the two goals were six hundred yards apart. Rules against betting all of one's property or breaking the arms, legs, and heads of the other players usually were enforced.

To the uninitiated the ballplay seemed to be a noisy free-for-all in which the shrill shouting, dangerously waving sticks, violent body contact, and vicious wrestling might cause permanent damage or death to the weak or careless. To the Indians it was sport and ritual. Each player had two sticks, each with a braided pouch at the end. The game master delivered a long speech, tossed a ball high into the air at midfield, and jumped out of the way as each player frantically attempted to catch the ball in the pouch of one of his sticks and carry it beyond the goal of the opposing team. When a team scored twelve times, the game ended. Often the spectators would run onto the field, slowing the game. Usually the contest lasted about two hours, at the end of which the players would rush to the river for a chilly bath, which was a purification rite. Returning to the field in proper dress, the victors received recognition and prizes for their valor. Thomas, stripped to the buff, sometimes participated in the game himself; more often he staged a ballplay as entertainment for some visiting dignitary.[17]

The Cherokee women were spectators at the ballplay, but they participated in the Green Corn Ceremony. When the tender corn first appeared, women, in what amounted to a religious festival, presented it for sacrifice to the fire. Forty or fifty days later, when the corn was ripe, the Cherokees held a ritual dance in celebration of fertility and the cycle of life. First, the men circled the dance ground and, on a signal, discharged guns, signifying thunder, while the women performed a Corn Meal Dance. There was a feast in which everyone participated. Just before sundown, men and women danced in separate groups, then came together to do the Trail-Making, Booger, Eagle, and Bear dances. The Corn Dance came just before dawn, followed by the Running Dance, after which the celebrants were supposed to run around the mountain and return to their homes. The Green Corn Dance was religious and social as well as entertaining.[18] Thomas often went as observer and participant, but he always seemed to enjoy the ballplay more.

Thomas respected the social and family structure of the Cherokees as much as he did their festivals and games. Men hunted, went to war, met in council, and participated in the ballplay. Women cleared and worked the small fields, collected firewood, cooked, sewed, and made baskets and pottery. As their society became more like that of the whites, their gender roles changed. By the 1830s men were beginning to do more of the farm work and to establish cultural dominance. In fact, Yonaguska's "adoption" of Thomas may have been evidence of a shift from a matrilineal to a patrilineal society. Women and men enjoyed considerable sexual freedom. Premarital sex, divorce, polygamy, venereal disease, and, less commonly, adultery, all existed among them. Sexual relations between unmarried Indian women and their white chief would have been acceptable to the Cherokee community.[19]

The facets of Cherokee culture that Thomas did try to change were alcohol consumption, education, religion, and poverty. He recommended temperance, although he contradicted himself by sometimes selling liquor to the Indians. He attempted to establish schools and occasionally hired an itinerant teacher for a short while, but most of these efforts had little success. He gave land for a Methodist church and imported Bibles and hymnals written in the Cherokee language, but the best he could derive from a Cherokee preacher was a synthesis of Christianity and conjuring, of faith and festival. Whenever white religion challenged Cherokee tradition, the tradition was likely to move a bit deeper into the mountains and there prevail. The membership rolls of the Echota Methodist Church and of its mission in Soco Valley were short; next to the names of several of the members is the notation, "turned out." Thomas therefore attempted to teach ethics unrelated to religion: he discouraged petty theft, murder, adherence to the ancient law of blood, and the imitation of evil white people. Although these troubles did not greatly beset the Indians, individual experiences of all of them did sometimes challenge his wisdom as their friend and chief.[20]

Thomas realized that, if he could help lift the Oconaluftee Indians out of poverty, many of their other adversities would diminish; in Washington and in North Carolina he labored to improve their economic status. A typical Cherokee family lived in a small one-room log cabin with a dirt floor, no windows, and a chimney made of sticks and clay. The family members engaged in subsistence farming, owned some livestock, hunted, and made most of their own clothes and utensils. Other necessities they purchased on credit from Thomas's stores.[21]

On January 10, 1845, at Thomas's request, the state legislature authorized the Quallatown and Cheoah Indians, with Thomas as their president, to organize the Cherokee Company. Ostensibly formed for the purpose of producing sugar and silk, which the state was encouraging by an act of 1836, the company hoped to do much more. The preamble to its charter elaborated on the Indians' legal rights and seemed to indicate that the organization would function mostly as a holding company for the land Thomas had purchased for them. When Governor William A. Graham questioned whether the company intended actually to produce silk and sugar, Thomas modified its bylaws sufficiently to get the governor's assent in 1847. The company produced no sugar or silk, although in the spring of 1848 Thomas did procure "a considerable quantity" of Chinese mulberry saplings for distribution to the one-hundred-acre leaseholders of company lands. Thomas was always elected president and remained the legal owner of the land.

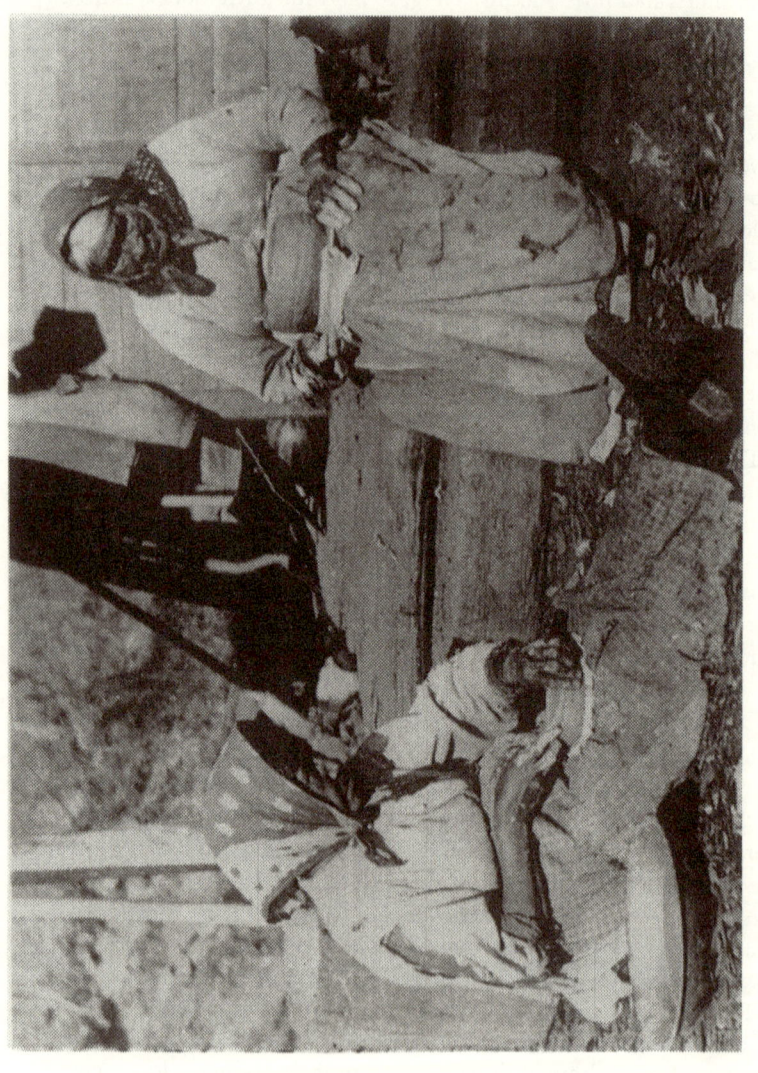

Women making pottery, 1888. Woman on right is the daughter of Yonaguska. Photograph by James Mooney. National Anthropological Archives of the Smithsonian Institution.

The company was nothing more than a valiant, but unsuccessful, attempt by the white chief to transfer ownership of the land to the Indians.[22]

If he could not guarantee their ownership of the land, Thomas at least attempted to guard their use of it. Timber was an important cash crop; the thievery of it had caused friction among Cherokees in the West. Thomas wanted that timber belonging to his friends in the Qualla Boundary protected. In 1850 he published a notice prohibiting the illegal cutting of timber on their lands: "All persons are forewarned from entering the Indian Boundary for the purpose of cutting saw logs — or wood of any kind — as the law will be put in force against those offending. The Indians claim the right of pay for timber cut — and it must be done."[23]

Thomas mixed his roles as Indian chief and capitalist with a career in state politics. Although he was a relative of Zachary Taylor's and an admirer of Henry Clay, he was a Democrat with views similar to those of John C. Calhoun. Like most western North Carolinians, he favored internal improvements and increased representation for their region in the state legislature. Thomas's own commercial ties were often directly with Calhoun's South Carolina, particularly the port of Charleston. Although North Carolina was dominated by Whigs in the late 1840s, many of them diverged from the national Whigs. Thomas sometimes agreed with those Whigs who favored social reforms, but he was not tempted to join that more popular party.[24]

Thomas's interest in politics dated from 1840, when he had intended to run for the state senate as a Democrat but was prevented by a train accident from returning home in time to do so. Probably because the Whigs were so strong in his district, he sat out the election of 1842, and he was in Washington working for the Indians in 1844 and 1846. In 1846, however, he was serious enough about his possible candidacy to set forth his views to the people of the Fiftieth Senatorial District. That district, 60 miles wide and 140 miles long, included Haywood, Macon, Cherokee, and, after 1850, Jackson, counties — all of which had been carved out of the large Haywood County as the population had increased.

In 1846 Thomas stated his views. He wanted the state to build a railroad from the capital in Raleigh across western North Carolina, through his property, to the Georgia state line. As the owner of thirty-four thousand acres he had purchased from the Cherokee Cession

Typical Cherokee cabin in the 1880s. Note ballplay sticks on front of cabin. Photograph by James Mooney. National Anthropological Archives of the Smithsonian Institution.

lands in North Carolina in 1835, Thomas was particularly sympathetic with the plight of others who had bought similar lands. Since many of them had been hard hit by the depression of 1837, Thomas wanted the state to be lenient in collecting its payments. Although his own lands were not in danger of foreclosure, those of many of his neighbors were. One of the strongest pitches he could make to constituents in his district was a promise to get the state to build a railroad through their area.

Thomas was also interested in the welfare of his district and in general reforms for the state. He called for a penitentiary in which criminals would support themselves by their own labor, a law to increase the amount of property that could be sold for debt to fifty acres or a town lot, the creation of a new county out of parts of Haywood and Macon counties, and a pay limit of eight dollars per day for state legislators. He strongly defended state rights. He believed that a good system of public education was essential if citizens were to understand and exercise their privileges under a republican government. Such a system, he said, would enable farmers, mechanics, and merchants to be represented in the legislature, thus removing the business of forming laws from the lawyers and making legislation more practical and relevant to all of the population.[25]

Thomas helped to develop a constructive program for the Democratic Party in his state. For several years after the Whig Party came into existence, the Democrats had no such program. They had been content merely to condemn the Whigs, to advocate low taxes and economy in government, and to limit the functions of the state to protecting the lives and property of its white citizens. By advocating reforms, Thomas was borrowing some ideas from the Whigs, particularly their interest in internal improvements and public schools.[26] He was also making the Democratic party more competitive with its Whig rival, especially in the western part of the state.

During his 1848 campaign for the state senate, Thomas spoke in favor of abolishing the fifty-acre requirement to vote for state senators. Free suffrage was popular in Thomas's native area, and it was the major plank in the gubernatorial campaign of Democrat David S. Reid. Although Thomas preferred not to discuss national politics during his local campaign, when pinned down he supported the Democratic administration of James K. Polk, the reestablishment of the subtreasury plan, the tariff of 1846, the Mexican War, and distribution among the

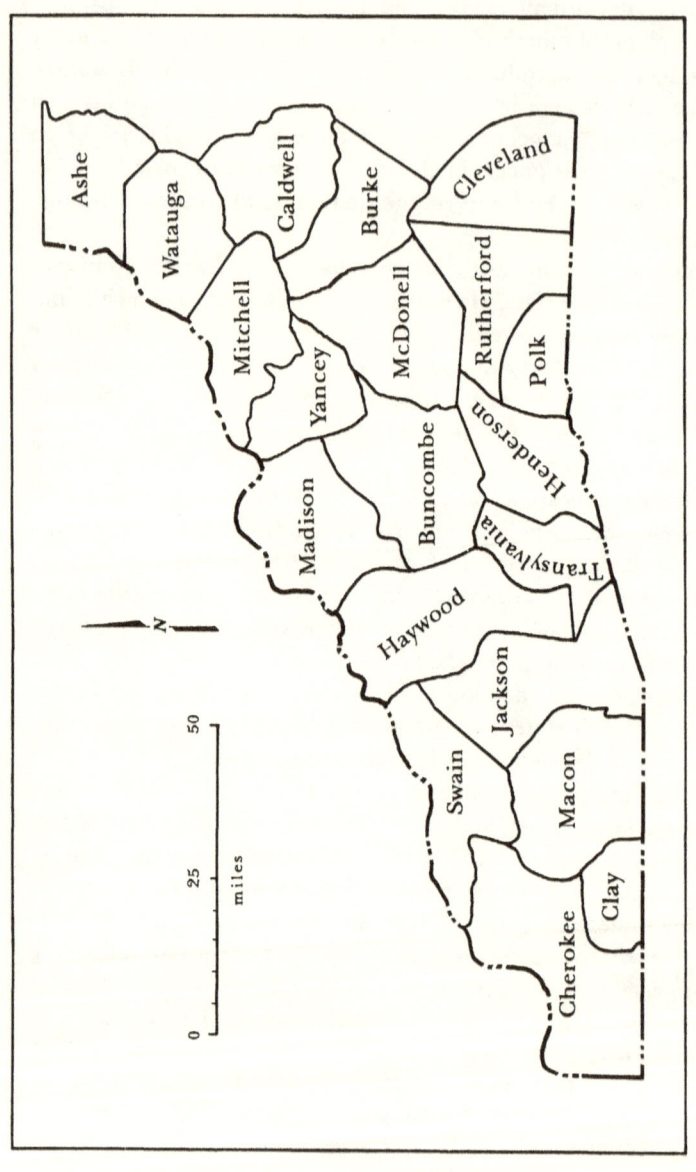

Western North Carolina counties in 1872. Based on a map in John L. Cheney, Jr., ed., *North Carolina Government, 1585–1974: A Narrative and Statistical History* (Raleigh: North Carolina Dept. of the Secretary of State, 1975), 694. Map by The University of Tennessee Cartographic Services Laboratory.

states of monies collected from the sale of national public lands. Thomas defeated the Whig incumbent Michael Francis by a large majority to become the first Democrat elected from his district in eight years. The Democrats held a slight majority in both houses, but Charles Manly, the Whig candidate for governor, defeated David S. Reid in a very close race. Thomas was reelected to the state senate every two years through 1860, after which he left politics to fight in the Civil War.[27]

Meeting in Asheville in August, the Democrats named Thomas to be a presidential elector. Thomas declined, arguing that he did not have the time and that he could not vote for the Democratic candidate Lewis Cass because, he said, Cass would not be likely to "recollect privates in the democratic ranks, like myself." Furthermore, he commented that he would not shed any tears if his cousin, Whig candidate Zachary Taylor, were elected. Four years later, however, when Thomas was again named a presidential elector, he voted for Democrat Franklin Pierce.[28]

Upon his arrival in Raleigh in the fall of 1848, Thomas began a fourteen-year career in state politics. The sketchy journals, limited newspaper coverage, and scarce personal correspondence make it difficult to re-create a comprehensive account of that career, but there are some clues to how he thought, debated, and voted. He was loyal to the people who had elected him, worked for the Indians, and looked for opportunities to enhance his own financial interests.

In a handwritten, undated booklet of political notes made while he was in Raleigh, Thoms revealed how he blended politics with his personality. The fact that he was an orphan still weighed heavily upon the new state senator; he sought heroes among other orphans. He scribbled in his political notes: "General [George] Washington was an orphan boy. [H]is father Augustus died when he was ten years old." Then, Thomas added, Washington once said that if forced into public life, he would "act with a sole reference to justice and the public good." On the next page, Thomas noted that, likewise, "Thomas Jefferson was left an orphan boy by the death of his father at the age of 14. His father Peter was from Wales."[29]

If Thomas wished to emulate the careers of Washington and Jefferson, he did not say. Yet, after listing the internal improvements in his state, he noted that "General Washington was in favor of internal improvements by the state of Virginia." With regard to other matters, Thomas approved a plan to carve a new county out of Haywood and

Macon, change the state constitution to extend the suffrage, limit the paid days a legislator could serve to thirty per session, and provide free schools. When the Mexican War began, he thought the United States was justified in fighting it. "The Mexican Army . . . murdered our citizens," he wrote. The war was just and honorable, "and I hope for the good name of my country that such will be the judgment of all Christendom." He felt strongly that the "Duty of members of the State Legislature is to confine their acts strictly to the business authorized by their appointments, not to step beyond that to meddle with the duties of members of Congress."[30]

When Thomas listened to the legislature in its 1848–49 session debate the question of establishing an asylum for the insane, he could not have known what significance that legislation would have for his later life. Dorothea Lynde Dix, a humanitarian reformer from Massachusetts, spent ten weeks in North Carolina in the fall of 1848 visiting jails, private homes, and homes for paupers, trying to determine how many insane people lived in the state and what kind of care they received. As a result, she prepared a forty-eight-page memorial to the state legislature, saying that she "was the voice of the maniac whose piercing cries" needed to be heard. The Whigs favored such an institution, but the Democrats feared the cost. Enough Democrats were moved by Dorothea Dix's pleas that the bill passed on January 16, 1849.

How Thomas voted is not recorded, but 90.5 percent of the Whigs voted yea and 86.4 percent of the Democrats voted nay. Named for the Massachusetts humanitarian, the hospital, located on a scenic hill near Raleigh, accepted its first patients in 1856. Ten years later, Thomas was to be admitted to the hospital which he probably helped to found. Ironically, his own political party opposed it.[31]

The other political matters with which Thomas concerned himself were less ironic than the asylum bill, but they reveal his curiosity about the major issues of his day. In Washington during the debate over the Compromise of 1850, Thomas heard the speeches of Henry Clay, Daniel Webster, and John C. Calhoun. The compromise, largely written by Clay, was endorsed by both Webster and Calhoun. It authorized the admission of California to the Union as a free state, the organization of the remainder of the Mexican Cession territory without provisions for or against slavery, the compensation of Texas for her claim to part of the Santa Fe territory, the abolition of the slave trade in the District of Columbia, and a new and effective fugitive slave law. Calhoun, who was extremely ill and tragically caught up in the defense of slavery even though most of the Christian world was abandoning it, still wanted to save the Union and guarantee the rights of the South as a minority in it. A follower of Calhoun, Thomas recorded that he listened "with much attention."[32] Back in the North Carolina Senate he said that, while he feared Calhoun was right in maintaining that the North would violate the compromise, he thought it should nevertheless be given a fair trial. An increasing number of Southern fire-eaters declared that the time had come to dissolve the Union, but Thomas did not agree with them. He voted against secession resolutions introduced in the state senate by William B. Shepherd on November 23, 1850.[33]

Expressing himself in the friendly Democratic *Raleigh Standard* of February 5, 1851, Thomas explained that he had voted against Shepherd's secession resolutions because all parties to the Compromise of 1850 had agreed to it. North Carolina would be better served by supporting the Compromise of 1850 and the Constitution of the United States, he said. Thomas reminded the senate that he represented a section of the state "where slave labor yields but small profits," but that his constituents would always defend the interests of any portion of the state. He hoped that it would not happen, but if North Carolina were ever forced to fight to maintain "civil and religious liberty," then he favored pledging "our *lives, fortunes,* and *sacred honor*" to defend her, if necessary fighting "the last battles in the Mountain passes of my native portion of the State."

Thomas was more interested in internal improvements than in the dissolution of the Union. In December 1850, he founded and became president of the Tennessee River Railroad Company. When the state legislature incorporated it two months later, it had capital stock of one million dollars and planned to construct a line from the intersection of the Tennessee state boundary and the Little Tennessee River to the point where the same river crossed the Georgia state boundary. Although the Whigs favored such a railroad, and Thomas feared they would use it as a means to elect the next governor, Thomas did not let partisan rivalry stop him from taking a stand for it.[34]

The construction and operation of railroads in the western part of his state was Thomas's principal new business interest in the 1850s. The Tennessee River and the Western North Carolina railroads were the two lines in which Thomas took the greatest interest. Through his efforts South Carolina, Georgia, and Tennessee all chartered lines to connect the Tennessee River Railroad. In 1852 Tennessee chartered the Knoxville and Charleston line; Georgia chartered the Blue Ridge Railroad; and South Carolina extended the latter from its terminus in Anderson, South Carolina, through Greenville to Columbia.[35]

After the legislature adjourned on December 27, 1852, Thomas set out for Washington, where he subscribed 1.2 million dollars worth of stock in his Tennessee River Railroad Company. The next spring he went to New York City to consult with Anson and Eli T. Bangs about their building a line from Anderson, South Carolina, to Knoxville, Tennessee. The Bangs brothers traveled by boat with Thomas to Charleston where they met Henry Gourdin, president of the Blue Ridge Railroad. On the night of May 30, 1853, the Charleston Chamber of Commerce lavishly entertained Gourdin, Thomas, and the New Yorkers. Gourdin contracted with the Bangses to build the line.[36]

After spending several days examining the site, the Bangses returned to Charleston, where Thomas had remained basking in the praise of Governor John L. Manning, Gourdin, and H. W. Conner, the president of the South Carolina Railroad Company. Thomas also hoped to make a profit from construction of the railroad. Bangs and Company contracted with him to furnish them materials for one section of the road at the rate of three cents per linear foot for mudsills and twenty cents each for crossties. One fourth of this money was to be paid in stock in the Blue Ridge Railroad; any other supplies Thomas acquired for them he would deliver at 10 percent commission, one half of which was to be paid in stock.[37]

Thomas returned to his native mountains, where he made speeches soliciting public support, accompanied engineers to construction sites, and raised money. South Carolina and Tennessee promised state aid, and some counties along the route offered modest assistance. Tennessee's aid was in the form of a promised loan to purchase rails after the completion of the roadbed. South Carolina provided a guarantee of the company's bonds in the amount of $1,250,000. Both North Carolina and Georgia declined to give assistance.[38]

The four companies formally merged into the Blue Ridge Railroad Company of South Carolina.[39] The proposed line, about 195 miles long, extended from Anderson, South Carolina, through Rabun Gap in northeastern Georgia, along the Little Tennessee River in Macon County, North Carolina, to Knoxville, Tennessee. The first half of the route lay through rough country. The survey called for thirteen tunnels, including one through Stump House Mountain in northwestern South Carolina that would be 5,800 feet long. In November 1853, Anson Bangs and Company started construction.[40]

The Bangs brothers, who seemed more interested in getting Thomas to help them acquire mortgage money than undertaking the difficult task of construction, soon abandoned their southern client. In 1854 they sold their interest in the firm to their partners, and the Directors of the Blue Ridge Railroad cancelled the contract with them on April 1, 1856. State aid from Tennessee and South Carolina dried up, and the bankrupt railroad was forced to stop construction. None of the tunnels and bridges had been completed, and only fifteen miles of track had been laid. A dream that Thomas had pursued for ten years evaporated.[41]

Thomas's hope for a railroad in the western part of his state, and a link with the west coast of the United States, now rested exclusively with the revival of the Western North Carolina Railroad. Chartered by the state legislature in 1852, it was supposed to run from Salisbury, North Carolina, across the Blue Ridge Mountains to some point on the French Broad River to be determined later. Nevertheless, when the state senate in its 1854-55 session voted on a bill to extend the line, Thomas was in a quandary. Uncharacteristically he voted against the bill because he suspected Democrats Zebulon Vance and David Coleman were scheming to have the line swing north through Madison County. Such a route would take it far away from Thomas's land and that of his constituents, thus weakening him politically. The bill to extend the railroad passed in spite of Thomas's negative vote. Vance, refusing to forgive Thomas for not supporting the extension bill, became his powerful enemy.[42] The General Assembly approved the route of the railroad — soon completed as far west as Morganton — to Asheville, but it postponed making a decision on the volatile question of where it would be built west of Asheville to the Tennessee line.

When the nation debated the Kansas-Nebraska Act in 1854 and 1855, Thomas was not greatly interested in the fate of Kansas, Nebraska, or slavery, but he was excited about the construction of a transcontinental railroad. Whether Kansas would someday be a slave state and Nebraska free or whether the railroad would be built via a northern or southern route did not seem to concern him, provided that the railroad be built. He wrote former Senator Thomas Hart Benton for information about the Pacific Railroad and suggested that it should be "central to the whole union," with trunk lines feeding into Tennessee and Kentucky. He could just envision Waynesville, North Carolina, he said, connected by rail with San Diego, California.[43]

In addition to the time he spent working for railroad development from 1846 through 1856, Thomas continued extensive speculation in land. In addition to the 55,000 acres he acquired for the Indians, he purchased many thousands more for himself. In 1847 he bought 1,400 acres, formerly owned by the Cherokees in Georgia, from Dr. Charles M. Hitchcock of the United States Army.[44] In 1850 he filed bonds of unknown value for 45,686 acres of state lands in western North Carolina. Dozens of extant deeds in the early 1850s reveal that he bought many tracts ranging from 50 to 640 acres.[45] In 1853 he bought, in 640-acre tracts for ten cents per acre, land extending from the Tennessee River at the state line to Macon County.[46] In 1854, he acquired 20,000 acres in Cherokee County for only five hundred dollars.[47] It was land made cheap by geography and geology.

Often Thomas resold his land at a profit. Early in 1855 he sold Dickagiskah 100 acres for an unknown price and gave him three years to pay.[48] Later that year he contracted with Mercer Fain and others to sell them 10,000 acres at the head of Scott's Creek for $10,000, payable in three annual installments with interest. In 1856 he acquired two grants in Jackson County, amounting to 25,486 acres, for which he paid the state $1,012. Four months later he sold James R. Love 30,000 acres for $7,300 in the same county.[49] James Terrell said that in 1856 Stekoa Fields and the 1,000 adjoining acres were valued at $5,000; the entire value of Thomas's land, including Stekoa Fields, in Jackson County that year was $28,075.[50] Incomplete records make it impossible to determine how many acres Thomas owned or how much they were worth. Certainly he held for himself, in addition to what he held for the Indians, more than 150,000 acres. Some of those acres were suitable for grazing, farming, or growing valuable timber, but many more were in terrain too rough to be of much value.

Since Thomas was in Raleigh, Washington, or elsewhere during much of the 1850s, the work of his stores was carried on by his clerks, James Terrell, George W. Hayes, M. L. Brittain, and George T. Mason. In their communications with Thomas they tended to mix business, news, and personal requests. Thomas trusted them enough that he did not, or could not, maintain strict supervision of their work.[51]

When Thomas himself was in western North Carolina, he kept busy with such diverse activities as serving as a justice of the peace in Haywood County, building local turnpikes, buying and selling a few slaves, and leasing land for an iron works.[52] None of these activities was either remunerative or a major interest.

The extent of Thomas's wealth remains elusive. As a large landowner with stores and other business enterprises, he was judged by his neighbors to be very wealthy. Thomas operated on credit, and the records of the 1840s and 1850s are filled with judgments brought against him for nonpayment of debts. The widow of J. W. King sued him for her share of the business at Murphy. Creditors from Georgia to Charleston to Philadelphia demanded payment. Occasionally some of his lands were sold at sheriff's sales, but none of these sales seems to have diminished his possessions in any significant way. His enemies accused him of staying in Washington to avoid paying his debts, an accusation he vigorously denied.[53] Were it possible to value his vast real estate holdings and to tally his assets and debits, the odds seem favorable that he operated at a profit. The odds seem equally as great that Thomas himself did not know exactly where he stood.

Despite time devoted to the development of his frontier investments, his work for the Indians, and service in the state senate, Thomas had an interesting and full personal life. In Washington he sometimes drank a little champagne, bought some good clothes and a fine foreign watch, and occasionally attended the theatre. Wherever he went, he kept an eye out for an attractive young woman. He smoked cigars. He read his Bible and went to church. Fishing was his favorite sport. In North Carolina he circulated among the people who called him their chief. He sometimes suffered with colds, diarrhea, and other illnesses, but he treated himself with Indian remedies and regained his health.[54] He was fifty-one and still a bachelor.

CHAPTER 5

The Chief in Love

WHEN CHIEF WILLIAM HOLLAND THOMAS MET and courted the beautiful young Sarah Love, he found the woman he wanted to marry. A member of a prominent family, and with impeccable manners and virtue, she was a lovely young woman with dark eyes and straight, black hair. Her family called her "Sallie," and she became the white chief's "dearest Sallie." He thought that he had found "one young enough for a bachellor to love," and he hoped "old enough to love a bachellor." One romantic winter evening early in 1857 in her father's large house at White Sulphur Springs, North Carolina, as they listened to "sweet" music, Sallie and Willie declared their love for each other.[1]

At fifty-one, Thomas proposed matrimony to Sarah Jane Burney Love, age twenty-four. She was the beautiful daughter of his onetime business partner and longtime friend, James Robert Love I. Sarah's mother, Maria Williamson Coman Love, had died in 1844 at thirty-nine. At the time Sarah was born on October 26, 1832, Thomas was in business with her father. Although their partnership soon dissolved, Thomas and Love occasionally had business dealings with each other, and they remained friends. In acquired land and wealth, Sarah's father ranked about equal with her would-be bridegroom. Thomas had watched her grow up, and after she reached her early twenties he developed a romantic interest in her.[2]

After their engagement Thomas journeyed to White Sulphur Springs, a mile from Waynesville, more and more frequently. In Sarah's presence he was polite, well dressed, and neatly groomed, although he did warn her that when returning from long trips by stage or horseback he could be dirty and disheveled. His hair, still dark and wavy, hung about midway to his shoulders. He was trim and energetic. Apparently Sarah did not object to his cigars, his age, or his past.

Fearing that Sarah's friends would tease her about being courted by an old bachelor, Thomas attempted to keep his visits secret. Sometimes he found it hard to believe that she could be interested in such an old man, but her blushes, glances, and many attentions bespoke her feelings. She rose early in the mornings to see him off when it was time for him to leave, and she was always near him at mealtime. He asked if she could still care for him when he was old and gray. She said that she could. When he proposed, and she accepted, he was filled with tender affection that he poured out to her in person and by letter.[3]

News of the courtship leaked out, however, for in February, Thomas's bachelor friend, Thomas L. Clingman, wrote him: "As to the dark eyed girl do not hesitate to go totally forward. I hope to get to your wedding soon."[4]

Even during his courtship, Thomas did not forget his Indian friends. In one of the first letters he wrote to his fiancée after their engagement, he told her that the Indians were a "proper field" in which she could practice some of her "Christian virtues." He hoped that she would write short Christian homilies for a newspaper he planned to establish at Quallatown. Such writings, he said, would do much good for "the small remnant of people who are now passing away, . . . and whose hearts were inclined to protect an orphan boy when he went among them." He assumed that her friends would be his and his also hers, "even the poor oppressed Indians." He concluded that he looked "forward to the time when we will ride through their settlement on our way to our mountain home when you will witness the affection of those people for their 'so called chief.'"[5]

The Love family had no objection to the impending marriage between Sallie and Thomas. In that family there were eight children, four boys and four girls. Sallie was the oldest of the girls. Because of their father's wealth, influence, and ambition, these children enjoyed numerous advantages. For their time and place, they received good educations. Their father employed a German master, Charles Loehr, to teach them music. Their mother, the daughter of Colonel James Coman of Raleigh, was a lady of genteel upbringing with a good education. Sallie's father was the son of Mary Ann Dillard Love and Robert Love, who were among the earliest and most successful settlers in western North Carolina. Through the Love family there ran a strain of gentility and family cohesiveness that was particularly attractive to the rugged frontier businessman who thought of himself as an orphan.[6]

Sallie and Willie were married on June 30, 1857, at the home of the bride's father in Haywood County. The Reverend Banister Turner officiated.[7]

The marriage of William Holland Thomas to Sarah Love attracted considerable attention. The groom, in his fifty-second year, was a state senator, a prominent businessman, a large landowner, the white chief of a Cherokee remnant, and, some had thought, a confirmed bachelor. The lovely and accomplished twenty-five-year-old bride was the daughter of one of the wealthiest and most respected families in the western part of the state. Whatever the cynics and jesters may have said, the subsequent drama of their lives together revealed that the marriage of Sallie and Willie was a true love match.

Nevertheless a Raleigh newspaper could not resist reporting the Thomas-Love nuptials in a humorous vein. Under the headline "News from the Mountains," the *Standard* reported on August 19:

> The attention of all bachelordom is particularly directed to the following deeply interesting item.—There is no such word as fail in the vocabulary of the patient and persevering:
> Married, at the residence of the bride's father, in Haywood county, on the 30th of June last, by Rev. Banister Turner, William H. Thomas, Esq., Senator from Jackson, to Miss Sarah Jane, daughter of James R. Love, Esq.

Thomas's bachelor friend Henry Gourdin of Charleston, with whom he had spent many hours discussing railroads, wrote that he was reminded of the proverb, "Old Birds are not to be caught with Chaff." Therefore he felt certain that Thomas had found himself a fine young lady. Yet he chided Thomas for giving no warning that he was about to take his leave from the "fraternity of old bachelors." Perhaps, Gourdin said, Thomas decided to take "french leave," thus avoiding the envy that his "happy and cheery luck" would stir in the hearts of those bachelors left behind.[8]

After the wedding, Thomas and his bride went to Stekoa Fields to live with his mother. The boy and girl Thomas had adopted had already grown up and left although Andrew Patton may still have lived there. How well Sarah got along living under the same roof in a relatively small house with her mother-in-law is unknown. Temperance Thomas was eighty-two when her son married, but she was still healthy and vigorous. Any friction that may have arisen between them went unrecorded. Sarah called her "Mother," just as her husband did, and

Sarah Love Thomas in 1867, ten years after her marriage to William Holland Thomas. The original portrait, 29 x 36 inches, was painted by W.M. Browning. Photographed by Susan Amos. Courtesy of Sara T. Thomas.

perhaps during his long absences from home the two women were comforting companions for each other.⁹

Accompanying Sarah to Stekoa was her personal slave, Caroline, about twenty-four. There is no mention of a dowry, but Sarah did make frequent visits back to the home of her father and siblings, and they continued to care for and visit her. When James Love died, in 1863, he left Sallie four more slaves and their children, two thousand dollars in cash, and 213 acres.¹⁰

As a young bride Sallie Thomas scarcely had time to be idle or discontented with her new life. She had been warned that her husband would often be away from home. He spent several months in Raleigh each even-numbered year as a state senator, periodically traveled to Washington to promote the welfare of the Lufty Indians, and frequently was on the road tending his business. Sarah took a major role in operating the house and overseeing his local business interests. Since her mother had died when she was only thirteen, and she was the oldest girl in her family, she probably had taken the lead in managing the household of her father. Also, she had seen her father and her brothers operate businesses identical to those of her husband. She was willing to work hard, and she was intelligent and practical.

Sallie was lonely and missed her Willie when he was away. She once wrote him in Washington that she imagined the nation's capital "to be at the fartherest extremity of the Union" and yearned for his return home. Her practical nature also revealed itself. "Above all things try and arrange your affairs so you can get out of debt," she wrote him at Raleigh in 1858, "for untill then you cannot get to remain at home." She apologized for annoying him about something she knew he was "*exerting every nerve to accomplish,*" but she did it, she said, because she knew he would "have no enjoyment" until he was "free from embarrassments." A week later she wrote that she hoped he would soon return home from Raleigh, because she found "no pleasure in being separated from a *kind* and *affectionate* Husband *so long.*"¹¹

Thomas seems to have disliked the enforced separations just as much as Sallie did. Three months after their marriage, he went to Washington to look after the claims of the North Carolina Cherokees. The three months he spent there seemed longer than the three years he had stayed there earlier. Having a wife at home to correspond with, he wrote her, was a "great protection against even the appearance of evil." He saw his old friends, but mostly he passed his time working for the Indians.[12]

In Washington, Willie bought Sallie a piano. He told her that he would convert a debt he was collecting into some kind of musical instrument "to keep you company at any time when I am absent, and to amuse me and my friends when they come to see me." He shipped the piano and other gifts by boat and rail to Athens, Georgia, where they were picked up by wagons Sarah sent for them. He also sent her sheet music, including Stephen Foster's "Willie, We Have Missed You."[13] In later years, listening to her play the piano for him became one of his favorite and most relaxing pastimes.

Thomas finally departed from Washington on the morning of March 8, 1858, taking six days to get home. At Baltimore he set sail on the steamer *North Carolina*. Seasick all night, he was relieved to disembark at Norfolk, Virginia, the next day. He crossed the Elizabeth River, then took the railroad from Portsmouth, Virginia, to Raleigh, where he visited with Governor Thomas Bragg for a few minutes. He hastened on to Charlotte, traveling at night, perhaps by rail. The next day he traveled in "an open box with the mail" to Asheville, where he spent the night with his brother-in-law, Dr. W. L. Hilliard. The next day, on back of a decrepit horse, he reached the home of his father-in-law, near Waynesville. He finally reached home and his beloved Sarah on March 14.[14]

Nine months later, on December 16, 1858, Sallie gave birth to their first child. He was born in the home of his grandfather at White Sulphur Springs. His proud parents named him William Holland Thomas, Jr. Thomas was in Raleigh serving in the General Assembly at the time of his son's birth.

Two weeks before delivering, Sarah wrote her husband that she wished so much he could have been with her that winter and hoped he would write to her at least twice every week. She shared with him the daily events of her life. She wrote that her father's health was improving and that he was "rising early, taking exercise, and but little medicine." As for herself, she had "a good many little ailments." Referring to her imminent delivery, she said, "Coming events cast their shadow before." She hoped that never again would her husband be away from her. "Nothing new or interesting has taken place since you left," she said. Her sister "Jo" Branner and "Mr. Branner" would be with them for Christmas. She reminded Thomas that it revived her "spirits particularly" to hear of his health and success. "Yours untill death, *Sallie*," she concluded.¹⁵

When his namesake was two weeks old, Thomas was still in Raleigh. Writing to his "Dear Sarah" early in January 1859, he explained that he was working on legislation to clear the way for the building of the Blue Ridge Railroad. When that line was completed, he wrote, he assumed that a free pass for life would be given to "your Willie and Junr, as well as the wife of the former and mother of the latter." He hoped that if she did not have an elegant carriage drawn by horses that she would "at least have a fine car with an iron horse to pull it which your Willie had a hand in causing to be constructed," and that that railroad car would at all times be "ready for your accommodation and the little company which you have always desired so much to go with you." He added that he was pleased for her to have "the little company," but he had "always feared the consequences upon your delicate constitution." He was relieved that she had endured the pregnancy and had delivered the baby in good health. He reminded her that proper exercise was essential to her well-being.

Perhaps thinking that he was rather old to be fathering a child, and maybe a bit fearful of being displaced in Sallie's affection, Thomas reminded his beloved wife that his spirit hovered above the "Little cottage" in which "was sleeping my own 'dear Sarah' *who had promised 'tho time should whiten the locks, and bedim the eyes of her Willie she would still love him, still cling to him, still be to him the warm hearted and affectionate Sarah, should fortune and all the world beside desert* him." He suffered "trials and anxiety" by being absent at "a time above all others" he should have been with her. He urged her to take good care "not only of yourself but also of your little Indian chief," and to pay his respects to her father and "the family blacks."¹⁶

Sallie and Willie intended for their "little Indian chief," or "Junaluska" as his father sometimes called him, to be their only child. Nevertheless, exactly two years later, on December 16, 1860, Sallie gave birth to a second son, James Robert. On October 3, 1862, their last child, a daughter named Sallie Love Thomas, was born. The old chief was fifty-eight at the time of his daughter's birth.¹⁷

The letters that passed between Sallie and Willie in 1858 and 1859 reveal a deepening of their love and increased dissatisfaction over their separations. "Fortunate for me," he wrote her in 1859 when he was struggling to pay his debts, "I married a woman who was capable of those exalted sentiments that serve as an anchor to my soul in the days of trial." Shortly before his marriage, Thomas had ceased to attend church because of his disillusionment with Protestant clergymen. In fact, before their wedding, he and Sarah had agreed to disagree on the subject of religion, but the example of his pious Methodist wife, he wrote her in 1859, had led him back into the Methodist fold.[18]

Sarah bore up without complaint under the burden of her husband's debts and absences. Her letters were full of tenderness, news of the family, business, good cheer, and even empathy for her husband's image of himself as an orphan. On November 2, 1859, she wrote him: "I trust that same Providence that took care of the little orphan boy when he slept alone on the mountain side, and watched over him during the many dangers of his varied life will still protect and watch over in mercy and bring him home to his dear wife." She reported that "Mother's health is good—mine was never better." She also urged that in his next letter he include a message for his mother. "She might think you were forgetting her *since you have got a wife.*"[19]

Thomas managed to balance his roles as son, husband, and father with his duties as chief and friend to the North Carolina Cherokees. Although he had turned most of the work dealing with Cherokee claims and payments over to James Taylor and James Terrell, he kept in close touch with the Cherokees and, on occasion, did attempt to get an individual claim honored. He wrote letters to and visited the appropriate officials in Washington. He sometimes signed a contract to purchase land for an individual Indian. The successes he had enjoyed in getting the government to honor the claims of his people almost a decade earlier he supplemented with a steady trickle of small new accessions of money and land. At the local level, in 1859, he pushed through the Quallatown council a reform that allowed the clerks of the different towns to issue marriage licenses and to keep a record of Indian marriages, births, and deaths. At the national level, in 1860, he had a friendly meeting with John Ross and felt reassured that the western Cherokees would not be able to make a new treaty with the United States that did not take into account the needs of the North Carolina Cherokees.[20]

Thomas understood that the future of the Oconalufty Indians rested largely with the state. Thus on December 1, 1858, in a speech before the state senate he made a special plea. The occasion was the death of Junaluska, and Thomas was supporting a bill to try to find a new residence for Junaluska's widow. Thomas reviewed the history of Indian-white relations in the state and attempted to win for the Indians a permanent home in North Carolina. The senator from Jackson County argued that past acts and laws, as well as the Indians' service to the state, obliged North Carolina to recognize their citizenship. The Indians, he reassured his colleagues, did not want to become involved in politics. They wanted only to live unmolested by the dominant white society. Since the federal government was no longer particularly interested in removal, Thomas realized that, if the state would leave his Indians alone, then they would remain. North Carolina never again attempted to evict the Lufty Indians, but for many more years the matter of their citizenship remained ambiguous.[21]

In the late 1850s Thomas gave more of his attention to his own business affairs than to those of the Indians. In addition to his established enterprises, he organized and became president of the Tuckasegee and Keowee Turnpike Company. Building turnpikes in western North Carolina was as important to him as building railroads. Since he provided much of the labor and some of the materials himself, this activity added to his indebtedness.[22]

Riding upon the prosperity he had enjoyed in the early 1840s, Thomas overextended himself financially. Money was particularly tight for him in 1858. He pressured those who owed him to pay. He borrowed $5,000 each from his neighbor William Johnston and from his father-in-law. For security on the latter he gave deeds to his Stekoa Fields farm and a family of five slaves. He confessed in his diary that he was "passing through many financial trials requiring much philosophy."[23] Philadelphia merchants won a judgment against him for $1,300, and he had been unable to pay Terrell his salary since 1855. Thomas raised some money by selling to Francis F. Oram of Ducktown half interest in sixteen thousand acres in Jackson County for $10,000. Despite forced sales and indebtedness, Thomas remained wealthy. In 1860 he owned personal property worth $27,500, real estate valued at $122,725, and thirty-eight slaves.[24]

As a North Carolina politician, Thomas worked hard for those less prosperous than he. When he was in Raleigh every other winter, he started each day with a cold bath, then often worked from 4:00 A.M. until 10:00 P.M. He introduced legislation to build turnpikes in western North Carolina, voted to abolish property qualifications for jurors, favored no annual pay increases for state superior court judges, argued that every free white male should be allowed to vote for state senators, supported Democratic candidates for governor, and always supported the welfare of the Lufty Indians. Though not a giant in the politics of his state, he was scarcely a silent member of the senate. Political service to the state was not lucrative; for the 1858–59 session, which lasted three months, he was paid $352.40.[25]

Two issues, both related to the Western North Carolina Railroad, inflamed Thomas during the few years before the Civil War. When the legislature had passed — despite Thomas's negative vote — the bill to extend the Western North Carolina Railroad west of Asheville, it had not specified where the route would be. Zebulon Vance and others from the state's northwestern counties favored building the line north of Asheville parallel to the French Broad River to the Tennessee state line at Paint Rock. Thomas, representing the southwestern counties, argued that the railroad should continue due west through Waynesville to Franklin, where it would intersect with his Blue Ridge Railroad, and continue to the profitable copper mines in Ducktown, Tennessee. The state ordered both sites surveyed in 1859. Thomas argued passionately that the southwesternmost counties of North Carolina were the "New England of the South," "the center of the Southern country," the hub to connect Charleston and Savannah with Louisville and Cincinnati, the Atlantic coast with the Mississippi River. It would also give his state access to the lucrative copper mines at Ducktown, he said. Ultimately, Thomas, who chaired the Public Works Board, won the point. In February 1861, the General Assembly finally approved the route Thomas wanted, but the Civil War delayed completion of the line for more than twenty years.[26] The war, too, provided a new stage for the hostility between Thomas and Vance to reach a white heat.

With the building of the railroad uppermost among his concerns, Thomas, during the gubernatorial campaign of 1860, followed the Democratic Party's line to oppose an ad valorem tax equally imposed upon slaves and other property according to their value. At first he had favored such a law as a means to raise revenue for internal improvements, but he reversed himself in 1860, claiming that the tax bill might jeopardize state support for the Western North Carolina Railroad. He thought eastern North Carolinians, who would have to pay more taxes, would not vote for their tax dollars to be spent on a western project. So strongly did he oppose the tax bill that he angrily walked out of a rally in Jackson County, where a speaker was arguing for it, declaring that the rally was not a fit place for a Democrat. Robert Vance of Buncombe County privately wrote to his brother Zebulon that "Bill Thomas will scare off hundreds out west by making them believe it will Kill the R.R."[27] Thomas and the Democrats won the debate; Democratic candidate John W. Ellis narrowly won the governorship. The Vance brothers had yet another reason to dislike Thomas.

In 1860, Thomas, like many Southerners, was as interested in the nation's presidential election as he was in state politics. The choice of Abraham Lincoln as the country's first Republican president prompted Thomas to speak out about the possibility of North Carolina's secession from the Union. He wanted to reorganize and arm the state militia for home defense. He hoped his state would not give in to "Black Republicanism" unless a convention of the people voted to do so. On December 21, 1860, the day after South Carolina had seceded from the Union, Thomas introduced two resolutions in the North Carolina Senate. The first said that the federal government had no power to coerce a seceding state; the second contended that the governor was correct to call for a convention of the people to decide the question of secession. Since most of the legislators had already left for the Christmas holiday, Thomas's resolutions were heard by few, and they were ignored by all. On Christmas Eve 1860, Thomas said that if the North attempted to use force to violate the constitutional rights of states that left the Union, then a convention of the people should decide whether North Carolina should secede.[28]

On the first day of January 1861, Thomas was still in Raleigh, thinking of Sallie, his two-week-old second son, his two-year-old "little Indian chief," and the future of the nation. South Carolina was already out of the Union, and he expected that the nation would split just as the Methodist Church had done in 1844. When writing to his young wife, he attempted to portray the breakup of the nation in a favorable light. He did not anticipate war but the emergence of two countries under similar laws with life in each virtually unchanged. The "mountains of Western North Carolina," he wrote Sallie, "would be in the centre of the Confederacy where the Southern people would congregate during the summer, and spend their money, instead of spending it [in the] north." Manufacturers would spring up to meet the needs of the South.[29]

Reassuring and optimistic in his private world, Thomas envisioned prosperity, not death and destruction. He was an old man with a young wife and a young family. With ambition and talent, he hoped that he could turn the impending revolution to his economic advantage, but he could not. Willie and Sallie, their two-year-old "Junaluska" and two-week-old Robert, a remnant of North Carolina Cherokees, and millions of Americans both North and South stood innocently on the precipice of violent change.

CHAPTER 6

Secession and War

"WE ARE UNDOUBTEDLY IN THE MIDST of a Revolution," William Thomas wrote from Raleigh on Christmas Eve 1860. South Carolina had been out of the Union for four days, and the other states of the Deep South were certain to follow. "The declaration of the Black Republicans," Thomas continued in a letter to his friend James Terrell, "that Mr. Lincoln will use the federal forces to coerce them [seceding states] back tends to increase the apprehension with regard to his administration."[1] Thomas was not an avowed secessionist, but he believed in the constitutional right of states to leave the Union without fear of military reprisal. His private remarks to Terrell were more pessimistic than his reassuring letter to his wife and his more moderate remarks in the state senate.

In January 1861 Thomas introduced six more resolutions in the senate. The first five blamed the Republican Party for the disruption of the Union and the destruction of public and private credit, denied the right of the federal government to make war against the seceded states, recommended that the people of North Carolina not submit to the principles of the "Black Republicans," and called for saving the Union by asking Lincoln to resign or the people in conventions to repudiate him. His sixth resolution stated that copies of the first five should be sent to the Congress of the United States and the legislatures of the thirty-three other states.[2]

In language and thought more heated than rational, Thomas gave his reasons for the new resolutions. He explained that the work of the abolitionists for the past quarter of a century had been "filled with falsehoods, slanders and libels." He cited particularly *The Impending Crisis*, a book by Hinton Rowan Helper, a North Carolinian who opposed slavery as detrimental to the economic well-being of poor whites.

Helper's incendiary book had been used by Republicans during the campaign of 1860. Southern Democrats had denounced and burned it. Thomas became more outraged as he spoke. He condemned Lincoln and other Republican leaders such as William H. Seward as traitors, proclaiming somewhat fantastically that the business depression of 1860 and 1861 was already severe and the direct result of Lincoln's election.[3] A few days later, in another speech, Thomas said that if the country did not repudiate Lincoln before he took office on March 4, the southern states remaining in the Union could expect tyranny and oppression.[4]

In a state where the two-party system was strong and most Whigs and many Democrats were still Unionists, Thomas's radical views attracted rebuttal. J. G. Ramsay, a representative from Rowan and Davie counties, expressed regret that "the Senator from Jackson had so many fears of a little man in Springfield, Illinois, called Abraham Lincoln." Ramsay continued that the professed patriot from Jackson had at one time considered Lincoln insignificant, but now the president-elect "had grown to gigantic proportions, at least equal to King Cotton or King George."[5]

Thomas seemed to like the reference to King George. It raised in his mind the image of one of his political heroes and fellow orphans, George Washington. Washington, he argued, was "a revolutionist, secessionist, and reconstructionist." The South, he continued, "occupied a position similar to that of the thirteen colonies before the Revolution."[6] Six days later, according to one Raleigh newspaper, when the state senate was debating a bill to send commissioners to the Confederate capital at Montgomery, Alabama, the firebrand from Jackson County threw some "random hot shot into the ranks of the Helperites, Lincolnites and Sewardites."[7]

Nevertheless the secession fever that was beginning to afflict Thomas—and that had already taken the seven states of the Deep South out of the Union—was not widespread in North Carolina. Slavery was not an important issue there. At least 70 percent of the people owned no slaves, and those who did owned relatively few. North Carolina was filled with men and women of modest means who were skeptical of movements and ideas of alien origin. So jealous of individual liberties were its people that it had been the next to last state to join the new nation after the American Revolution. With the state's peculiar history and geographical divisions, political unity was difficult to attain. The majority of North Carolina Whigs, like Edward Stanly, were nationalists who thought the Union was indestructible. Yet there were a few, such as Thomas L. Clingman, the United States senator from the mountain district, who leaned toward secession. The Democrats who controlled the governorship and the state in 1860 were likewise divided. Governor John W. Ellis, for whom Thomas had campaigned in 1860, advocated secession. Those Democrats such as Thomas who leaned toward secession but had not yet specifically recommended it were a minority. Soon, however, events outside the state drove them to become more outspoken.[8]

When Georgia seceded in January 1861, two of the four states that shared boundaries with North Carolina were out of the Union. Thomas feared that if Tennessee and Virginia joined the Confederacy, which he expected them to do, then North Carolina would be ruined economically if it did not do the same. Since North Carolina would be surrounded by foreign territory, he wrote Sallie, its citizens could not go anywhere without passports and could trade only through customhouses.[9]

As the pressure mounted, the politicians of North Carolina decided to consult the citizens. On January 29, 1861, the legislature passed a bill authorizing the people to decide on February 28 whether they wished for a convention. Thomas led a group that defeated an amendment to bar members of the legislature from serving in the convention. When the lawmakers adjourned on February 25, Thomas went home to campaign for the convention. In a close election, the citizens defeated the convention bill by a vote of 47,323 to 46,672.[10]

During the heated debate between Unionists and secessionists over the convention, Thomas took his first public stand in favor of secession. His approach was simplistic and emotional. He told his constituents that North Carolina must decide whether to serve the South or the abolitionists. "Our Southern Friends, both Church and State, have withdrawn," he wrote, "carrying with them the old Bible and old Constitution, . . . which the usurper Lincoln and his supporters propose to subvert, and form a military despotism." As for himself, Thomas continued, he stood "on the same platform of the Whigs of 1776, for the old Constitution, and for civil and religious liberty." He called for North Carolinians to meet in convention and secede. The other Democratic leaders in Jackson and Haywood counties agreed, but those in

Cherokee and Macon counties did not. Thomas's constituency defeated the call for a secession convention by a vote of 1,689 to 1,338.[11]

Despite their defeat on February 28, the twist of events was on the side of Thomas and the secessionists. Soon after Lincoln was inaugurated on March 4, he announced plans to send provisions to Fort Sumter in Charleston Harbor. At 4:30 A.M. on April 12, 1861, Confederate troops commanded by General P. G. T. Beauregard began to bombard the fort. It surrendered the next day. On April 15 Lincoln called upon the states still in the Union to raise 75,000 troops to put down the rebellion. These events almost immediately converted many Unionists in the upper South, including those in North Carolina, into secessionists. Governor John W. Ellis issued a call for all North Carolina legislators to return to the capital by May 1. Thomas probably heard the news about the fall of Fort Sumter, Lincoln's call for troops, and Ellis's call for a special session of the state legislature all in a letter addressed to him by James R. Love II on April 20, 1861. A first cousin to Sallie Thomas, Jim Love was a young attorney who shared Thomas's political views.[12]

Thomas arrived in Raleigh on May 1 in time to answer the roll call for the special session of the legislature. Since Governor Ellis and other secessionists had for several months been taking military precautions, Thomas found his state preparing for war. That special session quickly passed a bill calling for the election on May 13 of 120 delegates to a convention that would meet on May 20. It also authorized the governor to send military aid to Virginia, appoint a commissioner to the Confederate government, raise 10,000 state troops, and ask for 20,000 volunteers. A bill that Thomas had introduced authorizing the governor to have the bridges on the Western Turnpike repaired to facilitate the transportation of troops, provisions, and munitions was replaced by the bill calling for volunteers. Furthermore the legislature appropriated $200,000 to manufacture arms at Fayetteville, issued $5,000,000 in bonds for public defense, and agreed to accept at equal rank military personnel who resigned from federal service to enter state service. The legislature then adjourned for the elections to the convention.[13]

Immediately after that adjournment, Thomas hurried back to Quallatown where he called a council of the Oconaluftee Indians. Thomas explained to the Indians, whose treaties were with the government of the United States, the situation in the country as he understood it.

After discussion, the subchiefs said that they did not understand, but they would be loyal to Thomas and North Carolina. Chief Thomas therefore mustered two hundred Cherokees into state service, calling them the "Junaluska Zouaves" in honor of their recently deceased hero. Like many Southern political leaders, Thomas was more concerned about protecting his local area than he was with the entire state or Confederacy. He intended the Zouaves to be a home guard force. This colorful militia attracted the attention of the press. One Raleigh newspaper warned the "Northern barbarians, with A. Blinkum at their head," to guard their scalps when they heard the war whoop of the Cherokees. A Charleston newspaper announced that the "Zouaves" were excellent riflemen and "ready at a moment's notice."[14]

Of more immediate importance to Chief Thomas was his election to represent Jackson County at the secession convention. He was one of only four legislators chosen to the convention. Gathering in Raleigh on May 20, it elected secessionist Weldon N. Edwards as its president. He appointed other secessionists to chair the committees. He named Thomas as the chairman of committees on Amendments to the 33rd Section of the Constitution, on the Basis of Representation, on Justices of the Peace, and on Public Schools. Thomas was a member of three other committees, two of which were concerned with writing a new state constitution.[15]

On May 20, 1861, the convention unanimously ratified North Carolina's ordinance of secession. The surrender of Fort Sumter, the call for troops, and the secession of Tennessee and Virginia prompted the Unionists to fall silent. They sat quiet, calm, and depressed, according to their leader William W. Holden, while the secessionists shouted, rejoiced, and threw their hats into the air.[16]

Taking priority over the General Assembly, the convention met twice in 1861 and twice in 1862. Thomas attended the first three sessions, but he was in military service by the time of the fourth meeting. The General Assembly continued to sit, but not simultaneously with the convention.[17]

The immediate task of the convention was to raise a military force. With approval of the legislature, Governor John W. Ellis had already built up a large stockpile of armaments and had appointed three members to a military board charged with enlisting, equipping, and organizing from twenty to fifty thousand troops.[18]

The citizens of Thomas's four counties responded enthusiastically to Governor Ellis's call for soldiers. Volunteer companies in Haywood, Jackson, Cherokee, and Macon counties organized to support North Carolina and the Confederacy. They anticipated trouble not only with the government and troops of Abraham Lincoln but with those large numbers of citizens in western North Carolina and eastern Tennessee who remained loyal to the United States. James R. Love II was elected captain of the Haywood Rangers. His unit, plus several other companies, comprised the Sixth North Carolina Infantry Regiment. Three of Sallie Thomas's brothers were among its members. The Sixth Regiment was stationed at Camp Lee near Raleigh.[19]

Since the Sixth Regiment contained his in-laws, friends, and neighbors, Thomas greeted it warmly. He wrote his wife that her brothers were well. Robert had been elected lieutenant colonel, and some of his lady friends were paying him much attention. Matthew had brought his violin and, along with his cousin John, was serenading local belles. Thomas himself had chosen the campsite for the regiment in a beautiful grove near the city. He hoped, he told Sallie, to use his position to keep "our volunteers" in "healthy and comfortable locations."[20]

Thomas was proud of his work in the convention, especially his involvement in writing a new state constitution. "I regard it," he wrote Sallie, "as the most responsible position of my life." He thought that it was "of much more importance than any military position I could fill." Furthermore, he continued, he expected the North would propose peace without a fight. If England and France recognized the Confederacy, he continued, then "we shall . . . have in Western North Carolina one of the most prosperous countries in the world." Thomas's primary interest in secession was the economic advantage he hoped that he and his region might gain. He expected his mountains and valleys to be connected to the rest of the South by rail, to establish a center for manufacturing, and to become the "place where southern people will spend their summers, spend their money, educate their children, and very probably make laws for the nation."[21]

Despite such optimism, Thomas could not escape the realities of war. On June 19 he failed in an attempt to persuade the convention to recruit three regiments of volunteers in the western part of the state to defend the mountain passes. Angered by the defeat, Thomas accused his eastern friends of wanting a paid home guard for their region at the expense of the rest of the state. In language too strong for the newspapers to print, he warned the convention that it should not usurp powers the people never intended for it to have. The chairman called him to order for his "little unreportable colloquy." The traditional rivalry between the eastern and western parts of the state bent to the demands of the war, however; a few months later the state legislature permitted a regiment being formed near Asheville to remain west of the Blue Ridge Mountains to defend the western boundary of North Carolina and to assist Confederate forces in east Tennessee.[22]

Thomas feared that the impending war would be devastating to the Cherokees' long fight to get the state to grant them citizenship. Their treaties were with a government that the state had repudiated. He preferred for them to stay out of the war, but he realized that other North Carolinians would not tolerate their neutrality. He therefore decided to organize them himself and to be their self-appointed protector in wartime just as he had been for three decades.[23] He pondered how they might be affected by secession, protected from their enemies, and used in the defense of western North Carolina. Late in July, G. T. Jarrett, a cavalryman in Cherokee County, recommended that Thomas inquire of Confederate President Jefferson Davis his opinion on arming and mounting Cherokee soldiers. They could be used, Jarrett suggested, to accompany white rangers who would harass the enemy in the mountains of Kentucky before they reached Cumberland Gap, the passageway to east Tennessee and western North Carolina.[24]

Before Thomas could follow through on that suggestion, he needed to get the state to accept the Cherokees into its forces. In September he therefore introduced in the state senate a bill authorizing the governor to raise a battalion of Cherokees. When the senate approved the bill, without waiting for action by the house, Thomas wrote to Davis, whom he had met in Washington in the 1840s, telling him that he had an Indian battalion ready to serve the Confederacy. Davis replied that the Cherokees could be used to defend the coasts and swamps of eastern North Carolina.[25]

In the meantime, however, Thomas had underestimated his enemies in the state house of representatives. George W. Hayes, a onetime friend turned foe, member of the house, and commander of a cavalry unit, engineered the house's defeat of Thomas's bill to raise an Indian battalion. Hayes, who had two Cherokees in his unit, discriminated against them and discouraged others from joining. He said that he had rather be caught in a voting booth with a free black person than to associate with the Indians. Thomas argued that the Cherokees would enlist anyway and that they were, as he had been saying for more than twenty-five years, already citizens of North Carolina under terms of their treaties of 1817, 1819, and 1835. He tried to impress upon the Confederacy that such a Cherokee force could help stop Union soldiers attempting to pass southward through mountain gaps before they could reach the vital railroad and industrial center of Atlanta.[26] His promotion of the Zouaves and sustained enthusiasm for the economic progress that secession might bring to western North Carolina made Thomas sound like a Western or Northern businessman boosting his region to the emerging Confederacy.

Thomas took the approval of the senate, the interest of Davis, and his own concern about the Indians as authority enough to proceed to muster Cherokees into state and Confederate service. With their chief's approval, in October a Cherokee company began to form at Quallatown. It apparently absorbed the Zouaves, for no further mention of them appears. How Thomas financed this venture is unrecorded, but according to Terrell, he had $21,134.96 of the Indians' money in his possession at the outbreak of the war. The Treasury Department had given Terrell that amount to pay Indian claims, and Terrell said he turned it over to Thomas. Although Thomas probably disbursed it as intended, records to prove or disprove it do not exist.[27]

The Sixth Regiment, which had moved from Raleigh to western Virginia, continued to occupy Thomas's attention. He wrote Governor Henry T. Clark, who had become chief executive in July after Ellis had died, that if the Sixth Regiment should ever be withdrawn from Virginia, it should be combined with other companies being organized in western North Carolina to form a North Carolina Highland Brigade or Legion. Once the mountaineers were together in a single unit, he said in a thin argument, they could be removed from the coast during the hot season when the Union forces would be too afraid to attack it.[28] The state adjutant general liked Thomas's idea. When the chief again demanded that the state recognize Cherokee citizenship, however, the legislature refused, and the adjutant general withdrew his support. Nevertheless Chief Thomas continued to use willing Indians to defend the mountain gap and the road that connected Quallatown with east Tennessee.[29]

In the fall of 1861 Thomas was the first North Carolinian to announce for a seat in the Confederate Congress that would meet the next February in Richmond. Within a few days George W. Candler, a bitter political enemy from the western part of the state, entered the race primarily to prevent Thomas's election. Candler withdrew suddenly, however, when Allen T. Davidson, a lawyer, member of the secession convention, and president of the Miners and Planters Bank of Murphy, entered the fray. Candler and George W. Hayes, Thomas's former clerk and business partner who had turned political enemy, launched a vigorous campaign for Davidson and against Thomas.

As a part of his campaign, Thomas appealed to Governor Clark to protect the two Cherokees in Hayes's cavalry from mistreatment by their commander. The Cherokees, Jonathan Welch and F. M. Taylor, addressed a letter to the governor and sent it to Thomas to forward for them. They complained that Hayes treated them as badly as if they were free blacks. When forwarding their letter to the governor, Thomas included his own. He argued that Hayes was trying both to prevent the Cherokees from volunteering and to block his election to the Confederate Congress. Furthermore, he asserted, his opponent Davidson was as unfit to serve the new government as Hayes was to make military decisions. Thomas concluded with the suggestion that Governor Clark might do well to dismiss Welch and Taylor and advise Hayes not to accept any more Indians into his company.[30]

Governor Clark left Thomas alone to fight his own political battles. Since Candler did much of the campaigning for Davidson, he led the attack. In a face-to-face confrontation at Asheville, Candler accused Thomas of absenteeism from the senate, drunkenness on the senate floor, insensitivity to the defense of the eastern part of the state, and being in favor of keeping the majority of the people poor while he enjoyed affluence. Both the local audience and the newspaper that reported the exchange were clearly on the side of Candler and Davidson.[31] On October 30, 1861, the hostile *Henderson Times* contended that Thomas had vowed that, if Governor Clark removed a western regiment to Raleigh, he, Thomas, would introduce a bill to elect a new governor. Thus the governor, according to the jesting *Times,* should "tremble with the approaching tread of the infuriated Senator," and the people should shear this "Sampson" of his locks. There is no evidence that Thomas followed through with his threat.

In his speeches and in a published broadside, Thomas reminded the voters that Davidson was a Unionist who had once referred to the secession flag of South Carolina as "a dirty rag" and had snubbed the secessionists in his own state. Furthermore, Davidson had made no effort to raise the pay for Confederate volunteers or to protect the citizens in the western part of the state. Thomas claimed that when the General Assembly had been in session he was a good senator; he was present, he said, sober, and voting for measures that would guarantee the welfare and economy of the state. Thomas explained his views on secession and war. He wanted to prosecute the war vigorously but to end it as soon as an honorable peace could be agreed upon. The voters of the Tenth Congressional District, however, many of whom had remained Unionists, chose to send Davidson to the Confederate Congress.[32]

With no hope for a career in Confederate politics, Thomas slipped into the military life. He was past his mid-fifties and more interested in politics and economics, and he did not like being in the army. Nevertheless, early in January 1862, while home for the Christmas holidays, he met with the Indians at Quallatown to take charge of the company they had begun to form the previous October. By the end of the war four hundred of them, including practically all of the able-bodied males among the eastern Cherokees, entered Confederate service, but their loyalty was primarily to Little Will, their friend, chief, and leader. Others joined the Union forces or attempted to remain neutral.[33] Many whites, too, in the mountainous regions of North Carolina and Tennessee elected to remain loyal to the Union, thus complicating immensely the lives and maneuvers of their neighbors who went with the Confederacy.

Thomas returned to Raleigh in February to attend the third meeting of the secession convention. Writing to Sallie on February 16 after Confederate forces had been captured on Roanoke Island, he commented that an exchange of prisoners "will give us back our army, and relieve us from supporting their prisoners." He told her, too, that he was chairing a committee to investigate the condition of the military defenses of western North Carolina. He yearned for the convention to adjourn so he could hurry home. "I will then try to prove that our sheep have a shepherd, my children a father and my wife a husband to provide for them," he said.[34]

When the third session of the secession convention adjourned on February 27, 1862, marking the end of Thomas's service in elective office, he did not go home immediately. He went first to Columbia, South Carolina, where he met with the state executive council to present his plan to fortify the passes of the Smoky Mountains. Thomas reported back to Governor Clark that the South Carolina council concurred with his suggestion. Thomas also recommended that Clark present the plan to the Confederate secretary of war and ask him to put it into effect immediately. In the meantime, he said, as soon as he arrived home, he would establish his own defenses at the head of the Oconaluftee River on the road that stretched across the Smokies from Jackson County, North Carolina, to Sevier County, Tennessee. He promised that his Indian company, together with some mechanics, could defend the Oconaluftee pass. "Our mountain boys," he concluded, would remain "true to our Southern cause."[35]

Thomas remained in Quallatown only long enough to muster about one hundred more Cherokees into service, for he was soon off to Richmond. His mission was to promote the idea of using the Cherokees as allies. Since the Confederate Congress had already ratified treaties with the Five Civilized Tribes in Indian territory, promising to pay the annuities formerly promised by the United States, Thomas worked to get the eastern Cherokees included. Reversing his contention that the eastern Indians were separate from the Cherokee Nation, Thomas argued that the new treaty also applied to the North Carolina Indians, and he provided the Confederate Congress with a copy of the Mullay roll. Jefferson Davis had already advised the Confederate Congress to compensate the eastern Cherokees for their loyalty. The Confederate government agreed to assume the payments owed them under their treaties with the United States, but the war prevented it from doing so. In the meantime, the United States government stopped payment to all disloyal Indians, including those who considered Thomas their chief.[36]

Thomas's mission to Richmond was successful because no sooner had he returned home than he received word that the Confederate government would accept his Cherokees into its service. Instead of sending them to the eastern swamps, it now agreed to use them, as Thomas wished, as a home guard for the mountain passes in the western part of the state. On April 9, 1862, Thomas and his company of one hundred Cherokees and twelve white men entered the Confederate Army.[37]

General Edmund Kirby Smith, commander of the Department of East Tennessee, sent Major George Washington Morgan to muster Thomas and his Indian soldiers into Confederate service. Half Cherokee himself, Morgan had commanded the Tennessee Cherokees at the First Battle of Manassas, and supposedly he knew how to arouse the

Indians' war spirit. According to one report, when they were given a distorted account of a Southern victory at Shiloh, Tennessee, they let out a joyful war whoop. Truth to tell, however, the North Carolina Cherokees were probably more trusting of their white chief than they were of anyone else. They chose Thomas as their captain and James W. Terrell and Matthew H. Love as first lieutenants. For second lieutenants they selected Astoogatogeh, the grandson of Junaluska and translator of the New Testament into Cherokee; Peter Greybeard; R. C. McCalla; William S. Terrell; and David L. Whitaker.[38]

Thomas and his company of Indians and highlanders were stationed at Knoxville, Tennessee. The widespread disloyalty to the Confederacy there was as troublesome to its military officers as was the threat of a Yankee invasion. General Edmund Kirby Smith told his wife that Tennessee was "more dangerous and difficult to operate in than the country of an acknowledged enemy."[39] Smith could not even trust his own soldiers, especially if they were local volunteers. Many had joined only to escape persecution, and they often deserted or gave information to the enemy. No doubt he welcomed Captain Thomas and his unusual company as a small force upon which he could rely.

The trek from Quallatown to Knoxville, a short trip through rough terrain in bad weather, was the first test of the company's mettle. Departing on April 15, the Cherokees passed through Webster and Franklin, sending out messengers to nearby towns to invite other young braves to join them, and reached Valleytown, fifty miles from their origin, on April 19. En route Thomas and Morgan instructed the Indians in the ways of white warfare. They were good students. At Valleytown heavy rains delayed them for four days. When they resumed their march on April 24 they had great difficulty getting across Hanging Dog Creek. That night Thomas and Morgan slept at the house of Thomas's cousin, Andrew Colvard. The next night they camped on top of Unicoi Mountain on the Tennessee state line, then moved on to Madison and Sweetwater, where they made camp on April 26. Leaving James Terrell in command, Thomas and Morgan boarded a freight train for Knoxville. The next day Terrell loaded his soldiers into freight cars, while he rode in a dilapidated coach, bound for their assigned station.[40]

Thomas showed a good bit of spirit for the Confederate cause. He planned to raise a guerrilla force for local defense of the Carolinas, east Tennessee, and Virginia. Maintaining that President Davis had already agreed, Thomas asked Governor Clark for permission to enlist enough Indians and whites to form a battalion and to expand it later into a regiment that would serve for three years or the duration of the war. Morgan would assist him. He asked Clark to telegraph his answer to Knoxville, and he boasted that his current Indian company had the "reputation of being the most orderly company ever mustered out of the mountains."[41]

Late in April, Thomas's "orderly company" arrived in Knoxville where he and Morgan met the men at the depot. In columns two abreast they marched from the depot down Gay Street, the major thoroughfare, and on to Main Street. Crowds of curious townspeople, most of whom thought of Indians as warlike savages eager to take the scalps of their enemies, pushed in close to get a better look. Finally the Cherokees made their way to their camp, named Ogonstoka, which was Morgan's Indian name. They mustered into Colonel John C. Vaughn's Third Tennessee Regiment. Many distinguished citizens went to their camp to visit them.

The Indians created a sensation on their first Sunday when they conducted a service in their own language at the First Presbyterian Church. The Cherokee men sat to the left of the minister, and the pews in front and to his right were packed with white spectators. Their chaplain, Unaguskie, a grandson of Yonaguska, read eloquently from the Bible, preached, and prayed in Cherokee. The enraptured whites understood none of it and thus could not comment on his theology. They did note, however, that the music was characterized "by melody more than harmony" and was more primitive and "less artistic" than that to which they were accustomed.[42]

The festivities having ended, Thomas and his Cherokees settled into the boring life of a Civil War camp. About mid-May, they were ordered to Strawberry Plains, about fourteen miles from Knoxville, to guard the Tennessee and Virginia Railroad bridge over the Holston River. The bridge was about seventy miles south of the Virginia state line and the Shenandoah Valley and was located between the Cumberland and Great Smoky mountains. The valleys and gaps through which this railroad and its connectors passed from Virginia to Knoxville, to Chattanooga, and Atlanta, formed a route into the heartland of the South. President Lincoln wanted to invade through this area, but his generals did not. Nevertheless, Southerners feared a possible invasion by this route, and they were concerned that east Tennessee Unionists would try to break the railroad, thus cutting direct contact between Virginia and the western Confederacy.

Before marching to Strawberry Plains, Thomas on May 18 divided his men into two forces. Their assignment was important. East Tennessee had a large number of Unionists in it, and Lincoln was anxious for the Northern army to capture it.[43] Thomas wrote Governor Clark that he hoped to receive enough new volunteers to form a battalion, and he began to call his two Indian companies the North Carolina Cherokee Battalion.[44] The men suffered temporarily from measles, mumps, and various kinds of fever. One Indian, who had fallen asleep across the tracks, died under the wheels of a train. The Cherokee soldiers broke the monotony of camp life with short forays away from camp and sometimes a vigorous ballplay. Occasionally Thomas staged a ballplay, with the contestants dressed only in their birthday attire, to entertain white visitors.[45]

Throughout the summer of 1862 the Indian companies remained at Strawberry Plains, where they were determined to do their part to thwart any Union plan to invade east Tennessee. From battle at Shiloh, Tennessee, in April and the occupation of Corinth, Mississippi, in June, the Northern army marched toward Chattanooga, which nestled on the Tennessee River near the Georgia state line southwest of Knoxville. General Kirby Smith joined General Braxton Bragg there to defend the city. Thomas played a minor role at Chattanooga. He and about forty Indians, ordered to the front by Smith, scouted the Union side of the Tennessee River. Thomas personally captured a lost Michigan soldier, "an intelligent and gentlemanly man," whom he turned over to Confederate authorities. The Indians said that since Thomas had taken the first prisoner, they should each take one. They did not get the chance, however, because they were sent to a battle about twenty miles south of the city, only to find that it had ended by the time they arrived. Believing that Cumberland Gap was in danger, Thomas and his men returned to Knoxville and Strawberry Plains to resume guarding the railroad bridge across the Holston River.[46]

Back at Strawberry Plains in late June, Thomas met handsome young William W. Stringfield. The twenty-five-year-old son of a local Methodist minister had been in Confederate service since 1861. He and Thomas met because Thomas was boarding at his mother's house, which was located within sight of the railroad bridge that Thomas's men were guarding. "I liked the old man fairly well," Stringfield wrote;

"he told mother and [my] sisters that he had better things in store for me than I was then doing—enforcing the Conscript law."[47] The provost marshal of east Tennessee assigned Stringfield to be assistant provost marshal in the counties where as a lad he had traveled with his father, dated young women, and made many other friends, most of whom were now Unionists. When he had threatened to resign from service as a result of this unhappy appointment, the provost marshal had reassigned him as a mustering officer reporting to the Knoxville office. Thomas asked him in his new capacity to travel to Cherokee County, North Carolina, to recruit new troops. When he arrived there, Stringfield found Thomas's old political enemy, Colonel Allen T. Davidson, trying to discourage men from joining Thomas's force. Supported by Thomas's good friend, William C. Walker, Stringfield presented to Davidson his credentials to recruit for Thomas, proceeded to do so, and within a week had enlisted five hundred volunteers. Three of the five companies formed by the volunteers joined Thomas's North Carolina Cherokee Battalion, and the other two joined "Bill" Walker's battalion.[48] Stringfield later became a very important person in Thomas's life. He married Sallie Thomas's younger sister, Maria, came to know the old white chief and his family well, and after the war wrote a comprehensive account of his and Thomas's military service.

On July 19, the day Stringfield mustered in the new volunteers at Valleytown, Thomas's command reached battalion strength. He was promoted to the grade of major. Thomas now commanded two companies of Indians and six of whites. It was clear that Thomas now wanted to command a legion—a small force of infantry, cavalry, and artillery under a single commander—not simply a guerrilla band as he had first stated.[49]

Thomas spent that summer with the citizen-soldiers who were his officers, neighbors, friends, and relatives. Apparently he had little time to visit Sallie, his two young sons, and his infant daughter Sarah. Busy with her young family, Sallie remained at Stekoa Fields, awaiting letters from her Willie, news from others who had seen him, and occasional visits.

Thomas passed his time paying and equipping his men and increasing the size of his command, especially enlarging Lieutenant Colonel William C. Walker's force to battalion size. Their weapons were archaic squirrel-guns with bored barrels to permit the use of larger bullets. The men also carried loose powder, bar lead that could be shaped into bullets, percussion caps, and steel-tipped spears. Terrell thought bows and arrows would have been more effective and was relieved when, later in the war, his men were supplied with improved rifles. On August 21 Thomas acquired ten thousand dollars to pay a bounty, or bonus, to recruits. By September those men were ready for action.[50]

That action came in a skirmish on September 13 through 15, 1862, at Baptist Gap, about ten miles north of Rogersville, Tennessee, near the Virginia state line. When the Confederates received information that Union soldiers were preparing to move through gaps south of the Cumberland Mountains from southwestern Virginia into eastern Tennessee, General John P. McCown, who had replaced Kirby Smith as commander of the Department of East Tennessee, ordered Thomas's two Indian companies and others to protect the area. First Lieutenant William S. Terrell led the Indians into Baptist Gap on September 13; there they were ambushed by members of an Indiana Regiment. On September 15, Terrell ordered Second Lieutenant Astoogatogeh and his men to charge the Yankees. Astoogatogeh, a grandson of Junaluska, was killed, thus inflaming the other Cherokees to attack and drive the Indiana soldiers from the valley. The departing Northerners reported hearing blood-curdling war whoops instead of familiar rebel yells. As they glanced over their shoulders, they witnessed the grisly spectacle of Indians cutting away the scalps of several of their dead and wounded comrades.[51]

A writer for a nearby newspaper, the *Greenville Banner*, reported on September 15 that "renegades" and "deserters" would be scalped as readily as Union soldiers: "There is now a regiment of Indians lurking through the mountains to catch all renegades. They already, as we learn, have caught and scalped several." The writer urged the men of east Tennessee to escape such a fate by being "good soldiers" and facing "the music like honest men."[52] The writer's enthusiasm to use the threat of scalping to frighten his readers into being loyal to the Confederacy was nothing more than propaganda that had the side effect of giving the Indians an undeserved reputation for cruelty.

The rare ferocity with which the Cherokees fought and won at Baptist Gap raised the question of their savagery in battle. James Terrell, who knew them well, claimed they brought back many trophies. Unionists in east Tennessee liked to call them savages. Certainly the few Hoosiers who witnessed the scalping regarded them with fear. Stringfield, who was not there, later said that the Indians took only two or

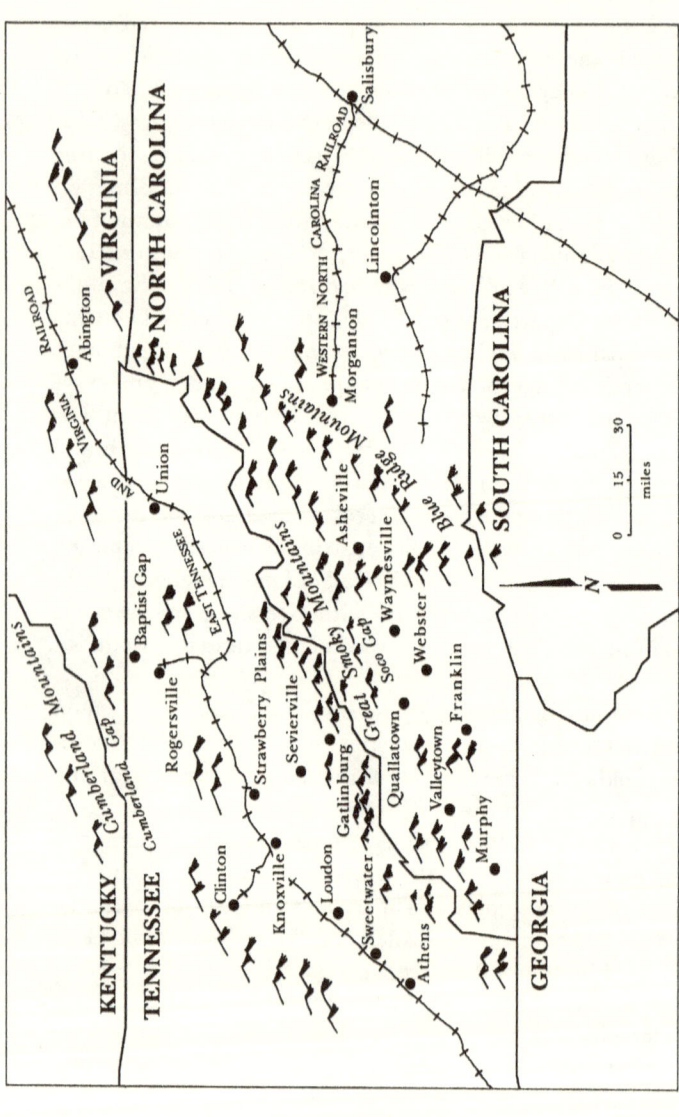

Western North Carolina and east Tennessee in the nineteenth century. Based on map on endpapers in Vernon H. Crow, *Storm in the Mountains*. Map by The University of Tennessee Cartographic Services Laboratory.

three "Federal scalps" and then returned them to be buried with the soldiers. Thomas, who was not there either, was "hurt by the affair," Stringfield said.

Proud of the distinctiveness and prowess of his warriors, Thomas did not want his Indians to be known as savages. Indeed, he had spent half of his life arguing in the halls of government that they were civilized people deserving all the rights and privileges of citizenship. When a woman at Knoxville had asked the Indians to bring back some scalps, Thomas had mildly rebuked her. Whatever military propaganda might have been gained by the image of savage Confederate soldiers, Thomas was not willing to use it. He had not yet won for his Indian people the rights and protection he thought they deserved, and he could not afford for any of them to have the reputation for savagery. The scalping at Baptist Gap was at most an isolated episode. Perhaps it was even less savage than the bushwhacking among whites that sometimes occurred in east Tennessee. The sight of their brother Astoogatogeh falling in battle had stirred within his fellow warriors the ancient law of blood, but the Cherokees who claimed Thomas as their chief were not a warlike people. Terrell's account to the contrary is difficult to explain; if he exaggerated the number of scalps the Cherokees took, however, it was intended as a compliment to them. The general character of Thomas and his officers, the lack of reference to scalping in the memoirs of Northern soldiers, and the rare and minor participation of Cherokees in battles suggest that the Indians in warfare were little different from their white counterparts.[53]

In September 1862, however, few people knew or cared what was happening in a remote pass south of the Cumberland Mountains. The eyes of the nation and of the world turned to Sharpsburg, Maryland, where on September 17 at Antietam Creek the Union Army claimed a victory. Five days later, President Abraham Lincoln, who had been waiting for such a favorable military turn, issued the preliminary Emancipation Proclamation. Phrased in terms that freed very few slaves, it nevertheless undercut European intervention and transformed the war in the popular mind into a conflict to end slavery, thus giving the North the superior moral cause. That event, added to the North's greater military might, rendered the Confederacy doomed.

Ten days after Antietam, Thomas got his wish to become commander of a legion. By order of General John P. McCown, Thomas was named colonel of a legion, often mistakenly called the "Sixty-ninth North

Officers in Thomas's legion: (1) William H. Thomas, (2) James R. Love II, (3) William W. Stringfield, (4) James W. Cooper, (5) R.T. Conley, (6) D.K. Collins, (7) James Conley, (8) William T. Welch. North Carolina Division of Archives and History.

Carolina Regiment." Thomas had under his command more than two thousand officers and men distributed among eleven companies of infantry, eight companies of cavalry, and one light battery of artillery. The first two companies of infantry were the Cherokees.

Thomas's lieutenant colonel was James R. Love II, a genial and talented man of about thirty years. He enjoyed the respect and trust of many who knew him. A tall, gentle, handsome man, he had served in the state legislature with Thomas. He was a first cousin to Thomas's wife. The older man called him Jim. An attorney educated at Emory and Henry College in Virginia, Jim Love sought a career in politics. He had fought with distinction in the Sixteenth North Carolina Regiment at Seven Pines and other battles in Virginia in the spring and summer of 1862. He also participated in the battle at Antietam before being ordered to report to Thomas in east Tennessee. A native of Haywood County, he was happy to return to his home.

The other officers in the legion included William W. Stringfield as major and James W., or "Jimmy," Terrell as assistant quartermaster. Many of the officers and men were people Thomas knew well. This enlarged fighting force, which subsequently added almost two hundred more Indians and six hundred more whites, included the most prominent whites and Cherokees from western North Carolina. It became known as "Thomas's Legion of Indians and Highlanders," or simply "Thomas's Legion."[54]

The exhilaration Thomas may have felt upon becoming colonel of his own legion was tempered by the fact that fate had swept him far adrift from the life he had wanted. He preferred to be at home with Sallie, their three small children, and his mother, and to continue his career in government and the economic development of his native region. The man who would have been a wealthy entrepreneur, a politician, a writer of constitutions, stood at the head of a small military command in the remote Appalachian South on the eve of its descent into a lost cause.

CHAPTER 7

Colonel Thomas

THE CIVIL WAR THAT BROUGHT DEATH, chaos, and change to the nation disrupted the life of Colonel William Holland Thomas at an advanced age. A civilian with no military training, he accepted his assignment with the same determination that had characterized his push for justice for his Indian people and his search for a wife. As colonel of the legion, he reported directly to Brigadier General Henry Heth, the commander of the Third Division of the Confederacy's troops in east Tennessee. Those troops were part of the Confederacy's western army that was poorly led by men who wasted time arguing among themselves.[1]

In the fall and winter of 1862 and 1863, Thomas's legion functioned, as he wished, as a home guard for east Tennessee and western North Carolina. On November 8, Thomas wrote Jefferson Davis from his headquarters at Strawberry Plains recommending that the Confederacy establish a line of posts, about fifteen miles apart and protected by guardhouses and Indian sentinels, to secure wagon communication between east Tennessee, the Virginia Railroad, and Kentucky. He also said that the Confederacy needed to put back into operation the Goose Creek Salt Works in southeastern Kentucky, which the Union army had dismantled in October. In addition to the salt, his troops needed "breadstuffs, bacon, beef, etc.," he told the beleaguered Davis, who apparently did not reply.[2]

Undaunted, Thomas turned to the new governor of North Carolina, Zebulon B. Vance. Since Vance was from the western part of the state, Thomas thought that, despite their long-standing disagreement over the route of the Western North Carolina Railroad, Vance might be particularly attentive to the needs of that region. He informed the governor that his legion was scattered along the railroad from Chattanooga to Bristol, enforcing conscription, disarming citizens, impressing property, forcing civil authorities to take a loyalty oath to the Confederacy, guarding bridges and blockhouses, and doing construction work. Because they could use more help, Thomas recommended that the governor use slaves in the defense of western North Carolina. If slaves were used to extend the Western North Carolina Railroad, he argued, their owners would benefit because fewer soldiers would be needed to defend the state. The situation was desperate, he said, because "deserters and renegades . . . by the hundred are taking shelter in the Smoky Mountains." If men between the ages of thirty-five and forty who lived west of the Blue Ridge Mountains were required to guard the mountain passes, then the Confederacy would be able to hold the "country encircled by the Blue Ridge and Cumberland mountains and . . . the heart of the south." To lose the passes and surrounding country, he said, would mean that "we sink under a despotism."[3]

Vance, who remembered Thomas's negative vote on the railroad extension bill in 1855, his own brother's criticism of "Bill Thomas" in 1861, and who was influenced by Thomas's political enemies, chose to ignore him, leaving him to the will of his military superiors. They chose to scatter the companies of his legion, sending them on different missions without consulting him. In January 1863, Heth ordered Thomas and his companies of Indians, along with General William G. M. Davis and other troops, to move from Strawberry Plains to Madison County, North Carolina, where they were supposed to curb the subversive activities of native Unionists. Before departing, Thomas confidently wrote to Sallie that he expected peace would become "much brighter" if the army did its duty. If he survived the war, he said, he would be content "to spend the remainder of my life in retirement surrounded by my family and friends."[4]

In the meantime, answering the immediate call of duty, Thomas and his Indians, under orders of General Davis, split off from the troops destined for Madison County and moved into Haywood, Jackson, and Cherokee counties, North Carolina, and Clay County, Georgia, where they undertook the odious task of rounding up deserters and tories.[5]

Jefferson Davis and the Confederate Congress understood that the Cherokee Indians were rendering a useful service. On January 12, 1863, Davis addressed the Congress, reporting that "relations with the Indians generally continue to be friendly."[6] One month later, on February

Railroad bridge at Strawberry Plains, 1864, in Union hands. Brady-Handy Collection, Library of Congress.

12, the Confederate House of Representatives passed a resolution calling for a full report on the status of the eastern Cherokees. Commissioner of Indian Affairs S. S. Scott submitted a report based upon information that had been supplied to him by Thomas and Terrell. The Confederate Congress thereupon appropriated $19,352.36 to pay the eastern Cherokees the interest due to them from May 23, 1860, through May 23, 1864. Although no payment was ever made, the Confederate government at least attempted to respond in good faith to the needs of its Indian allies.[7]

When Thomas returned to Tennessee in March, he discovered that more changes had been made with his legion. General Daniel S. Donelson had replaced Smith as commander of the twenty-five thousand troops in the Department of East Tennessee, and Donelson had placed the Thomas legion in the brigade of Brigadier General Alfred E. Jackson. Such action stripped Thomas himself of practically any authority except that which Jackson chose to give him. The fifty-six-year-old Jackson was ill-humored, disliked by his men, and singularly unpopular with the Indians and mountaineers who were loyal to Thomas. Thomas claimed that, when President Davis had given him permission to organize a legion, he had promised that it would never be attached to a brigade. He also feared that the Indians and highlanders would become discontented under an officer who did not understand them. The instant hostility that sprang up between Jackson and Thomas lasted for the duration of the war.[8]

Even before being forced to submit to Alfred E. Jackson, Thomas was disillusioned with the unwillingness of his superiors to adopt his ideas. During November 1862, under the authority of Smith, Thomas had enlisted one hundred miners and sappers in his service. These men had no military status and were averse to bearing arms for the Confederacy, but they were good engineers, working as carpenters, blacksmiths, gunsmiths, and in other support services. Thomas had an ingenious plan to solve two problems at once: he was using local citizens who would not bear arms for the South and keeping them so busy building bridges and other necessities for the Confederate troops that they would not be likely to support the other side. One of the first orders that Jackson gave to the miners and sappers was that they should bear arms. Most of them immediately deserted.[9]

Thomas was doomed to a difficult spring and summer in 1863. In April, one of his men and a former clerk, Joseph Keener, wrote to

Vance that "the military school at Strawberry Plains under Col. Thomas is a great curse to the country." Although there were many good fighting men in the legion, they often went home, and Thomas did nothing to check the desertions. He thought Thomas should be removed to some distant post where he would not be such a "flagrant" outrage on the people and the government and that an able commander should be sent in his place.[10] Apparently Vance ignored the complaint, but such a letter further eroded the reputation of the white chief whom the governor clearly did not like.

In addition, Thomas was the subject of debate in the western North Carolina press. The Hendersonville newspaper, as Thomas explained to Sallie, continued "its old trade of lying about me." At least, he said, he took some comfort from the fact that he was not the only "humble citizen" being "assailed by that contemptible dirty sheet."[11] The *Asheville News* defended him on June 11, 1863, arguing that the *Henderson Times* was "vindictive and spiteful towards every man who took an early stand against the tyrannical usurpations of the Lincoln despotism." Furthermore, its attacks on Colonel Thomas were unfounded, for anyone who knew him could testify that he was an able and excellent commander, loyal to the South, and had spent many months away from home on difficult and dangerous assignments.

Thomas endured numerous other discomforts and dangers that summer. The disloyalty of so many citizens and the increasing presence of armed bands made the lives of those who defended the Confederacy doubly difficult. By late summer Confederate control of the region was waning. Major General Simon Buckner took charge of the Department of East Tennessee, but Thomas's legion and Walker's battalion remained attached to Jackson's brigade.[12]

Thomas also worried about his family, property, and debts. He gave his power of attorney to his friend Mercer Fain and attempted to raise needed money by selling sixteen thousand acres of his land in Jackson County to three South Carolinians for ten thousand dollars. Since he had been absent from home for fourteen months, he was losing control over his finances. He wrote Sallie that he was lonely, wanted to go home, was suffering with sumac-poisoned ankles, and that the Indians yearned for home, too.[13]

Instead of going home, he went to Knoxville, where General Jackson ordered him sent to be tried for disobeying orders. On August 15, 1863, Jackson had Thomas arrested for insubordination. What order he disobeyed is not clear, but surely it dealt with Thomas's indifference to the desertions of the miners and sappers who refused Jackson's order to take up arms. Dealing with those deserters and others from among his troops was a difficult challenge for Thomas. They were often his favored Indians, friends, neighbors, and relatives. Sometimes he seemed more concerned about them than about the Confederacy. He was also sympathetic with the miners and sappers whom he had promised that they would not have to bear arms. The court-martial, however, did not take place because Union soldiers commanded by General Ambrose Burnside were already at the gates of Knoxville. The charges were apparently dropped, and Thomas went back to Strawberry Plains to command the Indians and highlanders.[14]

Thomas's inability to get along with Jackson and his arrest in the late summer of 1863 permanently altered his relationship to his legion. On September 1, 1863, Jackson named James R. Love II colonel of the companies of infantry in the legion, a position Love held until its surrender at the end of the war. This position was the one Thomas had been given when the legion had been organized on September 27, 1862. Thomas, however, retained his commission of colonel and often referred to himself and was referred to by others as the commander of the legion. In truth, however, except for brief periods, Thomas commanded only the two companies of Indians and highlanders and whatever other companies may have been given to him for a particular mission.

The troubles that plagued Thomas during the summer of 1863 coincided with the deterioration of the Confederacy. In July, General Robert E. Lee and his Army of Northern Virginia, suffering heavy casualties, had been forced to retreat from Gettysburg. On July 4, General John Pemberton, after withstanding a thirty-day siege imposed by General Ulysses S. Grant, surrendered Vicksburg, Mississippi, to the Union. With the Mississippi River secured for the Federals, powerful Northern armies could proceed from the West toward Chattanooga and Atlanta. What was worse for Thomas, on September 1 an invasion force led by General Ambrose E. Burnside marched unopposed into Knoxville. Unable to hold that city, the Confederates abandoned it. The next day, September 2, Union troops moved into Strawberry Plains.

On the night of September 2, acting under orders from Buckner, Thomas and his two companies of Indians and a hundred or more highlanders retreated to the Smoky Mountains.[15] In the fall, Burnside gained control of east Tennessee, although the Confederates held various posts and depots, vainly hoping to drive him from Knoxville. At Chattanooga, on November 23 through 25, Grant, who had been given command of the Union armies in the West on October 16, smashed the Confederates under the command of General Braxton Bragg. A simultaneous Confederate defeat at Knoxville solidified Union control of east Tennessee. Grant considered sending thousands of Union soldiers northward through the mountain country, but after surveying the wretched roads, he decided against that plan.[16]

When Thomas and his Indians and mountaineers retreated on September 2, they left behind the legion, which was ordered by General Jackson to move in the direction of Abingdon, Virginia. Burnside sent a cavalry force to pursue Thomas as he passed through Sevierville, Tennessee, but Thomas did not stop to fight. Thomas continued through the high Smokies, losing only one Indian as a prisoner. Finding the roads too rugged, the pursuing Union cavalry abandoned the chase. Thomas securely blockaded all roads behind him between Paint Rock in Madison County, North Carolina, and Ducktown, Tennessee.[17]

The comfort Thomas may have taken upon finding himself in North Carolina and sometimes at home with his family did not remove him from the demands of the war. More than 350 men from his legion who hated General Jackson and contended that they were needed to protect their families had already absented themselves without official leave.[18] The situation in western North Carolina involving tories and deserters was, if possible, even worse than in Tennessee. In Murphy, the county seat of Cherokee, tories led by Captain Goldman Bryson drilled publicly and then sacked the town. In late October, Captain Campbell H. Taylor and about twenty-five of Thomas's Indians pursued Bryson. They killed him, but all of his men escaped. The next day some of the Indians were seen wearing parts of Bryson's bloody uniform as they patrolled the streets of Murphy.[19]

General Braxton Bragg thanked Taylor, praised the Cherokee soldiers for their loyalty, and gave Thomas permission to recruit two more companies of Indians.[20] General Robert B. Vance, brother of the governor and commander of the Western District of North Carolina, promised to request at once that the remainder of the legion be brought back from Tennessee. Vance, however, distrusted Thomas. He urged Thomas to make certain that Lieutenant Colonel William C. Walker reported to Thomas and that Thomas in turn reported "weekly" to Vance. Many of the men in Walker's battalion were from Cherokee County, and they were deserting in large numbers. Aware of Thomas's weakness in dealing with deserters, General Vance warned him that it was "very important to arrest every deserter," because "deserters become our worst enemies."[21] After relaying the message to Walker, Thomas relieved him from duty with Colonel James R. Love II and reassigned him to defend the citizens of Cherokee County, where both he and Walker had vested interests.[22]

Thomas had no time to waste in argument with his superiors in North Carolina because on November 29, General James Longstreet, then commanding Rebel forces in east Tennessee, ordered Thomas with all of his command to move by way of Ducktown to join General John C. Vaughn at Cleveland, Tennessee. Longstreet told Thomas to bring all the soldiers he could who were absent without leave from Confederate service, and all beef cattle, horses, and mules that were not absolutely necessary for food and farming at home. Before Thomas could act, however, Longstreet retreated toward Virginia. Thomas marched his troops to Gatlinburg, on the Tennessee side of the Smokies, perhaps in response to a suggestion from General Vance that he guard the entrance to the mountain passes on their western side. Before leaving Stekoa Fields for Gatlinburg, Thomas—who feared the return of Bryson's raiders—asked Mercer Fain to look after his property at Murphy, which he hoped Colonel Walker and a home guard would be able to protect from robbers.[23]

In a bizarre episode, several of Thomas's men, who were on a scouting mission near Sevierville, were captured by Unionists and tossed into jail. The infuriated Thomas rushed two hundred more of his men to Sevierville, broke into the jail, and released the prisoners. He also captured sixty Unionists and six Federal soldiers and confiscated the latter's guns and ammunition. Union authorities in Knoxville dispatched Colonel William J. Palmer and the Fifteenth Pennsylvania Cavalry to retrieve the "stolen property." On December 10, Palmer surprised Thomas and his men as they cooked breakfast in their camp on a steep wooded ridge. For several hours Thomas's Rebels fired at the Yankee soldiers who milled about in their old camp where some of the hungry Federals devoured corn cakes that the Indians had left frying in cast-iron skillets over open fires. Realizing that his gunfire was ineffective, Thomas retreated deeper into the Smokies. Casualties included three wounded Indians and three wounded Federals. In addition, Palmer took one prisoner, sixteen horses, eighteen muskets, two boxes of ammunition, salt, meal, dried fruit, blankets, and other supplies. He destroyed the crude camp buildings, "returned most of the horses to their loyal owners," and dispersed a "number of squaws" who had arrived the previous day. Palmer was frustrated to have captured nothing more of the white chief than his hat.[24]

Thomas later noted that at least the enemy understood that the Indians would fight and that in the mountains they would not be easy to subjugate. Thomas went with the Cherokees to Quallatown where they hoped to pass the winter. Thomas spent Christmas 1863 at Stekoa Fields with his family.[25]

The Christmas peace did not carry over into the new year. On January 3, 1864, young Columbus Walker buried his father. Lieutenant Colonel William C. Walker, commander of the Walker battalion of Thomas's legion, had been shot in cold blood when he rose from his sickbed at his home in Cherokee County to see strange men demanding that his wife grant them admission to the house. Walker was, as James Love said, "a good man, a good citizen, and a good soldier." He was also a close friend to Colonel Thomas. His only crime had been to be a loyal Confederate officer in a county where Unionists, tories, and bushwhackers did not agree with the Southern cause. Thomas, who himself had received death threats, became seriously concerned for his own safety. He organized what he called a "Life Guard," a corps of twenty large Indians to be his bodyguards. They were not in the Confederate Army; they were loyal exclusively to Thomas. Thomas believed that the Confederate cause was as good as lost, and his difficulties with General Jackson and Governor Vance had dampened his spirit. He nevertheless remained faithful to the Confederacy.[26]

Early in January 1864, General Robert Vance, a political enemy of Thomas's and a brother to Governor Zebulon Vance, answering an order from Longstreet, prepared to cross the Smokies in the dead of winter to unite his troops with those in east Tennessee. His route would be an unfinished road that Thomas had been constructing through Indian, or Oconaluftee, Gap to connect Webster, North Carolina, with Sevierville, Tennessee. The path was so steep, narrow, and rugged that wagons and artillery would have to be dismantled and carried by men on foot through the pass and down the mountain to the other side. Thomas advised against attempting the trip, but Vance was eager to please Longstreet and pressed on. He left his headquarters at Asheville on January 8, journeyed to Quallatown, where he had sent orders to Thomas and his Indians to be ready to join him. On January 12, after heroic effort, the men reached Gatlinburg. There Vance divided his force, consisting of Thomas and 125 infantry Indians and 375 cavalrymen commanded by Lieutenant Colonel James L. Henry.

Leaving Thomas, the Indians, Henry, and almost 200 cavalrymen at Gatlinburg, Vance selected 180 of the best-equipped mounted men to proceed with him to Sevierville. He ordered Henry to join him later at Schultz Mill. On the thirteenth, Vance captured seventeen Federal supply wagons. He stopped the next day at Schultz Mill to rest and feed the teams. Henry and his men were not there. Unaware that the same Colonel William J. Palmer who had chased Thomas from a nearby ridge the previous year was still in the area, Vance did not post pickets. After learning that the wagons had been taken, Palmer, with a force of less than 200 men, charged Vance's men, completely routed them, and captured Vance himself and fifty of his men. The loss of the supplies was a serious blow to the Confederacy.[27]

The capture of Robert Vance caused trouble for Thomas. Vance, and later William Stringfield, attributed it to Henry's deliberate refusal to obey orders and meet Vance at Schultz's Mill. Since Henry was subordinate to Thomas, rumor soon accused Thomas also of disobedience. General Joseph E. Johnston ordered both men court-martialed, the trial to be held in Asheville on February 23. Jefferson Davis intervened, the charges were dropped, and no trial was held. Davis said that, since Vance was in prison, there could be no practical value in placing the blame on officers whose services were still needed.[28]

Upon hearing about Robert Vance's capture, Thomas returned to the North Carolina side of the Smokies, where he reported to Colonel John B. Palmer. Thomas knew that the help he had received from Jefferson Davis would not cause his enemies in North Carolina to disappear. In fact, Governor Vance had already received a letter from one of Thomas's critics saying that Thomas, who deserved to be hanged, was a false-hearted Unionist whose rascality had contributed to the capture of the governor's brother. One week later, Thomas himself wrote to Vance, explaining some details about the capture of the governor's brother and asking to have his legion reunited under his command.[29] What the governor thought he did not say. He knew that his brother was in a Yankee prison, that Thomas had been twice court-martialed but not tried, and that Confederate control of the western part of his state was surely doomed. He also knew that Thomas had been his and his brother's leading opponent in the debate over the ad valorem tax and the route of the Western North Carolina Railroad.

Thomas, however, was at the moment too busy trying to elude the enemy to worry about the governor. On February 2, at Quallatown, the Fourteenth Illinois Cavalry under Major Francis M. Davidson, who had been ordered to destroy Thomas's force, surprised the Indians and highlanders at Deep Creek, a tributary of the Tuckasegee River, about ten miles west of Quallatown. After more than an hour of fighting, the Union commander claimed that his troops had killed 137, captured 22 Indians and 32 whites, wounded the rest, and that only 50 had escaped. The Confederates claimed that they had lost only 2 killed and 18 as prisoners.[30]

The Northerners claimed that the Battle of Deep Creek was a great victory in which they had wiped out Thomas's Indian companies. They escorted the Indian prisoners to Knoxville, "flattered and feasted" them, and promised them magnificent things if they would abandon the Confederacy and join the Northern side. "They were promised their liberty and *five thousand dollars in gold,* if they would bring *the scalp! of their Chief, Col. Wm. H. Thomas!*" one North Carolina newspaper reported with exaggerated glee. The Indians consulted among themselves, it continued, and agreed to the proposition. When they were released, however, they returned to Thomas's camp, "told him all, and have since been on the warpath — *after Yankee scalps!*"[31] Thirty North Carolina Cherokees, however, did fight for the Union. When they returned home after the war they were treated as outcasts by the Confederate Cherokees.[32]

Thomas himself seemed almost amused by the incident. He said that the enemy had suffered about twelve killed or wounded whereas the Indians had lost only five men. Colonel John B. Palmer reported only two killed and twenty or thirty captured.[33]

The Battle of Deep Creek, and the subsequent invasion of Cherokee County by the First Wisconsin Cavalry, captured the attention of many men in Thomas's legion who were still scattered in Tennessee. Almost forty of them, including James Love, James Terrell, and William Stringfield, petitioned Governor Vance for permission to leave Jackson's brigade and return to Thomas in North Carolina. Their services were needed at home, they said, and besides, they did not like Jackson. Vance denied their petition. He said that troops never did well near home, but he promised that he would write to Jefferson Davis in their behalf.[34]

In the meantime, the Indian civilians were beginning to starve. Some women and children were eating weeds and bark. Unable to get help from Colonel Palmer or Richmond, Thomas wrote directly to the governor and Council of South Carolina for aid. Thomas reminded the South Carolinians that his troops were protecting their state, too, and that united action would be needed if the Yankees were to be defeated. Thomas received some corn meal and flour from South Carolina, but it was not enough. Thomas himself purchased between eight and nine thousand dollars worth of bacon, flour, rice, and other food for his people. It was still not enough, and some of them moved into South Carolina and Georgia where conditions were not quite as harsh.[35]

Thomas sometimes appeared to break down under the pressures of the war. He was old and tired, his life often threatened, his friends suffering, his home and family in danger, his finances in disarray—and the Confederacy was certain to fail. He was sometimes physically uncomfortable and sick. He could not take orders from his superiors. Those near him occasionally questioned his mental stability. In 1864, Dr. W. L. Hilliard, his brother-in-law by virtue of marriage to one of Sarah's sisters, noticed that sometimes he seemed to be laboring under "some peculiar mental excitement—that his mind was a little out of balance." But Thomas always seemed to snap back to reality, regain his optimism, and pursue his goals without fear. Early in March, James Love, who admired and wished to help him, wrote to his parents that "Thomas has improved wonderfully both physically and mentally, and is thoroughly impressed with the justice of the cause for which we are contending."[36]

The war demanded that Thomas muster whatever inner strength he had. The same month that Love reported that Thomas was much improved, the desertion problem in the legion escalated. Enlisted men and officers left their posts in Tennessee to go home to North Carolina. Thomas's close friends Jim Love and Jimmy Terrell, who did not wish to see Thomas get into more trouble with Jackson, both urged Thomas to send them back. The intransigence of both Governor Vance and General Jackson, however, as well as his natural inclination, caused Thomas to let them stay. Thus, for the third time, Alfred E. Jackson, who was himself believed by some to be suffering from "diseased nerves," court-martialed Thomas. On May 11, 1864, he charged Thomas with receiving twenty-one deserters from the Sixty-fifth North Carolina Regiment between September 1863 and April 1864. He accused him of improper conduct by having published a false statement that he was authorized to receive into his command all dismounted cavalrymen, thus encouraging desertions by men who wanted to leave Tennessee to go home. Jackson also accused Thomas of promoting disorder and lack of discipline among the troops. The trial was scheduled for late September. About the same time these charges against Thomas were drawn, however, Jackson was relieved of his command and sent to the Army of Tennessee, from which he was again removed because of a nervous condition. By the end of the war he was a staff officer.[37]

Thomas continued to have problems with deserters and critics. On June 25, 1864, William Hicks of Webster, North Carolina, sent Governor Vance a long complaint about his "neighbor, . . . Col. Thomas." He said that he had been robbed by some of Thomas's "pets," or deserters, and that the colonel was building up "a little kingdom . . . of deserters, vagabonds, out-laws and rascals." Every "true Southerner" should oppose this "Mogul of the Confederacy," Hicks said. "For God's sake," he continued, "transfer his Kingdom to the sea coast and let us have some body here of the true grit." Unless Thomas and his "refuse [are removed] we lose Western North Carolina," Hicks concluded.[38] Vance did not reply, but this new attack on a man he already did not like represented what he was beginning to see as a trend.

Thomas remained with his command at Quallatown. Except for one foray into Tennessee to chase Union guerrillas near Loudon, he passed the summer on his home turf. Awaiting a possible trial and aware of the criticism that he was not a loyal Southerner, he affirmed his loyalty to the South in almost every letter he wrote to a military officer. In truth, he always was more loyal to his small region and to his men than he was to the Confederacy or even to the state. On July 8, 1864, he wrote Confederate Adjutant and Inspector General Samuel Cooper that it was unfair for his section, "having least interest in the institution of slavery," to bear more than its proportion of the burdens of war. His men too often went without pay and provisions, except for what he could provide, he said. He yearned for the mountains to be a place where religious and civil liberty prevailed.[39]

Neither Cooper nor anyone else was able to send Thomas much help. In August, Thomas wrote again, his handwriting unusually neat, his appeal calm, and his arguments rational. It appeared to be a letter to which he had given much thought and which he had revised and recopied. He explained that his headquarters were within nineteen miles of enemy lines. He had learned from Union deserters that the Northerners planned to secure the Virgnia salt works, to reinforce the Northern army in Virginia, and to press eastward across North Carolina to the Blue Ridge Mountains. The enemy was paying a bounty to "induce our citizens and soldiers to join them." Many North Carolinians and east Tennesseans had become "copperheads," or people who wanted peace without saving the Union, who were hiding in the Smoky Mountains. "They would come out and join me if they could do so in safety. They are mostly men who have served out their three years in the Confederate Army and conscripts that have not been in the service. Would it be advisable to take them in?" Thomas asked. If they joined the enemy, western North Carolina would be lost.[40]

In other ways, too, Thomas, tried to prove that he was not guilty of the atrocities of which Hicks and others had accused him. He ordered one of his subordinates not to let his "men raid on the citizens of Tennessee," but to keep them "as much as possible in camp or out scouting."[41]

Thomas's desperate efforts to improve his reputation, get help from Richmond, and have his legion reunited under his command all ended in failure. In May, at about the time Thomas was charged with disloyalty, General William E. "Grumble" Jones sent the legion into Virginia, where its infantry and artillery companies joined General Jubal A. Early in his campaign through the Shenandoah Valley. They swept through the valley into Maryland, winning several victories and getting to within five miles of Washington, D.C. There they were checked by Northern forces, and soon General Philip Sheridan reclaimed the valley, now a barren ruin, for the Union.

Thomas waited in his Smoky Mountain retreat, supplying his men at his own expense with goods from Georgia and South Carolina. He hoped that Love's First Regiment would soon appear to help him. He obeyed nobody's orders but his own, struggled for survival in a land of tories and bushwhackers, and took in deserters as he saw fit. In western North Carolina, by late summer 1864, the people's hearts were no longer in the war. In mid-September Thomas was arrested and sent to Greensboro for trial, the charges being those that had been brought against him the previous May 11.[42]

The court-martial and trial of William Holland Thomas in October 1864 attracted very little attention. Such charges and trials in the final months of the Confederacy were common. Only Stringfield wrote directly about the proceedings at Thomas's trial, and he did it from memory many years later. There were five charges against Thomas. The first three were those that had been listed at the Headquarters of the Sixty-fifth North Carolina Regiment on May 11: receiving deserters, "conduct unbecoming an officer and a gentlemen" by falsely encouraging desertions, and conduct prejudicial to correct military discipline. To these were added two more: incompetency and disobedience.

Thomas must have pleaded not guilty, perhaps arguing that he had done nothing other than what was logical and necessary to survive and win the war in an area where disloyalty to the Confederacy was often worn in public as a badge of honor. William W. Stringfield thought Thomas was an honest man and a good military commander who suffered from mental stress and the conniving of his enemies. Even Confederate Assistant Secretary of War James A. Campbell had written a year earlier: "To allow those who belong to other organizations than those in which they enlisted . . . seems to me a measure of prudence under the existing circumstances." The court, however, was not convinced and found Thomas guilty. Unwilling to accept that verdict, early in November, Thomas boarded a train for Richmond where he would appeal personally to his friend Jefferson Davis.[43]

According to Stringfield, who received a letter from Thomas, Jefferson Davis reversed the whole matter. Exonerated, Thomas decided to use his time in Richmond to turn President Davis and Secretary of War James A. Seddon to his viewpoint. He asked Seddon to reissue an order for James Love's First Regiment of the legion to be returned to North Carolina. When Seddon did so, Thomas wired the news to Love, who immediately prepared his men for the long journey home. Then Thomas went a step further; he tried, with no success, to get the Confederate Congress to pass a law that would allow tories who returned to their homes to be forgiven for their disloyalty. Such a law, he argued, would unite the South and frighten the North into stopping the war. His absurd argument was perceived as such by the members of the congress, and they ignored him.[44] His asking for such a law based on such an argument suggests that he had either lost touch with reality or that his enemies who had accused him of disloyalty perhaps had some good reason. It could have been a manifestation of his later mental illness. The most likely answer is that what Thomas really wanted was for his friends and neighbors in the western North

Carolina mountains to return to peace, harmony, and prosperity regardless of what became of slavery and the Union.

Governor Vance feared the influence Thomas might have with Jefferson Davis and Secretary of War Seddon. On December 13 he wrote Seddon, informing him that the troops under Colonel John D. Palmer, if properly led, could protect western North Carolina from the enemy, deserters, and tories. "Col. Thomas is worse than useless," Vance wrote; "he is a positive injury to that country." Thomas's command, Vance contended, was "a favorite resort for deserters . . . who do no service," and Thomas himself "is disobedient of orders and invariably avoids the enemy when he advances."[45] Vance's attack was surely motivated by Vance's belief that Thomas was responsible for the capture of his brother and by his longstanding political hostility toward the former senator from Jackson.

Vance's condemnation of Thomas apparently took Seddon and Davis by surprise. Seddon forwarded the letter to Davis with the comment that he had thought both Thomas and Palmer "particularly efficient." He suggested that perhaps a brigadier general should be appointed to unify the command. Davis replied that Brigadier General James G. Martin was in charge of that district.[46] Martin, an able military commander, graduate of West Point, hero of the Mexican War and several Civil War battles in Virginia, took charge of the Western North Carolina District on August 16. After considering all aspects of the Thomas affair, he decided to leave the old white chief undisturbed. He wrote to Robert E. Lee that Thomas was not a military man but a person for whom "many allowances are to be made." Since Thomas had no supplies, no pay for his troops, and so few troops in his command, Martin saw no reason to make any changes.[47]

The decisions made by Thomas, Martin, Seddon, and Davis in the winter of 1864–65 were no doubt determined by the desperation that had settled over the Confederacy. Although many Confederate military and civilian leaders were not yet ready to admit it, the sweeping victories of the Union armies in 1863 and 1864 had pressed the Confederacy to the point where little remained but the time and place of surrender. In January 1865, acting with authorization from Seddon, Thomas frantically recruited men in his section of the country where the Southern conscription act could not be enforced, swelling his legion's ranks to about one thousand, or 60 percent of Martin's fighting force.[48]

Confederate veterans of Thomas's legion in 1901. North Carolina Division of Archives and History.

In February, William Stringfield, who commanded a battalion of Thomas's legion, reported to Thomas that he had so few arms, ammunition, and necessities for life, that should the enemy appear, he and his men would have no choice but to run and hide.[49] In March, Union Colonel George Kirk and his raiders, after wreaking havoc in Waynesville, penetrated as far as Soco Creek en route to Quallatown to attempt to capture Thomas. Stringfield and the Indians and highlanders stopped them in a battle that raged for several hours. Kirk escaped.[50]

On April 9, 1865, Robert E. Lee surrendered to Ulysses S. Grant at Appomattox Courthouse, Virginia. In the next four weeks the Civil War in the Smoky Mountains of North Carolina ground down to its inevitable conclusion.

The Union forces then converging on western North Carolina included Colonel George Kirk's raiders, who were sacking any hamlet too weak to protect itself; General George Stoneman's troops, who had captured Salisbury on April 17; and Colonel Isaac M. Kirby's brigade, which arrived from Tennessee and camped on the outskirts of Asheville. Kirby heard a rumor that Thomas had "800 infantry, 400 Indians, one four-gun battery, and about 450 calvary" stationed at Quallatown and was preparing to raid the Knoxville and Chattanooga Railroad at Loudon or Charleston, Tennessee.[51] In truth, Thomas had only about 300 Cherokees with him and was not about to raid anyone. His only advantage was whatever fear the Union forces had for his legion.[52]

The final events that led to the surrender of Thomas and his legion began on May 3. By then, Martin had heard the news from Appomattox and had joined with Colonel James R. Love in a retreat from Asheville toward Waynesville. Lieutenant Colonel Stringfield had surrendered at Knoxville on May 1 and had been imprisoned. The town of Waynesville was little more than a dirty hamlet of fifteen to twenty dwellings. It was occupied by Colonel William C. Bartlett of the Second North Carolina Mounted Infantry, a tory regiment under General George Stoneman's command. During the night of May 6, Thomas arranged his Indians on the ridges surrounding the town. He ordered them to build as many fires as possible to make it appear to the Yankees that they were surrounded by thousands of Rebels. As the fires blazed, the Cherokees danced their ancient dances and shattered the night with blood-chilling war whoops.[53]

The next day, May 7, under a flag of truce sent out by Bartlett, the Confederate officers Thomas, Love, and Martin, with their bodyguards, walked into town for a conference. According to one report, Thomas became boisterous, dominated the talk, and told Bartlett that if he did not surrender he would unleash his Indians upon the entire Yankee regiment and have them scalped. Bartlett attempted to avoid Thomas, and the account of Thomas's conduct may have been exaggerated. On May 9, after two days of talks during which the Confederate surrenders in Virginia and eastern North Carolina were mentioned, the exhausted disputants agreed to the same terms that Lee and Grant had accepted one month earlier. The Confederates, including about 500 whites and 200 Indians in Thomas's legion, laid down their weapons and went home. Since Thomas's private bodyguards, about twenty large Indians, were not Confederate soldiers, but in his personal employ, he succeeded in his demand that they be allowed to keep their guns.[54]

Colonel Thomas presented quite a spectacle when he walked into Waynesville on May 7, 1865, surrounded by his Indian bodyguards. He was dressed exactly as they, stripped to the waist, painted and feathered in the style of a warrior ready for battle. He was half a foot shorter than most of his guards. Considering his peculiar history as both a white man and a Cherokee Indian, such a form of dress probably seemed natural for him. His unusual appearance, however, and his boisterous demands on his captor, raised anew the issue of his mental stability. Writing thirty-five years later that "Col. Thomas . . . lost his mind after the war," his friend William Stringfield said, "I think he was a little off at this time from his actions—he and his Indians were painted and feathered in good old style."[55]

CHAPTER 8

In a Mad Man's Cell

COLONEL WILLIAM HOLLAND THOMAS'S DREAM of returning to a happy, prosperous family nestled in a sylvan paradise was not to come true. When he traversed the short distance from Waynesville, where he had surrendered, to the modest house at Stekoa Fields, where Sallie and the children waited, he was an old man weakened in body and mind, angered by defeat, and uncertain of what fate awaited him and the few hundred Cherokees who still called him chief. Despite a strong determination to return to a normal life, Thomas was never able to regain full physical and mental stamina or recoup his financial losses.

Thomas hoped to resume his career in politics, but as an ex-Confederate colonel he was certain to be regarded with suspicion by the new political regime. In May 1865 President Andrew Johnson, who had succeeded to the presidency upon the assassination of Lincoln, appointed William W. Holden as provisional governor of North Carolina. When Holden received a report of opposition to his government in Haywood and Jackson counties, he suspected that Thomas and his brother-in-law, Dr. Samuel L. Love, might be attempting to cause trouble. The governor's distrust of Thomas was not justified, however; Thomas signed an oath of loyalty to the United States in 1865.[1] Since Thomas fell into the category of Southerners whose prewar taxable property exceeded $20,000 in value, he had to petition President Johnson for an individual pardon. He had known Andrew Johnson for twenty-five years, he said, and he was confident that the president would restore the seceded states to their constitutional rights and privileges. Thomas applied for his pardon, received it about the middle of 1866, and was thus restored to citizenship and the privilege of participating in politics.[2]

Nevertheless, Thomas's effort to return to politics came to naught. After the war, Thomas considered himself a moderate and was chosen as an alternate delegate to the National Union Convention. That political convention, which met in Philadelphia in August 1866, hoped to unite those Democrats who had followed Stephen A. Douglas in 1860 with moderate Republicans in order to defeat the radical Republicans.[3] Thomas did not attend the convention, nor was it successful. However, his selection as an alternate delegate and willingness to attend suggest that the war had not turned him into an extremist.

Likewise, Thomas was not upset by the end of slavery. He owned about fifty slaves at the time they were set free in 1865 by the Thirteenth Amendment to the Constitution, but the loss of that human property made little difference to him. He wrote Sallie, who was visiting her family in Waynesville, that only a few blacks remained on the farm. He said that, although he had offered homes to Aunt Rose, Ann, and Caroline, they preferred to move. Their departure would be no "pecuniary injury," he said. "If they can do without us we probably can do without them."[4] Two years later, Thomas hired one of his former slaves, Major Bartlett Wells, who had served him in camp during the war, to work for him as a free laborer at the rate of ten dollars per month.[5] A few years later, Caroline, who had been Sallie's slave at the time she married Willie, returned with her two children and contracted to work for Thomas and Sallie in return for "food and raiment for myself and two children" and fifty dollars per year for the services of her oldest son until he reached age twenty-one.[6]

Thomas had often used free labor before the war. Resuming that system and the project he had put down to enter military service, he went to work on the road through Indian Gap in October 1865. First he removed the obstructions he had placed across it during the war. Then he began to extend and repair it, expecting that it would be opened for use by wagons within a week. Since he anticipated that friendly relations would be restored between North Carolina and Tennessee, he planned to have a trade route ready.[7]

Struggling to reestablish his businesses and to pay his debts, Thomas signed one contract with James W. Terrell to resume joint operation of the tannery at Quallatown and another with Abraham Mingus to operate on halves a grist mill there. Thomas was the sole owner of a wagon repair shop. As his ability to function rationally became more and more impaired, Thomas, as he had done for many years, began to depend on Terrell. Thomas's creditors, especially those in the North, were anxious to collect. "We are desirous of hearing from all of our old friends," wrote a firm in New York, "and learn of their welfare, prosperity, etc. and wish also to remind them of their indebtedness due us." Thomas could not pay; he sank deeper into debt, owing William Johnston and his son Robert at least $33,887.11 by 1867.[8]

The Indians who returned from the war, as well as those who never went, fared—if possible—even worse than their white chief. Besides excruciating poverty, their most immediate problem was an outbreak of smallpox. One of the Indians who had deserted to the Union side brought the disease home. The nature of his illness was not known until after his death, by which time he had infected others. When Thomas recognized it, he sent his wife and children to Waynesville where she had relatives and where the children could be vaccinated. He remained at home to try to help the Indians. He asked Dr. John Mingus for an ounce of asafetida and "at least two gallons purified whiskey" to be used as a preventive against the disease. He sent for a doctor from Sevier County, Tennessee. Although the doctor worked for twelve days, vaccinating and treating the Indians, his vaccine was ineffective. The Indians distrusted white medicine, and some treated themselves with plunges into the ice-cold river, which in every case was fatal. An estimated 125 of them died in the fall and spring of 1865–66.[9]

Other problems the Cherokees confronted were hunger, factionalism, crises in leadership, and the difficult legal questions concerning their relationship to the defeated state and reunited nation. Among their numbers were Cherokees who had fought for either the Confederacy or the Union, for neither, or for both. The esteem, even reverence, that most of the Quallatown Indians had for Thomas was not shared by all eastern Cherokees. Some even wished to go west to escape the harsh life in North Carolina. Thomas's friend James Taylor, a man of mixed blood who was well educated and loyal to Thomas, and James Terrell, who had served him well since they met when Terrell was a teenager, assumed much of the work that Thomas had done. George Bushyhead, who did not trust Thomas, emerged as a rival leader who thought Thomas was motivated only by self-interest.

The North Carolina General Assembly, on February 19, 1866, passed a law acknowledging the right of the Cherokees to remain in the state, but not granting them citizenship. This act made them eligible for federal money that had been promised in 1848 and again in 1855, and it indirectly rewarded those who had served the state during the war.[10] Being allowed to remain in North Carolina in 1866, however, did not alleviate the Cherokees' troubles. The relationship of North Carolina and the other former Confederate states to the remainder of the nation was yet to be determined. The Indians still needed the advice and help of their white chief.

Thomas, however, was not able to give his Indian people help, because in March 1867 he was declared insane and sent to the asylum in Raleigh. The mental aberrations noted by W. L. Hilliard and James Love during the war had not disappeared. Sometimes he was lucid; sometimes he was not. He had frightening outbursts of violence. On one occasion, as he stood behind Sallie holding a hatchet over her head, he ordered her to play the piano—the very piano he had sent her as a gift from Washington shortly after their marriage.[11] Perhaps it was that occasion, or some other, that caused Sallie to summon her brothers Robert and Samuel, and the sheriff, for help. As Sallie wept, her brothers delivered her demented husband into the care of the sheriff, who had him transported to Dix Hill—then called the "lunatic asylum"—in the state's capital. Ironically, his children now suffered the fate that had bedeviled him all of his life: they had no father.

The asylum in which Thomas found himself was the one he and other North Carolina politicians had provided in response to the appeal of Dorothea Dix in 1848. Thomas's first commitment lasted less than a month. His caretakers quieted him and attempted to determine whether he was insane. At first, he expressed considerable anger toward those who had committed him. Shortly, however, he calmed down, ate and slept properly, and engaged in intelligent conversations. On April 8, the superintendents declared him sane and allowed him to return to his home in Jackson County. They charged him twenty-five dollars for his board at the asylum.[12] Jim Love, who saw him on his way home, thought him improved but not restored.[13]

His bittersweet return to Stekoa Fields marked the beginning of a troubled decade for Thomas and his family. When he was lucid, he was slow to make decisions and virtually helpless to do anything about his debts. Often crippled with a bad ankle, he was generally miserable. When he was not lucid, Sallie took care of him, sometimes resorting to having him physically restrained. She attempted to operate the businesses near their home herself, but usually she depended upon Terrell and others to help her. The fate of the Cherokees, too, remained entwined with that of Thomas. In 1867 he resigned as their chief. After several years of bitter factional strife, Flying Squirrel emerged as principal chief. The complete disentanglement of their lands and business from Thomas's required time and litigation.[14]

In May 1867, both Terrell and Thomas thought that Thomas was competent to do business.[15] Thomas sent notes to Cherokees calling them to meetings and dances and exhorting them to avoid liquor. He gave them supplies from his stores on credit. He bought land in Jackson County that had once belonged to Indians, and he borrowed money from Robert B. Johnston, a son of William Johnston, his principal creditor.[16] In 1868 he partially settled an old account with the widow of his former partner at Murphy, Johnson W. King, and later traded off a note from his business associate Robert Rose for three hundred dollars. For reasons unstated, but surely for indebtedness to his partner, he gave his share in the store at Quallatown to Terrell. His credit ran out, and although William Johnston granted him an extension in 1868, the next year his creditors converged upon him.[17]

The crisis of Thomas's indebtedness, and its impact on the land he held in his name for the Indians, reached a climax in 1869. Thomas's creditors, especially the elderly William Johnston and his son Thomas, demanded that his lands be sold to pay his debts. Since thousands of acres registered in Thomas's name belonged, in fact, to the Indians, they too became fearful of losing their property. James Terrell advised Sallie Thomas, who was acting for her incapacitated husband, to employ a local attorney and to send someone to Washington to work for a settlement of the business affairs between the Indians and her husband. Since Sallie could afford to do neither, Terrell agreed to work for her at his own expense. He employed Nicholas W. Woodfin of Asheville as her attorney, and he made the trip to Washington himself.

Terrell understood Thomas's business affairs as well as it was possible for anyone to understand them. Terrell told Woodfin that he knew the Indians owed Thomas enough money for Thomas to pay his debts to the Johnstons. James Taylor calculated that the Indians owed Thomas $40,000 in addition to their accounts at the store. The Cherokees could pay nothing, however, unless they acquired what was due them from the government. Terrell also understood that, since North Carolina had granted the Cherokees the right to live in the state, they were eligible to collect many thousands of dollars under the laws of 1848 and 1855 for which Thomas had lobbied. Thomas was entitled

North Carolina Hospital for the Insane, Raleigh, 1857. North Carolina Division of Archives and History.

to a 10 percent commission on anything the Indians collected. Terrell had worked for a decade as a disbursing agent among the Indians and was entitled to his own commission.[18]

William and Sarah Thomas needed any help Terrell could provide because in June the Johnstons levied all of Thomas's lands in Jackson, Macon, Cherokee, and Clay counties. Since Thomas had borrowed money from them to purchase the land, they regarded the property as collateral on the loan, not knowing that almost half the acreage was intended for the Indians. Thomas owed them $33,887.11 in 1867. Since they knew that Thomas was broke, could not collect debts owed to him, and had lost his mind, they attempted to retrieve their money in the only way possible. Acting for them in August 1869, the sheriff of Cherokee County sold 115,407 acres of Thomas's land. The Johnstons bought it for less than $9,000. Of those acres, at least 50,000 belonged to the Cherokees.[19]

In the meantime the legal and financial status of the Cherokees had improved. On July 27, 1868, Congress recognized the North Carolina Cherokees as a distinct tribe, provided for a new census to be taken, and arranged for those eligible for money under the laws of 1848 and 1855 to be paid. In December the Indians who had been loyal to Thomas met in council at Cheoah and drew up a constitution. In 1869 the government paid those on the new roll $48,540, but since much of it went to make payments to lawyers who claimed to represent them, the Indians collected only about $32,000.[20]

The Johnstons knew the Indians had the money. They said that if the Indians would pay them $30,000, which was almost $4,000 less than Thomas owed them, then they would deed to the Cherokees the land they claimed and return the remaining acres to Thomas. The Indians, acting on advice from Terrell, accepted the offer and made a down payment of $6,500.[21] The secretary of the interior, however, who had been influenced by George Bushyhead and others of Thomas's enemies, suspected that Thomas and the Johnstons were collaborating to defraud the Indians. Both he and the commissioner of Indian affairs wanted enabling legislation to charge Thomas and the Johnstons with fraudulent transactions with the North Carolina Cherokees. In July 1870, Congress passed a bill authorizing the Cherokees to institute suits against agents of their band. On October 26 of the next year, the council of eastern Cherokees reported to the Board of Indian Commissioners that they had been "greatly and grossly wronged" by Thomas;

he had claimed, they alleged, that he had invested all of the federal money he had collected for them in lands for them, but those lands had been sold to satisfy his private debts.[22]

The complicated matter of landownership among the Cherokees, Thomas, and the Johnstons was finally resolved through two suits the Cherokees brought against the whites in 1873. No bad feelings existed among any of the parties involved. Apparently Thomas, the Indians, and the Johnstons regarded the suits only as a business matter that had to be settled. The first suit, *Eastern Band of the Cherokee Indians vs. William H. Thomas, William Johnston, and James W. Terrell*, was the more important, because it attempted to force Thomas to account for the money he had collected for them between 1836 and 1861. The suit named Johnston because he had taken title to the lands Thomas had bought with the money, and it named Terrell because he had served as disbursing agent from 1853 through 1861. The second suit, *Eastern Band of Cherokee Indians vs. James W. Terrell, William H. Thomas, William Johnston, A. J. Murray, and J. B. Allison*, named Terrell as the defendant and several men who had functioned as sureties on his bond as disbursing agent. In the spring of 1873, Terrell and Thomas D. Johnston, son of William Johnston and a prominent attorney in Asheville, went to Washington to collect as much evidence as they could to document the prewar transactions between Thomas and the Cherokees.[23]

When the United States Circuit Court for the Western District of North Carolina at Asheville, with Judge Robert P. Dick presiding, took up the suits in May 1873, Thomas was present. Since his return home in April 1867, he had been in and out of the asylum, but most of the time he had been home. In 1871, while resting at nearby White Sulpher Springs, he had written his Indian friends a long letter warning them not to trust George Bushyhead's "*liars, Swindlars,* and *vagabonds.*" He urged them to remember what a struggle it had been since 1838 to remain in their homes and to trust no one who might want to take their lands or urge them to emigrate west. Some of their friends, he said, had deserted them and were worshipping "the *golden calf*," like the Israelites in the Bible. He, as always, wanted them to remain in their "native country, the garden of Eden of the Red man." Since he had spent three months at the springs, doctoring himself with sulphur water and Indian remedies, he wrote, "a kind Providence has nicely restored my health." He knew an attorney in Washington who would help them, he said.[24]

The true condition of Thomas's mental state at the time he wrote that letter cannot be known, but it suggests that, healthy or sick, his attitude toward the Indians was consistent. The government officials and his enemies, who did not know the story of his adoption by Yonaguska and life as both a Cherokee and a white man, were simply not correct when they accused him of conspiring with others to defraud the Indians. Certainly he had wanted to earn his commissions, but he was more concerned for the welfare of the Indians. During the hearing he demonstrated that he was sincere in his wish for the Indians to have the land he had purchased for them.

In May 1873, Terrell, who had been Thomas's closest associate since 1852, learned for the first time something of the intensity of feeling the old white chief had for his people. On one occasion, when the trial had recessed and Terrell was riding home with him, Thomas seemed to be in his right mind. He talked freely about the Indians, recalling everything that had been said in court, and asked Terrell if he had said anything that might be prejudiced against the Indians. Terrell became very impatient with Thomas and asked him why, after all he had done for them, in his old age he would allow a few Indians to disgrace and destroy him. Terrell accused Thomas of being more solicitous of the welfare of the Indians than he was of his own children.

After listening patiently to his friend, Thomas replied that the great body of Indians wished him no harm and that in his youth he had with enthusiasm taken up their cause, enjoyed their loyalty, and promised them homes and protection "in the land of their nativity." Thomas made his point so poignantly that Terrell thought that, if the Indians were ever driven from their homes, Thomas would not survive it. Thomas continued that it was true that the Indians were indebted to him, but if the government paid them what it had promised, all parties could be satisfied.[25]

At the trial itself, the plaintiffs in the first suit alleged that Thomas had collected many thousands of dollars between 1836 and 1861, and instead of investing it for them, had bought land in his own name. Furthermore, William Johnston had acquired the same land at sheriff's sales as payment for debts Thomas owed him. In the second suit, the plaintiffs contended that Terrell had undisbursed funds that he or his sureties should distribute as the law intended. The attorney for the defendants presented hundreds of pages of deposition from Terrell as well as dozens of land deeds, mortgages, and contracts between Thomas and individual Indians that Terrell had collected. Thomas's answer, which had been prepared for him, was that he had not collected $200,000 as alleged, that he had paid individual Indians monies he had acquired for them, that he had bought land for the Indians with the understanding that they would pay him whenever they received their federal money, and that the total cost of the Indians' lands up to 1850 was more than $49,000. The incomplete though voluminous records, the impossibility of defining the boundaries of the property in question, and the necessity to depend upon witnesses whose memories were not reliable made it impossible to reach an easy verdict. The cases were carried over to the next year.[26]

When the court took up the cases in the spring of 1874, Thomas was again present. In May all parties agreed to combine the two suits and submit them to binding arbitration. The arbiters were John Henry Dillard of Greensboro, Thomas Ruffin, Jr., of Hillsboro, and General Rufus Barringer of Charlotte—all prominent citizens known for their ability and sense of fairness. Their verdict would have to be approved by Judge Robert P. Dick, the secretary of the interior, the commissioner of Indian affairs, and the Department of Justice. The arbiters got to work in August, moving from Asheville to Waynesville to Quallatown and back to Waynesville, as they found it convenient, to interview more than 150 witnesses and examine hundreds of documents.[27]

The United States Department of the Interior sent Francis N. Dony as a special agent to protect the property and the rights of the Cherokees. After working at his task for six days, Dony wrote that "To unravel the entanglement and decide what was Indian land, and what was not, seemed insurmountable." He soon learned what many others before him had discovered: when dealing with the eastern Cherokees, he needed the help of Thomas. In order to deal with Thomas, however, he admitted that "it was necessary to indulge his idiosyncrasies and patiently bide" his time. Once, as they rode together, with no one else present, Dony found that the "so-called lunatic" spoke calmly, accurately, and rationally about his dealings with the Cherokees, and, to Dony's amazement, defended the very people who had brought suit against him. Dony was convinced that Thomas wanted the Indians to win their case and to have their lands.[28]

When the arbiters interviewed Indians and others at Quallatown, however, Thomas was both their best and worst witness. According to Terrell, "When the trial began at Quallatown in August 1874 the mildest description that can be given of the state of Col. Thomas' mind was that he was a raving, furious maniac." While a jury of inquest was deliberating in the room, "Thomas was raving at the door and could easily have been heard half a mile." Nevertheless, "his memory of facts seemed good." At that hearing, however, Thomas turned against his friend Terrell and threatened to have him put in the penitentiary for producing documents in Thomas's defense against the Indians.[29] The best witness for the plaintiffs was the defendant himself.

In October 1874 the arbiters reached their conclusion, and it was accepted by the judge and government offices. They decided that Thomas had indeed acquired thousands of acres for the Indians, which he had paid for in part with money that was theirs and in part with money that was his. For the seventy-three thousand acres that the surveyors said were in Qualla Boundary and a number of individual tracts, the Indians still owed Thomas $18,250. From that amount the Indians could deduct the $6,500 they had paid Johnston, plus interest it had earned since September 1869, bringing the total to $8,486. The Indians owed a balance of $9,764.

The arbiters also decided that Terrell owed the Indians $2,697.89 that he had incorrectly, but without malicious intent, diverted to Thomas as their attorney. They could also deduct this amount from their balance, leaving $7,066.11 which they must pay to the Johnstons as Thomas's creditors in order to have clear title to their lands. The Indians must pay the Johnstons 6 percent interest on the money due until the debt was paid. Since the arbiters concluded that Thomas still owed the Johnstons $18,335, they appointed Terrell and Thomas D. Johnston to act as commissioners to sell any of Thomas's property not encumbered by the Indians to satisfy that debt. Thomas was to be paid a 10 percent commission on the monies accruing to the eastern Cherokees from their share of the sale of western lands.[30]

The Indians got their land, the Johnstons got their money, and Thomas was left impoverished. There is no evidence that he ever collected the commission that was promised him on the sale of western lands, although Terrell estimated the commission to be $50,000 and made a valiant effort to collect it for him. As his other lands were sold to pay his debts, Thomas was left with only the house and farm at Stekoa Fields, and he retained these largely because of the sympathy of his creditors.[31]

No one was more sympathetic with Thomas than the Indians.

Meeting in council on November 16, 1874, they passed resolutions giving him thanks and highest praise. They acknowledged that for nearly forty years, he had managed their business, purchased lands for them with his private funds, introduced the Christian religion among them, and cared for their orphans and infirm. The passage of the title to their lands in 1869 to the Johnstons was no fault of Thomas, they said. They regretted that the suits had placed them "in apparent antagonism to him who had for so many years been our steadfast friend and protector." They would be happy for him to receive "ten percent of such funds as may hereafter accrue to us as our *pro rata* share of the sale of western lands." As the ultimate proof of their devotion, they adopted Thomas's adopted daughter Angelina Sherrill and her two children, and the two sons and daughter he had with Sallie "as members of the Eastern Band of Cherokees."[32]

The amiable parting of Thomas and the eastern Cherokees marked the end of an era in the lives of both. Thomas's affection for them remained intact for the balance of his life, but he was almost seventy and mentally and physically incapable of rendering the service he had once given them. Since North Carolina had agreed in 1866 to allow them to remain in the state, and the United States in 1868 and again in 1886 recognized them as separate from the Cherokee Nation, they were more secure in their homeland than they had been since 1835. In 1875 the federal offices that dealt with Indians began to treat the Eastern Band as permanent residents of western North Carolina. Although their legal, economic, and social problems were scarcely ended, in forty years they had made considerable progress with the help of their white chief.[33]

The lives of Sarah and William Thomas during the ten years after his first commitment were filled with tenderness, love, pain, suffering, and courage. Sarah was determined to keep her husband at home; she came to depend more and more upon help from her brothers and sisters. After her youngest sister, Maria, married William W. Stringfield in 1871 and settled with him in the Love family home at Waynesville, they were her closest confidants. Since Maria's father was dead, Stringfield had asked permission from the Thomases to marry Maria. From his first meeting with the old colonel at Strawberry Plains in 1862, he had held Thomas in high esteem and genuinely wished to help him.[34]

The isolation of Stekoa Fields, the state of their father's health, and financial difficulties necessitated Sarah's sending her three children to stay for long periods of time with the Stringfields in Waynesville or her brother-in-law, W. L. Hilliard, in Asheville. The two boys, William, Jr., and James Robert, usually went to Waynesville, and Sallie went to her uncle's home in Asheville. Hilliard once wrote Sarah that he would watch over Sallie "as faithfully as I do my own daughter."[35]

Sarah passed much of her time caring for her husband at home or traveling with him to White Sulphur Springs, where he seemed to be more comfortable, but she eagerly wrote her siblings for news about and from her children. She wrote Stringfield in January 1871 that she was anxious to see her little boys.[36] She urged Maria and her husband to make sure that her son Willie studied because she hoped that eventually he could get a business education and a job as a store clerk. She was delighted when Willie, who was about fifteen, "made a profession of religion" in the fall of 1873, and she hoped he would remain faithful. Willie had never been baptized, she said, because his father did not believe in the doctrine of infant baptism. Colonel Thomas was willing for his namesake "to join the church, if he thinks he can make a *good member and not* bring any reproach on the church or himself."[37] Occasionally, however, Willie felt unwanted, did not get along well with the Stringfield children, and went to his Uncle Matt Love's house. Sarah tried to right matters the best she could, and usually she was successful.[38]

The Thomases' daughter, Sallie, lived in Asheville as she entered her adolescence. Shortly after Christmas 1874, she wrote her mother that she was sorry she had not been able to send her "Pa" any tobacco but to tell her brother Willie to supply him with plenty of it.[39] A few years later, when she was about fifteen and attending a school in Asheville at the expense of Uncle Hilliard, she wrote her mother with enthusiasm that her "Pa" would be pleased to know that she would soon be finished with her arithmetic, and that she would "do anything to please you both." She also sent a message to her brother Jimmie that "he must go to school and make a man for I've found out that if you don't paddle your own canoe you will be apt to sink."[40]

The long separations from her children, the illness of her husband, and the struggle to survive economically, however, pushed Sarah Thomas to the point of desperation. She confided her feelings of helplessness to her sister Maria. "I have not a home free of embarrassments in which to lay my head," she wrote. Her husband was "going down to the grave, under a load of physical disease and mental anxiety," and her children were "growing up like wild weeds in rich soil." She now referred to her husband as "Mr. Thomas" or "Col. Thomas," reserving the name Willie for their son. She said that when she and Mr. Thomas had discussed their troubles, he had taken a "hearty-cry," but she knew that if she cried her "eyes out it will not *gather up spilt milk.*" In this letter, which she intended for no one but her sister to read, she said, "My heart aches within me, when I think of the coming future."[41]

Well might Sarah Thomas's heart have ached, for the burdens that were bringing down her husband were her own. In addition to his nervousness, occasional violence, and drift into a world of fantasy, he suffered severe pains in his legs and one ankle that sometimes crippled him. He had complained of similar pains since the beginning of their marriage, but not until his old age did they debilitate him. In letter after letter, Sarah commented on the trouble he had. "One of his legs which pained him most," she wrote in 1871, "has broken out, and now has a running sore on it." In 1872, she wrote her sister, "Mr. Thomas, his leg has been paining him a good deal for several days." The next year she said that he suffered so "greatly with his leg he can't stand many more such attacks." Thomas himself, in a flight of fantasy, said he had suffered an ankle wound when his horse had fallen into a bog after the Battle of Malvern Hill, Virginia. Thomas, however, was not at Malvern Hill.[42]

Thomas's mental condition seemed to deteriorate more rapidly after the court trials of 1873 and 1874. He turned with a vengeance upon his friend Terrell, who was under court order to sell Thomas's lands to pay his debts. Thomas threatened to have him put in the penitentiary and posted handwritten notices in every mill, store, and blacksmith shop that he had no agents or attorneys.[43] One visitor to Quallatown described him as "a maniac chained to the floor."[44] The legend arose that Sarah had a stone room built connected to the house where she kept her husband chained and locked up during his violent rages.[45] Even when he was not restrained in some manner, Thomas's behavior often caused Sarah and her family much anxiety. Shortly before Christmas 1876, her brothers Matt and Bob went out to make arrangements to send Thomas to the asylum. As Maria reported to her husband, "Sister Sarah would not allow it."[46]

Although determined to care for her husband, Sarah herself was often ill. In August 1876 she wrote her oldest son, Willie, that "your

Sarah Love Thomas (Mrs. Alphonso C. Avery),
daughter of Sarah Jane Burney Love Thomas and William Holland Thomas.
Courtesy of Sara T. Thomas.

mother has almost been in eternity for several times during the last few weeks, and if I have a recurrence of the same disease it may prove fatal, as I am in quite a delicate and critical situation." She admonished him to be a good boy and to perfect his mathematics and grammar. She worried how she would educate her second son, Jimme. "I think my brothers and friends, if I have any, are very unmindful of me in my present condition," she wrote.⁴⁷ A few months later, Maria wrote how sad she was about "Sister Sarah's illness," and that "Col. Thomas is even worse than he has been heretofore." Sarah needed the "constant attention of a Physician all the time."⁴⁸

Chief Thomas's beloved "Sallie" died on May 15, 1877. She was forty-five. Thomas was away from the house working on a turnpike at the hour of her death. The nature of her final illness is not known. The day after her death, W. L. Hilliard sent her grieving husband a telegram, saying he very much regretted that she had allowed her case to go without treatment, but he felt certain that she had gone to heaven to be with her relatives.⁴⁹ Whether Thomas was able to attend Sallie's funeral is not known, but she was buried near her mother-in-law on a hillside at Stekoa Fields. Temperance Calvert Thomas, in her one hundredth year, had been laid to rest there after her death on October 1, 1874.

For ten years Sarah alone had stood between Thomas and permanent commitment to the asylum. Within a week of her death, her brothers again had him committed. Terrell, still his friend, was much pained when he learned that Thomas was forced to travel in a wagon with a convict to the railroad depot where he was placed on a train for Raleigh.⁵⁰

Thomas's first order of business upon finding himself once again in what he called the "Lunatic Asylum" was to try to get out. He appealed directly to the governor, who was none other than the same Zebulon Vance who had been a political enemy since 1855 and who had thought Thomas less than useless during the Civil War. "I arrived at this place last Friday and by false representations of an ignoramus of a sheriff have been deprived of my liberty and lodged in this miserable Bastile under the charge of 'lunacy,'" Thomas wrote. He accused his brothers-in-law, Robert and Samuel Love, and the justice of the peace who had heard his case, of committing him in order to escape debts they owed him.⁵¹

When Vance did not reply to Thomas's first appeal for help, Thomas kept trying. He wrote again on July 30, arguing that his constitutional rights were being denied him, that he was being treated with "silent contempt," and that it would be a sad state of affairs if "an old democrat who has grown gray in the service of his country" had to appeal elsewhere for help.[52] Thomas did not know that in the meantime his friend William Stringfield had written Vance: "If you can conveniently and in good taste call on, or show Col. Thomas . . . any favors, the kindness will be highly appreciated by not only his friends and kindred — but by all our western people."[53]

Vance gave no help. On August 11 he wrote Thomas that his commitment had been in accord with the law. Thomas responded on September 21, saying that his conduct for three months "proves that no mental disease has attended me." Thomas begged Vance to come to see him personally and decide if he were insane. "It does seem hard," he continued, "that a man who has served the public as long as I have should be . . . wearing out [his] remaining days in a mad man's cell."[54]

Except for brief visits to the Stringfield home in Waynesville, Thomas passed the remainder of his years "in a mad man's cell." He suffered from old age, the death of his wife, the loss of his property, the impact of the war, and very poor physical health. No medical report giving a diagnosis of the cause of his illness has been found, but the circumstantial evidence suggests that it was the tertiary stage of syphilis. Thomas's physical and mental complaints were typical of those of such patients: sores that would not heal, crippled legs or ankles, mental delusions, and periodic outbursts of violence. Although he did not say what Indian remedies he had used, the Cherokees had several treatments for sores or ulcers and at least one for syphilis. Since Thomas lived for so long after contracting the disease, if this theory is correct, he must have contracted it after the age of forty-five; men and women who contracted it at an earlier age usually lived for only a few years in the tertiary stage. Thomas married late in life and was sexually active for about twenty years before his marriage. Furthermore, the statistics for late-nineteenth-century asylums indicate that from 25 to 33 percent of the patients were diagnosed as insane by reason of untreated syphilis.[55]

Because of the reformer Dorothea Dix and progressive politicians such as Thomas, the care of the mentally ill in the United States had progressed significantly since the Civil War. Nevertheless, the term "asylum" rather than "hospital" was appropriate for what went on inside. The diagnosis and treatment of mental illness was still in a primitive stage. Patients were often locked up and nothing else done. The staff members were usually political rather than professional appointees. Various restraining devices and liquid bromides were administered, but there is little evidence that they contributed to a cure. The most innovative treatment at the time was called "moral therapy." It consisted of having a sympathetic attendant spend time talking with individual patients about their interests, treating them as human beings, encouraging them to keep regular schedules consisting of proper diet, personal cleanliness, religious practice, and recreation. Because of overcrowding, every patient did not get that kind of care, nor would they all necessarily have responded to it. There was a tendency also to ignore the older patients.[56]

Although Thomas accepted his fate, he yearned to be well and to be free. He wrote his son that he kept up with current events, was infuriated by the assassination of President James Garfield in 1881, and passed most of his time reading books and newspapers. The building, called Dix Hill, where Thomas lived was located on an elevation one mile southwest of Raleigh; it was an imposing structure with an attractive entrance and plenty of windows for light and ventilation.[57] The view from inside, however, was quite different from that of the passerby.

While Thomas lived at the asylum, the management of his personal and business affairs was assumed by others. The house and farm at Stekoa Fields were rented, which provided his only source of income. That source dried up when his older son married and settled there.[58] In 1878 a probate judge in Jackson County appointed Dr. W. L. Hilliard to be Thomas's guardian. The next year Hilliard petitioned that Stekoa Fields not be sold under execution because it would not bring enough to pay Thomas's debts, and its sale would leave him and his family destitute.[59] Terrell, who claimed that he put Thomas's welfare above that of his own family, continued to deal with unsettled suits for debts and to identify, evaluate, and sell Thomas's property as required. He sold about $20,000 worth and received a 10 percent commission. His compensation for the many years he spent working for Thomas was very low.[60]

When Thomas returned to the asylum in 1877, his children were not able to give him much help. The two boys, William Holland, Jr., and James Robert, ages nineteen and seventeen, continued in the care of Maria and William Stringfield. Sarah Love, age fifteen, remained with Dr. Hilliard in Asheville. All had to request money for their needs from Terrell. Some years later, however, the children did become interested in their father's affairs. James, a farmer living near Whittier, became his guardian in 1889, and William, Jr., and his family moved into the home place. Sarah took a more personal interest in the history of her "Pa." Despite his long absences during their childhood and later prolonged illness, all three seemed to have had genuine affection for him. They distrusted Terrell and Thomas Johnston and eventually sued them for mismanagment of their father's resources, a charge they could not prove.[61]

In 1883 the fate of their hospitalized father took a new and somewhat positive turn. That year North Carolina opened the Western Insane Asylum at Morganton. On May 12, 1883, a special train pulled out from the depot at Raleigh for Morganton, loaded with those patients at Dix Hill who were natives of the western counties. When Thomas arrived at his new home, he found a spacious E-shaped building, with the administrative officers in the middle, and separate, comfortable wings for men and women. A mixture of Gothic and Romanesque architecture, it was located on a hill three miles from town and surrounded by 460 acres of pastures and farmland. The scenic views Thomas could see from there were very similar to those he knew at his home . The administrator was Patrick Livingston Murphy, a doctor whose campaign to educate the public about the mentally ill helped to bring about the use of the word "hospital" instead of "asylum." Thomas fared so well there that on May 22, 1884, he was sent home on probation. On August 9 he was discharged, but he had to be readmitted on October 24.[62]

From his residence at the Western Insane Asylum, today Broughton Hospital, the old former white chief of the Cherokees made his final contribution to the lives of the people who had considered him one of their own for more than half a century. In 1887 a young ethnologist from the Smithsonian Institution, James Mooney, then twenty-six, arrived in western North Carolina to research and collect information about the Cherokees. He soon learned about their famous white chief, who was not far away at Morganton. After interviewing many eastern Cherokees, James Terrell, and others, he decided to interview Thomas.

When Mooney first arrived at the Western Insane Asylum in 1889, Thomas was too disoriented to be of help. Mooney interviewed his

Western Hospital for the Insane, Morganton, ca. 1900. North Carolina Division of Archives and History.

doctor and gained access to his medical records. Mooney recorded in his notes that Thomas had been admitted to the hospital on May 12, 1883, that he was a widower, seventy-eight years old with a liberal education, and an Indian agent who had been insane for five years. At times, Mooney wrote, Thomas was completely himself, but at other times "subject to continued paroxysms of excitement when he is very noisy, abusive, and destructive." He was "not considered violent when properly managed." Daily entries in the record indicated that on some days he was violent enough to be restrained, but most of the time he appeared to be quiet, able to walk about the grounds or stay in his room and read. Occasionally he was treated with bromides, but beyond that Mooney's notes contain nothing about a diagnosis or treatment of his illness.

When Mooney returned the next year, however, he found Thomas rational, alert, and eager to talk. It had probably been many years since anyone had shown such interest in him as the young ethnologist did. Thomas talked to Mooney for several days, telling him the full story of his life among the Cherokees, from his adoption by Yonaguska to his resignation as chief in 1867. Thomas also told him about Yonaguska, Tsali, the Cherokees in the Civil War, Indian medical remedies, the troubles the Eastern Band had had in getting their money from the government, and his own personal history. When Mooney published his classic "Myths of the Cherokee" in 1900, it contained information that he had acquired from their old white chief. Thus, in his last years, Thomas contributed, however inaccurately, to the preservation of the story of their traditions and history.[63]

In his eighty-eighth year, Thomas found peace at last. He died at 2:30 A.M., Wednesday, May 10, 1893. Murphy sent a telegram to William Stringfield: "Colonel Thomas died this morning. Body will leave here Thursday. Wire explicit shipping directions." Hilliard wrote Maria Stringfield: "I trust that the dear old man, who has suffered so long in the flesh, has entered upon an eternity of peace and joy in reunion with loved ones gone before." The mourning family and friends buried their colonel and chief in the city cemetery at Waynesville. Relatives later removed the bodies of his wife and his mother from Stekoa Fields and reinterred them near his.[64]

More than half a century later, Colonel Thomas's descendants erected an appropriate marker for his grave. They pieced together a summary of the story of his life, had it cast in a bronze plaque, and attached it to the marker. A ridge in the Great Smoky Mountains National Park extending in a semicircle from Deep Creek following the curve of the Oconaluftee River bears his name. He is a character in Kermit Hunter's popular outdoor drama, *Unto These Hills*. More important, to the west near Cherokee, North Carolina, and in the surrounding counties, live the current generation of the sons and daughters of Yonaguska. They and their scattered relatives have managed to maintain many of their traditions as well as their memories and the human dignity that their white chief wanted them to have. The destiny of the small white boy who rode through imposing mountains to the Indian trading post at Soco Creek is an intricate part of the mystery of their past. Woven into the fabric of history, the worth of this most unusual Confederate colonel and Cherokee chief is at least as durable as the silent hills that shelter him.

Notes

ABBREVIATIONS

DU — Manuscript Department, William R. Perkins Library, Duke University, Durham, N.C.
GPO — Government Printing Office, Washington, D.C.
NA — National Archives and Records Administration, Washington, D.C.
NAA — National Anthropological Archives of the Smithsonian Institution, Washington, D.C.
NCHR — *North Carolina Historical Review*
NCDAH — North Carolina Division of Archives and History, Raleigh, N.C.
OR — *The War of the Rebellion: A Compilation of the Official Records of the Union and Confederate Armies.* 128 vols. Washington, D.C.: GPO, 1880–1901.
RG 75 — Record Group 75: Records of the Bureau of Indian Affairs, Letters Received, 1824–81. National Archives and Records Administration
RG 93 — Record Group 93: Revolutionary War, Compiled Military Records. National Archives and Records Administration
RG 123 — Record Group 123: United States Court of Claims. National Archives and Records Administration
UNC — Southern Historical Collection, Louis Round Wilson Library, University of North Carolina at Chapel Hill
WCU — Special Collections, Hunter Memorial Library, Western Carolina University, Cullowhee, N.C.
WHT — William Holland Thomas
WHT Papers micro. — William Holland Thomas Papers on microfilm, Newspaper Department, William R. Perkins Library, Duke University

CHAPTER I
Little Will and Chief Yonaguska

1. James Mooney, Notes on 1890 interview with WHT, Mooney Papers, NAA; WHT Genealogy, Charles E. Bird Collection, WCU; Notes on Thomas

Family Genealogy, WHT III Collection, WCU; James Mooney, "Myths of the Cherokee," *Nineteenth Annual Report of the Bureau of American Ethnology* (Washington, D.C.: GPO, 1900), 160; Mrs. Alphonso C. Avery, "Col. William Holland Thomas," *North Carolina University Magazine* 29, no. 5 (May 1899): 291; Revolutionary War, Compiled Military Record, Thomas, Richard, 11th Va. Regt., RG 93, NA; John H. Gwathmey, comp., *Historical Register of Virginians in the Revolution* (Richmond: The Dietz Press, 1938), 767; John P. Arthur, *Western North Carolina: A History from 1730 to 1913* (Raleigh: Edwards and Broughton Co., 1914), 580.

2. WHT Memorandum and Diary 1834-35, p. 31, WHT Papers, WCU; Avery, "Thomas," 291; Thomas Family Bible, cited in Mattie Russell, "William Holland Thomas, White Chief of the North Carolina Cherokees" (Ph.D. diss., Duke University, 1956), 1.

3. *A List of Warrants Issued to the Officers and Soldiers in the Continental Line*, # 789, NCDAH.

4. Avery, "Thomas," 291; WHT Genealogy, Bird Collection.

5. William C. Allen, *Annals of Haywood County, North Carolina* (N.p. 1935), 35; Allen T. Davidson, "Reminiscences of Western North Carolina," *Lyceum* 1 (June 1890-May 1891): 4-5; Arthur, *Western North Carolina*, 137, 293; Avery, "Thomas," 291; WHT Memorandum and Diary 1834-35, p. 31, WHT Papers, WCU.

6. Horace Kephart, *Our Southern Highlanders: A Narrative of Adventure in the Southern Appalachians and a Study of Life among the Mountaineers* (1913; reprint, Knoxville: University of Tennessee Press, 1976), 171-72, 278-79.

7. Register of Reservations under the Cherokee Treaty of 1817, WHT Papers, DU; John R. Finger, *The Eastern Band of Cherokees, 1819-1900* (Knoxville: University of Tennessee Press, 1984), 10-11; George E. Frizzell, "The Legal Status of the Eastern Band of Cherokee Indians" (M.A. thesis, Western Carolina University, 1981), 8-10; Charles C. Royce, "The Cherokee Nation of Indians: A Narrative of Their Official Relations with the Colonial and Federal Governments," *Bureau of American Ethnology Fifth Annual Report* (Washington, D.C.: GPO, 1887), 212-28; Duane H. King, "The Origins of the Eastern Cherokees," in *The Cherokee Indian Nation: A Troubled History*, ed. Duane H. King (Knoxville: University of Tennessee Press, 1979), 166; George Dewey Harmon, *Sixty Years of Indian Affairs: Political, Economic, and Diplomatic, 1789-1850* (Chapel Hill: University of North Carolina Press, 1941), 150-52; George E. Frizzell, "The Native American Experience," in *The History of Jackson County*, ed. Max R. Williams (Sylva, N.C.: Jackson County Historical Association, 1987), 42.

8. Ben Oshel Bridgers, "A Legal Digest of the North Carolina Cherokees," *Journal of Cherokee Studies* 4 (Winter 1979): 22.

9. Charles M. Hudson, *The Southeastern Indians* (Knoxville: University of Tennessee Press, 1976), 125-32.

10. Wilbur G. Zeigler and Ben S. Grosscup, *The Heart of the Alleghanies; or,*

Western North Carolina (Raleigh: A. Williams and Co., 1883), 20-22; Allen, *Annals of Haywood*, 50.

11. Hudson, *Southeastern Indians*, 131.

12. Mooney, "Myths," 239-40; Hudson, *Southeastern Indians*, 132-34, 144, 147.

13. Allen, *Annals of Haywood*, 35-36, 38, 40, 107, 109, 114; Royce, "Cherokee Nation," 181, n. 5.

14. Albert Ray Newsome, ed., "The A. S. Merrimon Journal, 1853-1854," *NCHR* 8 (July 1931): 319; Allen, *Annals of Haywood*, 39-42; John H. Wheeler, *Historical Sketches of North Carolina, from 1584 to 1851* (Philadelphia: Lippincott, Grambo, and Co. 1851), 2:204.

15. Interviews by Mattie Russell with Mrs. Sara Thomas Campbell and Judge Felix E. Alley, both in Waynesville, N.C., n.d.; Col. Wm. H. Thomas, one-page handwritten sketch by unknown author, Gladys Avery Tillett Papers, folder 1218, UNC.

16. Arthur, *Western North Carolina*, 39, 137, 643-44; Felix Walker, "Memoirs of a Southern Congressman," *Journal of American History* 1 (Jan.-March 1907): 51-60; Davidson, "Reminiscences of Western North Carolina," 5; F. Hampton Walker to WHT, 31 May 1821, WHT Papers, DU.

17. Mooney, "Myths," 160; Avery, "Thomas," 291-92; William Holland Thomas, *A Letter to the Commissioner of Indian Affairs, upon the Claims of the Indians Remaining in the States East* (Washington, D.C.: Buell and Blanchard, 1853), 9.

18. Mooney, "Myths," 160; James Terrell to G. F. Ivey, 29 Jan. 1906, Terrell Papers, WCU; Kephart, *Our Southern Highlanders*, 39; Ed Trout and Olin Watson, *A Piece of the Smokies: A Pictorial History of Life in the Smoky Mountains* (Maryville, Tenn.: the authors, n.d.), illus. 66.

19. Mooney, "Myths," 16-17, 108-9, 160.

20. Mooney, "Myths," 160; Answer of WHT to the bill of complaint of the Eastern Band, 28 June 1873, James Taylor Papers, DU; Charles Lanman, *Letters from the Alleghany Mountains* (New York: G. P. Putnam, 1849), 107; WHT, *Letter to the Commissioner of Indian Affairs*, 10; Frizzell, "Native American Experience," 42.

21. Reservations under the treaties of 1817, 1819, and 1835, WHT Papers, DU; Theodore F. Davidson, *Reminiscences and Traditions of Western North Carolina* (Asheville: Service Printing Co., 1928), 8-9; Mooney, "Myths," 162; Terrell to Lyman C. Draper, 27 Sept. 1873 and 11 May 1874, Draper Collection, State Historical Society of Wisconsin.

22. Quoted in Mooney, "Myths," 163.

23. Terrell to Draper, 27 Sept. 1873, Draper Collection.

24. Willnotah, "The Life and Memory & Death of My Brother Yonah, Guskuh," 21 Feb. 1844, WHT Papers, WCU. Written in Thomas's hand, this "biography" of Yonaguska may have been dictated to him by Yonaguska's brother, but it probably is Thomas's memoir of Yonaguska.

25. Mooney, "Myths," 160; Avery, "Thomas," 291-92; WHT, *Letter to the Commissioner of Indian Affairs*, 9; Depositions, Legal Notes, etc., 1827-43, WHT Papers, DU; Arthur, *Western North Carolina*, 580.
26. Walker to WHT, 31 May 1821, WHT Papers, DU.
27. Col. Wm. H. Thomas, family sketch, Gladys Avery Tillett Papers, UNC.
28. Mooney, "Myths," 161, 526; WHT to J. W. King, 8 July 1839, WHT Papers, WCU; Lanman, *Letters*, 115; James G. McGregor Ramsey, *Annals of Tennessee* (Charleston, S.C.: Walker and James, 1853), 88.
29. Fragment of docket of reservations under the treaties of 1817, 1819, and 1835, Taylor Papers, DU.
30. Avery, "Thomas," 292; Certificate from the Land Commissioners, 16 Oct. 1820, and State Treasurer, Cherokee Lands Sale Book 1820-1830, p. 1, both in NCDAH; Mooney, "Myths," 161.
31. Mooney, "Myths," 161; Order to the Sheriff of Jackson County to Sell Thomas's Land, 7 Feb. 1862, and J. W. King to WHT, 9 May 1839, both in Terrell Papers, WCU; interview by Russell with J. Scroop Styles, Asheville, N.C., n.d.; Fragment of a History of Stekoih Fields, WHT Papers, WCU.
32. Mooney, "Myths," 205; interview by Russell with W. H. Thomas III, n.d.; W. Clark Medford, *Mountain People, Mountain Times* (Waynesville, N.C.: the author, 1966), 19; interview by Godbold with Robert Varner, Whittier, N.C., 29 Nov. 1985. Common variations of the spelling of "Stekoa" are "Stekoih," Stecoah," and "Stecoe." The farm was on modern U.S. Highway 19 where Highway 441 turns off toward Cherokee, North Carolina. The farm was on the south side of the Tuckasegee River, on the border of Jackson and Swain counties. The house currently on the site dates to before 1900, and one of the interior rooms was possibly once part of Thomas's original house. The cold-storage cellar and log pipes are still there.

CHAPTER 2
Businessman in Indian Country

1. On the emergence of the American frontier businessman, see Daniel J. Boorstin, *The Americans: The National Experience* (New York: Alfred A. Knopf, 1965), 115-23.
2. Statement by Thomas and Welch regarding expenses, ca. 1833; Contract between Love and WHT, 22 April 1834; Love to WHT, 16 Nov. 1833, all in WHT Papers micro., DU.
3. Henry B. C. Nitze and Henry A. J. Wilkins, "Gold Mining in North Carolina and Adjacent South Appalachian Regions," *North Carolina Geological Bulletin* (Raleigh: Guy V. Barnes), 10 (1897): 28.
4. Indian Credit Book 1819-1829, WHT Papers, DU.
5. For a discussion of mountain merchants, see John C. Inscoe, *Mountain*

Masters, Slavery, and the Sectional Crisis in Western North Carolina (Knoxville: University of Tennessee Press, 1989), 40-44.

6. Land certificate, 14 Sept. 1824, WHT Papers, DU.

7. Statement of Terrell relative to WHT slaves, 26 March 1842, WHT Papers, DU. Incomplete records of WHT land purchases are in WHT Papers, WCU.

8. WHT Journal 1829, typescript privately owned, cited in Russell, "Thomas," 50. On the Constitution of 1827, see Mary Young, "The Cherokee Nation: Mirror of the Republic," *American Quarterly* 33 (Winter 1981): 507.

9. Mooney, "Myths," 117.

10. Cullen Joe Holland, "The Cherokee Indian Newspapers, 1828-1906; The Tribal Voice of a People in Transition" (Ph.D. diss., University of Minnesota, 1956), 117-20.

11. Willnotah, "The life and Memory & Death of my brother Yonah, Guskuh," 21 Feb. 1844, WHT Papers, WCU; Mooney, Notes on 1890 interview, Mooney Papers, NAA; Mooney, "Myths," 163; Lanman, *Letters*, 106-7; Zeigler and Grosscup, *Heart of the Alleghanies*, 33; Terrell to Lyman C. Draper, 27 Sept. 1873, Draper Collection; King, "Origins of the Eastern Cherokees," 167.

12. Wheeler, *Sketches*, 205; WHT to James Graham, 18 Oct. 1838, WHT Papers WCU; Lanman, *Letters*, 108.

13. Wheeler, *Sketches*, 206; testimony of fourteen white residents of Haywood and Macon counties, 31 Jan. 1836, WHT Papers micro., DU; WHT to William Wilkins, 3 March 1845, RG 75, NA; Terrell to Draper, 27 Sept. 1873, Draper Collection.

14. Wheeler, *Sketches*, 206.

15. Stokes to Cass, 15 May 1832, and Gen. Alexander C. Macomb to Stokes, 18 July 1832, both in Letterbook 1830-32, Montford Stokes Papers, NCDAH.

16. Gen. John Coffee to Secretary of War Lewis Cass, 27 Feb. 1833, RG 75, NA. For the number of square miles, see William G. McLoughlin, *Cherokee Renascence in the New Republic* (Princeton: Princeton University Press, 1986), 107.

17. Willnotah, "The Life . . . of Yonah, Guskuh," Terrell Papers, WCU.

18. William G. McLoughlin and Walter H. Conser, Jr., "The Cherokees in Transition: A Statistical Analysis of the Federal Cherokee Census of 1835," *Journal of American History* 64 (Dec. 1977): 680; Walter H. Conser, Jr., "John Ross and the Cherokee Resistance Campaigns, 1833-1838," *Journal of Southern History* 44 (May 1978): 192.

19. Mooney, "Myths," 161; Anna Critts Kilpatrick and Jack Frederick Kilpatrick, eds., "Chronicles of Wolftown: Social Documents of the North Carolina Cherokees, 1850-1862," *Bureau of American Ethnology Bulletin* (Washington, D.C.: GPO), 196 (1966); Finger, *Eastern Band*, 67.

20. Eastern Cherokee Census Roll, 1835, RG 75, NA.

21. Ronald N. Satz, *American Indian Policy in the Jacksonian Era* (Lincoln: University of Nebraska Press, 1975), 99-100; Conser, "John Ross and Cherokee

Resistance," 193; Royce, "Cherokee Nation," 249, 251, 279-82, 289; Mooney, "Myths," 122-23; *Senate Doc.* 120 (25 Cong., 2 sess.), 124; Finger, *Eastern Band*, 16-17.

22. Royce, "Cherokee Nation," 253-57; Mooney, "Myths," 123; Finger, *Eastern Band*, 17; Richard Peters, ed., *The Public Statutes at Large of the United States of America: Treaties between the U.S. and Indian Tribes* (Boston: Little and Brown, 1846), 7:4-6; Felix S. Cohen, ed., *Handbook of Federal Indian Law* (Washington, D.C.: GPO, 1945), 54-56.

23. Schermerhorn to WHT, n.d., attached to WHT to Schermerhorn, 28 Aug. 1845, WHT Papers micro., DU. See also Terrell to G. F. Ivey, 29 Jan. 1906, Terrell Papers, WCU.

24. *Senate Doc.* 120 (25 Cong., 2 sess.), 535, 620.

25. Terrell To G. F. Ivey, 29 Jan. 1906, Terrell Papers, WCU; Power of Attorney from 237 Cherokees of Haywood and Macon counties to WHT, 30 Jan. 1836, WHT Papers micro., DU; WHT to E. Herring, 4 July 1836, RG 75, NA.

26. WHT to Schermerhorn, 25 March 1836, RG 75, NA. See also *Senate Doc.* 120 (25 Cong., 2 sess.), 620.

27. Statement by WHT, 26 May 1836, containing undated contract with Major Ridge, et al., WHT Papers, DU.

28. Undated [ca. 26 May 1836] contract between WHT and Major Ridge, et al., WHT Papers, DU. See also Laws on Treaties relating to Cherokees in N.C., RG 75, NA.

29. WHT to Quallatown Indians, 15 Feb. 1845, Sibbald Smith Papers in Records of the *Eastern Band of Cherokees vs. William Holland Thomas, et al.* See also Kenny A. Franks, *Stand Watie and the Agony of the Cherokee Nation* (Memphis: Memphis State University Press, 1979), 26, 29, 35.

30. Sharlotte Neely, "Acculturation and Persistance among North Carolina's Eastern Band of Cherokee Indians," in *Southeastern Indians: Since the Removal Era*, ed. Walter L. Williams (Athens: University of Georgia Press, 1979), 154-58.

31. Memorial of 9 Sept. 1836 in Thomas's hand but signed by Joseph Keener and seven others, Edward Bishop Dudley Papers, NCDAH.

32. Quoted in Lanman, *Letters*, 109-10. A journalist who visited Quallatown in 1848, Charles Lanman talked with Thomas and various Indians. He recorded this speech by Yonaguska a dozen years after Yonaguska supposedly had given it. The speech was probably told to him by Thomas and reflects the view Thomas wanted Lanman and his readers to have. See Frizzell, "Native American Experience," 45.

33. Memorial to Dudley, 3 April 1837 [WHT's handwriting], Dudley Papers. See also George Dewey Harmon, "The North Carolina Cherokees and the New Echota Treaty of 1835," *NCHR* 6 (July 1929): 245, 247; *Senate Doc.* 408 (29 Cong., 1 sess.), 9; and King, "Origins of the Eastern Cherokees," 168-70.

34. Finger, *Eastern Band*, 18-19; *Laws of the State of North Carolina, 1836-37*, 30.

35. WHT to Thomas Moore, 30 Dec. 1836, Letterbook 1835-42, p. 30; WHT

to unknown addressee, 6 March 1838; WHT to John F. Schermerhorn, 1 Sept. 1838, Letterbook 1838-45, pt. 2, pp. 7-8, all in WHT Papers, DU. Statement of settlement with James W. Y. Walton, 12 June 1838, WHT Papers micro., DU. Mooney, "Myths," 161.

36. WHT Diary 1833-34, cited in Russell, "Thomas," 159, 193; I. F. King, "The Coming and Going of Ohio Droving," *Ohio Archaeological and Historical Quarterly* 17 (July 1908): 249; Arthur, *Western North Carolina*, 285-86.

37. WHT Diary 1833-34, p. 70, cited in Russell, "Thomas," 159, 192.

38. King Memorandum, 27 Feb. 1844, WHT Papers, DU.

39. Financial Statement from J. W. King to WHT, 9 April 1841, Letterbook 1830-40, WHT Papers, DU; J. W. King Propositions, 1 Jan. 1839, WHT Papers, WCU.

40. Agreement between WHT and Allen Fisher, 7 March 1834, WHT Papers, DU.

41. Contract between WHT and Keener, 28 May 1834, and WHT to H. P. King, 8 July 1839, both in WHT Papers, DU; *Journal of the House of Commons of the General Assembly of North Carolina*, sess. of 1862-63, pp. 3-4; Arthur, *Western North Carolina*, 186.

42. William L. Sherrill, *Annals of Lincoln County, North Carolina* (Charlotte, N.C.: Observer Printing House, 1937), 83. WHT Daybook 1832-33, Scott's Creek, 54. WHT to John Hoke, 4 April, 12 Sept., 22 Oct. 1838, 10 Aug., 23 Nov. 1840; WHT to William Dearing, 6 April 1837; WHT to Robert C. Wilson, 3 March 1837, all in WHT Letterbook 1835-42, pp. 39, 3, 71, 56, 47, 29, 37. Hoke to WHT and King, 11 DEC. 1838, and to WHT, 7 May 1835, 28 April 1838; List of notes against WHT held by Hoke Estate, 1846, all in WHT Papers, DU. WHT to Hoke, 8 Oct. 1842, WHT Papers, WCU.

43. WHT to J. W. King, 28 Jan. 1841, Letterbook 1835-42, pp. 62-63; WHT and Fisher Accounts 1835-39, Scott's Creek; WHT and J. King Account Book 1837-41, Quallatown, 17, 59; WHT Accounts and Inventory 1836-53, Scott's Creek, 143; Catalogue of Books, n.d., all in WHT Papers, DU.

44. Rules of Indian Store, 30 Jan. 1838, WHT Daybook 1838, WHT Papers, DU.

45. Speech of WHT in Charleston, 1853, WHT Papers micro., DU; *Report of Walter Gwynn, Chief Engineer of the Blue Ridge Rail Road Company, in South Carolina, . . . Held in Charleston, the 22d November 1856* (Charleston: Walker and Evans, 1856), 31-32.

46. Depositions of Ute Hyatt, 24 Aug. 1838, and of George W. Hayes, 26 Aug. 1838, both in WHT Papers micro., DU; WHT Account Book 1836-37, WHT Papers, DU; Deposition of Scroop Enloe, 23 Aug. 1838, WHT Papers, WCU; Royce, "Cherokee Nation," 256; *Senate Doc.* 120 (25 Cong., 2 sess.), 174, 622, 773.

47. Francis to Dudley, 17 July 1837, Dudley Papers. See also Davidson, "Reminiscences of Western North Carolina," 7.

48. WHT to Dudley, 1 Aug. 1837, and Testimonial from eleven men of Quallatown to Dudley, 26 July 1837, both in Dudley Papers.

49. Testimonials of Jesse C. Cockerham and Nathan Hyatt, and of George W. Hayes, 27 and 30 Aug. 1837, WHT Papers, DU.

50. Dudley to WHT, 12 Aug. 1837, WHT Papers, DU.

51. WHT to Farrar and Robinson, 25 May 1837; Farrar and Robinson to WHT, 9 Feb. 1837; WHT to Major Delaney, 13 Oct. 1837; WHT to Committee of the Cherokee Nation, n.d., with their reply of 24 Jan. 1837; Licence issued to WHT by William F. Collins, Jan. 1837, all in WHT Papers, DU. Mooney, "Myths," 221, 127. Royce, "Cherokee Nation," 283. Jerry Clyde Cashion, *Fort Butler and the Cherokee Indian Removal from North Carolina* (Raleigh: State Department of Archives and History, 1970), 11.

52. Cunningham to William Lindsay, 12 Jan. 1838, and WHT to Dudley, 29 Oct. 1837, both in WHT Papers, DU.

53. WHT to Dudley, 29 Oct. 1837, with testimony of Cunningham attached, WHT Papers, DU.

54. Petition of Haywood County Men, 6 April 1837, WHT Papers, DU. WHT to Dudley, 29 Oct. 1837, and 25 April 1838, Dudley Papers. Testimonies relative to WHT, 3–6 Jan. 1838; WHT to Clark, McTier, and Co., 24 July 1838; WHT to Dudley, 25 April 1838; WHT Ledger 1839-43, Murphy, N.C., 96; WHT Cash Book 1837-72, Calhoun, Tenn., 6-21, 124; WHT to Schermerhorn, 1 Sept. 1838, all in WHT Papers, DU.

CHAPTER 3
Let My People Stay

1. Cashion, *Fort Butler* 32–33. See also Royce, "Cherokee Nation of Indians," 255.

2. Jones to John Ross, 20 Nov. 1837, in *The Papers of Chief John Ross*, ed. Gary E. Moulton (Norman: University of Oklahoma Press, 1985), 1:550.

3. Killion to Dudley, 5 Jan. and 25 March 1838, and WHT to Dudley, 25 April 1838, both in Dudley Papers.

4. Wool to Secretary of War B. F. Butler, 3 June 1837, RG 75, NA.

5. Thomas wrote his account of the Tsali episode in the form of a pamphlet, *Argument in Support of the Claims of Cherokee Indians Remaining East of the Mississippi River* (Washington, D.C.: n.p., 1839), 18–20, WHT Papers micro., DU. Other significant primary accounts include: WHT to Scott, 7 March 1846; R. Jones to Commissioners of Indian Affairs, 12 Jan. 1839; List of Cherokees who served in capturing Charley and others, n.d.; Crawford to WHT, 2 Aug. 1844, all in WHT Papers, DU. Scott to James Monroe, 6 Nov. 1838; A. J. Smith to C. H. Larned, 5 Nov. 1838; Larned to Scott, 5 Nov. 1838; Foster to Scott,

4 Nov. and 3 Dec. 1838, all in RG 75, NA. Cherokee Field Notes, File 2497, Mooney Papers, NAA.
The best secondary account of Tsali is John R. Finger, "The Saga of Tsali: Legend vs. Reality," *NCHR* 56 (Winter 1979): 1–18. Other secondary accounts include Finger, *Eastern Band*, 20–26; Horace Kephart, *The Cherokees of the Smoky Mountains* (1936; rev. and ed., John R. Finger, Gatlingburg, Tenn.: Great Smoky Mountains Natural History Association, 1983), 28–33; King, "Origins of the Eastern Cherokees," 165–66; Paul Kutsche, "The Tsali Legend: Culture Heroes and Historiography," *Ethnohistory* 10 (Fall 1963): 329–57; W. Clark Medford, *Great Smoky Mountain Stories and Sun Over Ol' Starlin* (Waynesville, N.C.: the author, 1966), 26–37; Mooney, "Myths," 131, 157–58; and Grace Steele Woodward, *The Cherokees* (Norman: University of Oklahoma Press, 1963), 12–13. On the Cherokee law of blood, see John Phillip Reid, *A Law of Blood: The Primitive Law of the Cherokee Nation during the Early Years of European Contact* (New York: New York University Press, 1970), 73–80.

6. Census of North Carolina Cherokees 1840; Supplementary Report of Cherokee Indians Remaining in N.C. 1835–40; WHT to Wilson Lumpkin, 20 Sept. 1839, all in WHT Papers, DU. Nathaniel C. Browder, *The Cherokee Indians and Those Who Came After: Notes for a History of Cherokee County, North Carolina, 1835–1860* (Hayesville, N.C.; the author, 1973), 73–87; Finger, *Eastern Band*, 29; Morris L. Wardell, *A Political History of the Cherokee Nation, 1838–1907* (1938; reprint, Norman: University of Oklahoma Press, 1977), 11–12.

7. WHT to Poinsett, 2 Jan. 1839, RG 75, NA.

8. WHT to Nicholas S. Peck, 22 April 1839, and WHT to Crawford, 21 May 1839, both in WHT Letterbook 1839-40, pp. 1, 8, WHT Papers, DU; Willnotah, "The Life . . . of . . . Yona, Guskuh," Terrell Papers, WCU; Cherokee Field Notes, File 2497, and Notes on 1890 interview with WHT, both in Mooney Papers, NAA; Mooney, "Myths," 163; Lanman, *Letters,* 110; Ruth Y. Wetmore, *First in the Land: The North Carolina Indians* (Winston-Salem, N.C.: John F. Blair, 1975), 159.

9. H. G. Robertson, "The Eastern Band of Cherokee Indians, from 1835 to 1893," *North Carolina University Magazine* 31 (1901): 177; Chiefs of Bird Town to WHT, 21 Dec. 1854, WHT Papers, DU; Kilpatrick and Kilpatrick, eds., "Chronicles of Wolftown."

10. Powers of Attorney from Qualla and Buffalo Town Indians dated 27 Feb., 1 April 1839, 23 July 1841, and 31 Aug. 1843, James Taylor Papers, DU; Powers of Attorney from Cherokees dated 21, 22, 23, 29 March, 10, 11 April 1839, and others, WHT Papers, DU.

11. WHT to John F. Gillespie, 1 July 1839; WHT to Allen Fisher, 24 July 1839; WHT to J. W. King, 28 June 1839; WHT to John Timson, et al., 10 June 1839, all in WHT Letterbook 1839-40, pp. 36, 48, 32, 20, WHT Papers, DU.

12. WHT to Poinsett, 9 Sept. 1839; WHT to Oconaluftee Indians, 4 June 1839; WHT to Gideon F. Morris and other Cherokees, 25 Sept. and 6 Nov. 1839; WHT to John Timson and other Cherokees, 6 Nov. 1839, all in WHT Letterbook 1839-40, pp. 16, 89, 115-16, WHT Papers, DU.

13. WHT to J. W. King, 8 July 1839; WHT to H. P. King, 29 July 1839; WHT to J. W. King, 28 Oct. 1839, all in WHT Letterbook 1839-40, pp. 50, 110, WHT Papers, DU.

14. WHT to James P. H. Porter, 18 Sept. 1839; WHT to George W. Churchwell, 29 Sept. 1839; WHT to Nicholas W. Woodfin, 5 Aug. 1839, all in WHT Letterbook 1839-40, pp. 76-77, 96, 116, WHT Papers, DU. Acting Secretary of War William W. Wilkins to President John Tyler, 6 Sept. 1844, WHT Papers, DU. WHT to Crawford, 12 and 25 July, 5 Aug. 1839; Crawford to Acting Secretary of War T. Cooper, 12 Sept. 1839, all in RG 75, NA. Richard W. Iobst, "William Holland Thomas and the Cherokee Claims," in King, ed., *Cherokee Indian Nation*, 190.

15. WHT to James W. Guinn, 20 Sept. 1839; WHT to Wilson Lumpkin, 20 Sept. 1839; WHT to Major Hinton, 21 Sept. 1839, all in WHT Letterbook 1839-40, pp. 79, 83, 91-92, WHT Papers, DU. Crawford to WHT, 8 July 1840, in Records of *Cherokees vs. Thomas*. Iobst, "William Holland Thomas and the Cherokee Claims," 192-93.

16. WHT to Hyatt, McBurney, and Co., 26 Sept. 1839; WHT to Clarke, McTier, and Co. and to E. D. Cook, 23 Nov. 1839, all in WHT Letterbook 1839-40, pp. 91, 137-38, WHT Papers, DU.

17. Wool to Commissioner of Indian Affairs C. A. Harris, 3 March 1837, in *Senate Doc.* 120 (25 Cong., 2 sess.), 788; WHT to Wool, 20 Nov. 1839, WHT Letterbook 1839-40, pp. 131-32, WHT Papers, DU; WHT Account Book 1835-37, WHT Papers micro., DU.

18. WHT to John Timson and friends, 20 Dec. 1839, WHT Letterbook 1839-40, WHT Papers, DU.

19. WHT to Crawford, 21 Jan. 1840, in WHT Letterbook 1839-40, p. 185; WHT to U.S. Attorney General Henry D. Gilpin, 25 March 1840; Gilpin to WHT, 26 March 1840; WHT to E. Hyatt, 10 Aug. 1840, in WHT Letterbook 1835-42, p. 46, all in WHT Papers, DU. WHT to Crawford, 30 July 1842 in Records of *Cherokees vs. Thomas*. Crawford to WHT, 8 July 1840, RG 75, NA.

20. Secretary of Interior Alexander H. H. Stuart to R. W. Johnson, 20 May 1852, in *House Misc. Doc.* 64 (32 Cong., 1 sess.), 30-31. For examples of settlements for individual Indians, see Crawford to WHT, 7 Feb. and 24 Oct. 1840, WHT Papers, DU, and WHT to Crawford, 20 Jan. and 1 May 1840, RG 75, NA.

21. Finger, *Eastern Band*, 31. For a detailed account of the second removal effort, see John R. Finger, "The Abortive Second Cherokee Removal, 1841-1844," *Journal of Southern History* 42 (May 1981): 207-26, and for a good summary of

Thomas's 1838-48 attempt to collect for his Indians, see Iobst, "Thomas and the Cherokee Claims," 181-201.

22. WHT to Collidge and Wyeth, 25 July 1840, WHT Letterbook 1835-42, WHT Papers, DU; Crawford to WHT, 8 July 1840, RG 75, NA; Royce, "Cherokee Nation," 256; John Ross, et al., to John Spencer, 6 June 1842, in *Papers of John Ross* 2:131.

23. Finger, *Eastern Band*, 32-33.

24. Hindman to Acting Commissioner of Indian Affairs Daniel Kurtz, 6 Dec. 1841, RG 75, NA.

25. Finger, *Eastern Band*, 33-34.

26. James Graham to William A. Graham, 6 April 1851, *The Papers of William Alexander Graham*, ed. James G. de Roulhac Hamilton (Raleigh: State Department of Archives and History, 1957-76), 4:66; J. Keener to William A. Graham, 31 May 1842, *Papers of William Alexander Graham* 2:319; William Rogers to WHT, 7 April 1842, WHT Papers, DU. See also Finger, *Eastern Band*, 35-40.

27. WHT to Crawford, 30 July 1842, in Records of *Cherokees vs. Thomas*. See also J. W. King to WHT, 1 July 1845, Terrell Papers, WCU.

28. WHT, *Letter to the Commissioner of Indian Affairs*, 13-14; Royce, "Cherokee Nation," 256; J. W. King to E. P. Sharp, 28 Aug. 1843, and WHT Letterbook and Accounts 1838-45, p. 237, both in WHT Papers, DU.

29. WHT to Crawford, 26 Feb. 1844, and Crawford to WHT, 21 March 1844, RG 75, NA; Green to WHT, 20 Jan. 1845, and Bill of Injunction filed by Duff and B. E. Green, 21 Sept. 1850, both in WHT Papers, DU; Royce, "Cherokee Nation," 300-301; A. L. Lougherty to Duff and B. E. Green, 5 Sept. 1850, in Records of *Cherokees vs. Thomas*.

30. WHT to Cherokees at Quallatown, 15 Feb. 1845, WHT Papers, WCU.

31. Ibid.

32. Wetmore, *First on the Land*, 159; Deed from Catchcart heirs to WHT, 7 Dec. 1840, Haywood County Deed Book F, 158, Haywood County Courthouse; WHT to Crawford, 30 July 1842, RG 75, NA; *House Exec. Doc.* 1 (43 Cong., 2 sess.), 64; Deed from Samuel Agnew to WHT, 14 May 1841, and Contract between WHT and Mullendore, 14 May 1841, both in Terrell Papers, WCU; Promissory notes from WHT to State of N.C., 30 April 1856, WHT Papers, DU; William Munn Colby, "Routes to Rainey Mountain: A Biography of James Mooney, Ethnologist" (Ph.D. diss., University of Wisconsin, 1978), 65; Mooney, "Myths," 158-62.

33. WHT to Allen Fisher, Jan. 1838, in WHT Letterbook and Accounts 1838-45, p. 344, WHT Papers, DU; (Raleigh) *N.C. Standard*, 8 Feb. 1851.

34. WHT Diary, 23 Sept. 1837, cited in Russell, "Thomas," 164. WHT Invoice and Daybook 1838-42, p. 7; WHT to John Hoke, 4 April 1838; WHT to unknown addressee, 6 March 1838; WHT to Clark, McTier, and Co., 24 July 1838; WHT Cash Book 1837-72, p. 5; WHT to John M. Clarkey, 31 Aug. 1838, all in WHT Papers, DU.

35. WHT Accounts 1836-53, p. 73; WHT Daybook 1839-40, p. 1; WHT Cash Book 1837-72, pp. 6-21, all in WHT Papers, DU.

36. King to WHT, 9 May 1839, Terrell Papers, WCU. King to WHT, 17 Nov. 1839, 15 June 1842, 25 Jan., 6 Feb., 9 March, 30 March, 12 Dec. 1844, 14 Jan., 24 Feb. 1845, all in WHT Papers, WCU.

37. Contract between WHT and Mount, 30 Dec. 1845; WHT to William R. King, 30 Dec 1845, both in WHT Papers, DU. Mount to WHT, 21 Sept. 1858, Terrell Papers, WCU.

38. WHT to Allen Fisher, 31 July 1839, in Letterbook 1839-40, pp. 54-55, WHT Papers, DU.

39. WHT to H. P. King, 9 Aug. 1839, in Letterbook 1838-45, WHT Papers, DU.

40. WHT to Schermerhorn, 10 June, 1, 13, 31 July, 15 Aug., 14 AND 28 Sept., 19 Dec. 1839, in WHT Letterbook 1839-40, pp. 18, 33, 45, 53, 62, 74, 98, 161, WHT Papers, DU.

41. WHT to H. P. King, 28 Sept. 1839; WHT to Fisher, 7 Oct. and 13 Nov. 1839; WHT to J. W. King, 19 Nov. 1839; WHT to James H. Bryson, 28 Nov. 1839, all in WHT Letterbook 1839-40, pp. 80, 30, 124, 132, 142, WHT Papers, DU.

42. The identity of Cudjo is confusing. A free black male by that name appears in the census of 1840 but in no subsequent censuses. The names "Cugo" and "Cudge" appear fairly often and may have been slaves who belonged to Thomas in the 1850s and 1860s. For a discussion of the problem of identifying Cudjo, see Russell, "Thomas," 231-33. Inscoe, *Mountain Masters*, 96-98, mentions only one person named "Cudjo" and portrays him as a trusted slave who "enjoyed privileged status just short of emancipation."

43. WHT to Price, Newlin, and Co., 24 July 1839, and WHT to William Patton, 29 May 1841, WHT Depositions and Legal Notes 1827-47; Contract between WHT and Fisher, 13 Nov. 1841, WHT Ledger and Indian Accounts 1840-58; WHT Ledger 1839-44; clippings from *Highland Messenger*, 30 Sept. 1842 and 20 Jan. 1843; WHT to Wurts, Musgrave, and Wurts, 14 Oct. 1844; Robert Rose to WHT, 3 Dec. 1844 and 8 Jan. 1845; WHT to Fisher, 16 April 1845; WHT to W. Whitaker, Jr., 4 June 1845; Duff Green to William L. Marcy, 19 Aug. 1848, all in WHT Papers, DU. WHT and J. W. King receipt to Austin Fry, 3 June 1845, Terrell Papers, WCU.

44. WHT Diary and Accounts 1839-41, p. 4, WHT Papers, DU.

45. Ibid., 14-18.

46. Ibid., 19-21.

47. Ibid., 22-24.

48. James W. Guinn to WHT, 16 June 1840; WHT to Henry Addison, 24 Nov. 1840, both in WHT Papers, DU.

49. Mark Colvard to WHT, 15 July 1841, Terrell Papers, WCU; WHT Diary and Accounts 1839-41, entry for 16 MARCH 1841, and Bill of Sale, 9 Jan. 1843,

between WHT and John Shuler, both in WHT Papers, DU; John C. Inscoe, "Mountain Masters: Slaveholding in Western North Carolina," *NCHR* 61 (April 1984): 149.

50. Receipt from WHT to John Love, 31 Jan. 1849; Contract between WHT and Abraham Wiggins, 25 May 1842; Promissory note from Raper to WHT, 8 June 1860; J. W. King to WHT, 4 Dec. 1843, all in WHT Papers micro., DU. Terrell to WHT, 5 Jan. 1860; Receipt from WHT to Johnston, 25 March 1843; Deed from Mercer Fain to WHT, 12 Jan. 1852, all in WHT Papers, DU. See also Inscoe, *Mountain Masters*, 90, 91, 96-98, 104.

51. WHT Ledger 1839-44 for Scott's Creek, 486, 494, WHT Papers, DU.

52. Contract between WHT and John B. Love, 13 July 1835, WHT Papers micro., DU.

53. WHT Letterbook and Accounts 1838-45, p. 344; loose pages from *Boston Guide to Health* [1843]; WHT Diary 1844-45, all in WHT Papers, DU.

54. Temperance Thomas to Mr. Mason, 4 Jan. 1847; WHT to H. P. King, 12 July 1839, in WHT Letterbook 1839-40, p. 42, both in WHT Papers, DU.

55. WHT Ledger 1839-40, pp. 42, 47, in WHT Papers, DU.

56. WHT Diary 1842-45, cited in Russell, "Thomas," 250-52.

57. Terrell Statement of 26 March 1842: WHT to Temperance Thomas, 12 July 1839, in Letterbook 1839-40, p. 44; D. Angeline Thomas to Samuel P. Sherrill, 29 Nov. 1848; Samuel P. Sherrill to WHT, 16 Dec. 1850, all in WHT Papers, DU. Sixth Census of the U.S., 1840, N.C., 5:113-14.

58. William P. Hyde to Bella A. Lockwood, n.d., letter contained in application #500, RG 123, NA, M1104, reel 6.

59. Supplemental Application for Minor Children, 9 Aug. 1907, application #13254, RG 123, NA, M1104, reel 131. This application was denied by the U.S. Claims Court when it acted on application #500 on the grounds that the Hydes did not offer sufficient proof that they were descended from Betsy Walker, a Cherokee woman listed in the Cherokee census of 1835. See also Shirley Hoskins, *Cherokee Blood, Vol. II based on Eastern Cherokee Applications of the U.S. Court of Claims, 1906-1909* (Chattanooga: the author, 1982), 2:98-99.

60. Contract between WHT and King, 1 April 1841, Terrell Papers, WCU.

61. WHT to Nimrod S. Jarrett, 11 Nov. 1839; WHT to Nicholas S. Woodfin, 6 June 1839, both in WHT Letterbook 1839-40, pp. 119-20, 17-18, WHT Papers, DU.

62. WHT Diary, 1, 2, 6, April 1842, 1 May 1843, cited in Russell, "Thomas," 262-63.

63. WHT Diary, 13 April 1850, 10 July 1845, 4 July 1844, cited in Russell, "Thomas," 259-60.

64. WHT Diary, *passim*, and entries for March-June 1845, cited in Russell, "Thomas," 259-62.

65. WHT Diary 1844-45, cited in Russell, "Thomas," 246, 259, 262.

CHAPTER 4
Both White and Cherokee

1. WHT to Quallatown Cherokees, 2 Feb. 1846, including Polk to Mason, 11 June 1845, and Mason to Polk, 19 Sept. 1845, WHT Papers, WCU.

2. Finger, *Eastern Band*, 45-46.

3. Commissioner of Indian Affairs William Medill to Secretary of War W. L. Marcy, 31 March 1846; WHT to Medill, 24 Aug. 1846; Message of the President, 13 April 1846, all in *Senate Doc.* 298 (29 Cong., 1 sess.), 2-18, 171-84. WHT to the President, 10 July and 6 Aug. 1846; WHT to Medill, 30 Nov. and 14 Dec. 1846, all in RG 75, NA. WHT to W. P. Mangum, 17 July and 24 Dec. 1846, in Willie Person Mangum, *The Papers of Willie Person Mangum*, ed. Henry Thomas Shanks (Raleigh: State Department of Archives and History, 1950-56), 4:421, 457-58, 527-28. WHT to Mangum, 2 March 1847, in Mangum, *Papers* 5:53. Harmon, *Sixty Years of Indian Affairs*, 194-95.

4. Finger, *Eastern Band*, 47; Iobst, "Thomas and the Cherokee Claims," 197-98.

5. WHT to Preston Starrett, 5 May 1848, WHT Papers, DU; *House Exec. Doc.* 63 (30 Cong., 1 sess.), 46; P. L. Clayton to WHT, 21 Nov. 1849, WHT Papers, WCU.

6. Duff Green to WHT, 26 Sept. 1848; WHT to Benjamin E. Green, 7 and 23 Nov. 1848, all in Green Papers, UNC. Power of Attorney to WHT, 26 Oct. 1848; WHT to Thomas Corwin, 28 April 1851, both in WHT Papers, DU. WHT to Cherokee Indians, 6 March 1850; WHT Papers, WCU. A. L. Loughery to Duff and B. E. Green, 5 Sept. 1850; Bond from WHT to Qualla Indians, 25 Oct. 1850, both in *Records of Cherokees vs. Thomas. House Misc. Doc.* 64 (32 Cong., 1 sess.), 19-28. WHT to P. Clayton, 20 Nov. 1850, WHT Papers, DU.

7. Numerous letters from U.S. Treasury Dept. agents to WHT, 1849, paying individual Indian claims, and WHT to P. Clayton, 23 May 1851, WHT Papers, DU. J. K. Rogers to Commissioner of Indian Affairs Luke Lea, 1 Sept. and 11 Nov. 1851, 12 Feb. 1852; WHT to Lea, 26 Feb. 1853; David W. Siler to Lea, 20 June, 6 July, and 17 Oct. 1851; Benjamin E. Green to Secretary of the Interior Alexander H. Stuart, 3 Nov. 1851, all in RG 75, NA. See also Finger, *Eastern Band*, 52-54.

8. WHT to Cherokee Indians at Buffalo Town, 8 March 1851, WHT Papers, WCU. Terrell to WHT, 28 Feb. 1850; Powers of Attorney from Indians to WHT, 1850, all in WHT Papers, DU.

9. William Holland Thomas, *Explanation of the Rights of the North Carolina Cherokee Indians* (Washington, D.C.: n.p., 1851), 1-18, copy in WHT Papers, WCU.

10. *House Misc. Doc.* 64 (32 Cong., 1 sess.), 3-18; *Cherokee Indian Claims, Eastern Band of Cherokees, Petitioner Docket* 282 (1906), Records of the Treasury Department, pamphlet in WHT Papers, WCU.

11. WHT, *A Letter to the Commissioner of Indian Affairs*, 1-46.

12. Terrell to Secretary of Treasury, 22 Aug. 1854, and Terrell to First Auditor, 28 Nov. 1854, WHT Papers micro.; DU. Settlements of WHT with individual Indians dated 26 April, 5, 8, 13 May 1855, and many more, WHT Papers, DU. WHT to George W. Manypenny, 9 June, 17 July 1855; WHT to Charles E. Mix, 4 Dec. 1855, all in RG 75, NA. See also Finger, *Eastern Band*, 55-56.

13. Finger, *Eastern Band*, 54-55.

14. Contract between WHT and Terrell, 6 Jan. 1854; Terrell to James R. Thomas, Sr., 27 March 1896, both in WHT Papers micro., DU. Terrell Reminiscences; Terrell to G. F. Ivey, 29 Jan. 1906, both in Terrell Papers, WCU. Kilpatrick and Kilpatrick, eds., "Chronicles of Wolftown," 84.

15. Taylor to WHT, 6 May 1857, WHT Papers, WCU.

16. Finger, *Eastern Band*, 46, 58-59. Taylor to Secretary of Interior R. McClelland, 26 June 1856; Taylor to G. W. Manypenny, 7 Oct. and 18 Dec. 1856; WHT to Taylor, 26 May 1856, all in RG 75, NA. Taylor to WHT, 6 and 19 Sept. 1856, 6 May 1857, 25 Nov. 1858, all in WHT Papers, WCU. Taylor to WHT, 20 July 1856, William W. Stringfield Papers, WCU.

17. Finger, *Eastern Band*, 74-80; Hudson, *Southeastern Indians*, 408-21; George William Featherstonhaugh, *A Canoe Voyage Up the Minnay Sotor; With an Account of the Lead and Copper Deposits in Wisconsin; of the Gold Region in the Cherokee Country; and Sketches of Popular Manners* (London: R. Bentley, 1847), 2:296; Lanman, *Letters*, 85, 96-97; WHT Diary, 4 and 5 June 1848, cited in Russell, "Thomas," 256; Charles M. Wiltse, *John C. Calhoun* (Indianapolis: Bobbs-Merril Company, 1944-51), 1:340; WHT to Duff Green, 29 Aug. 1848, Green Papers, UNC.

18. Theda Purdue, "Southern Indians and the Cult of True Womanhood," in Fraser, et al., eds., *Web of Southern Social Relations* (Athens: University of Georgia Press, 1985), 36-37; Ruth Y. Wetmore, "The Green Corn Ceremony of the Eastern Cherokees," *Journal of Cherokee Studies* 8 (Spring 1983): 47-50.

19. Kilpatrick and Kilpatrick, eds., "Wolftown Chronicles," 59-60; Perdue, "Southern Indians and the Cult of True Womanhood," 35-51.

20. Kilpatrick and Kilpatrick, eds., "Chronicles of Wolftown," 46-47, 59-60; Finger, *Eastern Band*, 63-67; Colby, "Routes to Rainey Mountain," 156-60; Young, "The Cherokee Nation: Mirror of the Republic," *American Quarterly* 33:502-24; WHT Diary, 28 May 1848, 2-6 Oct. and 7 Nov. 1850, cited in Russell, "Thomas," 254-55; WHT to Preston Starrett, 5 May 1848, Green Papers.

21. Finger, *Eastern Band*, 61.

22. Ibid., 44-45, 73-74; Charter of Cherokee Company, 4 Dec. 1846, WHT Papers, DU; *Laws of North Carolina*, sess. of 1836-37, pp. 40-43, and sess. of 1844-45, pp. 71-72; *House Exec. Doc.* 1, pt. 3 (41 Cong., 2 sess.), 897; George T. Mason to William A. Graham, 19 May 1847, Graham Papers, NCDAH; Receipt from D. McClelland to WHT, Terrell Papers, WCU; Deed from Thomas to

Cherokee Co., 22 May 1848, Jackson County (N.C.) Deed Book, E-5, pp. 418-19, Jackson County Courthouse.

23. 2 Oct. 1850, quoted in Kilpatrick and Kilpatrick, eds., "Chronicles of Wolftown," 10 and 11.

24. William J. Cooper, Jr., *The South and the Politics of Slavery, 1828-1856* (Baton Rouge: Louisiana State University Press, 1978), 168, 267, 285-87; Charles S. Sydnor, *The Development of Southern Sectionalism, 1819-1848* (Baton Rouge: Louisiana State University Press, 1948), 163-64, 277-80.

25. WHT, "To the People of the Senatorial District, Embracing the Counties of Haywood, Macon, and Cherokee, North Carolina," 22 July 1846, Broadside Collection, Rare Book Room, DU. See also WHT to B. E. Green, 22 June 1848, Green Papers; *Senate Journal*, sess. of 1848-49, p. 4, and sess. of 1852, p. 488; *Raleigh (N.C.) Standard*, 8 Feb. 1851; and WHT Landbook 1838-53, Murphy, 21-29, WHT Papers, DU.

26. Marc W. Kruman, *Parties and Politics in North Carolina, 1836-1865* (Baton Rouge: Louisiana State University Press, 1983), 5-6; Hugh Talmadge Lefler and Albert Ray Newsome, *North Carolina: The History of a Southern State* (Chapel Hill: University of North Carolina Press, 1963), 340; *Raleigh (N.C.) Standard*, 25 Feb. 1857.

27. WHT to B. E. Green, 22 June 1848, Green Papers; Lefler and Newsome, *North Carolina*, 340, 358-60; Inscoe, *Mountain Masters*, 142; *Raleigh (N.C.) Standard*,16, 23, 30 Aug. 1848; Directory of Members of the Legislature of North Carolina 1848-49, Broadside Collection, DU; *Senate Journal*, sessions of 1850-61; Terrell Reminiscences, Terrell Papers, WCU.

28. WHT to Duff Green, 29 Aug. 1848; WHT to B. E. Green, 7 and 13 Nov. 1848, all in Green Papers. *Asheville (N.C.) Highland Messenger*, 17 Aug. 1848.

29. Booklet of Political Notes, 25-26, WHT Papers, WCU.

30. Ibid., 2-5, 10, 11, 15, 23.

31. D. L. Dix, *Memorial Soliciting a State Hospital for the Protection and Cure of the Insane* (Raleigh: Seaton Gales, 1848). See also *Journals of the House of Commons of the General Assembly 1848-49*, 189, 225; Kruman, *Parties and Politics*, 59-60; Herbert Dale Pegg, *The Whig Party in North Carolina, 1835-1860* (Chapel Hill: The Colonial Press, 1969), 112-13; and Hugh Talmadge Lefler, ed., *North Carolina History, Told by Contemporaries* (Chapel Hill: University of North Carolina Press, 1948), 212-13.

32. WHT Diary, 5-6 Feb., 5, 7, 19 March, cited in Russell, "Thomas," 141; WHT, "To the Freemen of the Tenth Congressional District," 26 Oct. 1861, Broadside Collection, DU.

33. *Senate Journal*, sess. of 1850-51, pp. 27-28; WHT, "To the Freemen of the Tenth Congressional District."

34. *State Journal*, sess. of 1850-51, p. 55; copy of speech by WHT delivered in Charleston ca. 1853, WHT Papers micro., DU; Ulrich Bonnell Phillips, *A*

History of Transportation in the Eastern Cotton Belt to 1860 (New York: Columbia University Press, 1908), 179-202; Kruman, *Parties and Politics*, 75-76; WHT to James C. Dobbin, 24 Aug. 1854, WHT Papers, DU.

35. WHT speech in Charleston, ca. 1853; unsigned letter to the *Pickens (S.C. Courier*, 1 Sept. 1853; Contract between WHT and Henry Gourdin, 15 July 1853; Gourdin to WHT, 20 Nov. 1852, all in WHT Papers micro., DU. *Report of the President and Directors to the Annual Meeting of the Stockholders of the Blue Ridge Rail Road Company, Held in Charleston, the 22d November 1856* (Charleston: Walker and Evans, 1856), 3.

36. *Senate Journal*, sess. of 1852, pp. 464, 490; *Report of the Blue Ridge Rail Road Company, 1856*, 5; Henry Gourdin to Robert N. Gourdin, 12 Aug. 1853, Gourdin Papers, DU.

37. *Raleigh (N.C.) Standard*, 28 May 1853; WHT to B. E. Green, 24 June 1853, Green Papers; H. W. Conner to WHT, 3 March 1852, WHT Papers, DU; Contract between WHT and Anson Bangs and Co., 14 July 1853, WHT Papers micro., DU.

38. *Report of the Blue Ridge Rail Road Company, 1856*, 5; Anson Bangs and Co. to WHT, 27 Aug. 1853, 1853, WHT Papers, DU; *Raleigh (N.C.) Standard*, 31 Aug. 1853; Phillips, *Transportation*, 371-74.

39. Phillips, *Transportation*, 376; Contract between WHT and Gourdin, 15 July 1853, WHT Papers micro., DU.

40. Gourdin to WHT, 23 Oct. 1852, WHT Papers micro., DU; *Report of the Blue Ridge Rail Road Company, 1856*, 5; *Annual Report of the President and Chief Engineer to the Stockholders of the Blue Ridge Rail Road Company, at the Annual Meeting Held in Charleston, Nov. 6*, 1855 (Charleston: Walker and Evans, 1855), 17.

41. Bangs to WHT, 17 Aug. 1853, WHT Papers, DU; Bangs to WHT, 22 Sept. 1853, WHT Papers, WCU; *Report of the Blue Ridge Rail Road Company*, 1856, 7-28; Phillips, *Transportation*, 378-80.

42. *Asheville (N.C.) News*, 25 Jan. 1855; *Raleigh (N.C.) Standard*, 24 Jan. 1855; *Public and Private Laws of N.C.*, sess. of 1854-55, p. 257; letter from WHT in *Asheville (N.C.) News*, 16 April 1856; Arthur, *Western North Carolina*, 469.

43. WHT to Benton, 10 Jan. 1855, WHT Papers, DU.

44. Deeds from Hitchcock to WHT, 19 Aug. and 4 Sept. 1847; WHT to Hitchcock, 25 Nov. 1848, all in WHT Papers micro., DU.

45. Promissory notes from WHT to State of North Carolina, 30 April 1856, WHT Papers micro., DU; many deeds, dated 1854-56, in WHT Papers, WCU.

46. WHT to M. L. Britain, 4 April 1853, WHT Papers, WCU.

47. Deed from John B. Allison to WHT, 22 Sept. 1854, WHT Papers micro., DU.

48. Deed from WHT to Dickagiskah, 10 Jan. 1855, Taylor Papers, DU.

49. Promissory notes from WHT to State of North Carolina, 30 April 1856; Deed from WHT to Love, 6 Sept. 1856, both in WHT Papers micro., DU.

50. List of WHT Lands in Jackson County in 1856, Terrell Papers, WCU.

51. Mason to WHT, 2 March 1846; Ute Sherrill to WHT, 1851; Brittain to WHT, 4 Jan. 1854; Terrell to WHT, 22 Dec. 1856, all in WHT Papers, DU. Brittain to WHT, 4 Feb. 1854, WHT Papers micro., DU. Brittain to WHT, 14 May 1855, WHT Papers, WCU.

52. Depositions of Euchella and Flying Squirrel, 15 Aug. 1849, WHT Scrapbook; T. J. Cooper to WHT, 8 March 1856; William Johnston to WHT, 25 March 1853; Contract between WHT and Allen Fischer and Thaddeus D. Bryson, 27 Oct. 1853, all in WHT Papers, DU. For reference to Thomas as a justice of the peace, see Paul W. Wager, *County Government and Administration in North Carolina* (Chapel Hill: University of North Carolina Press, 1928), 57.

53. *J. F. Hoke, et al. vs. Wm. H. Thomas*, 1846; Jesse C. Cockerham to WHT, 4 Sept. 1846; Sheriff's deed to Hoke heirs, 23 March 1847; *S. W. and Nancy A. King Hyatt vs. Wm. H. Thomas*, 11 Sept. 1855, all in WHT Papers, DU. Felix Axley to WHT, 21 April 1846; *Nancy A. King vs. Wm. H. Thomas*, 29 March 1847, both in Terrell Papers, WCU. Felix Axley to WHT, 25 March 1846, WHT Papers, WCU. Sheriff's notice, 3 Sept. 1846; George W. Hayes to WHT, 17 Jan. 1847; *James R. Love I vs. W. H. Thomas and Thomas Raper*, 1849; Promissory notes from WHT to William Johnston, 28 Aug. 1853, all in WHT Papers micro., DU. Execution Dockets of the Superior Court of Jackson County, 1852-59, 1853-59, Jackson County Courthouse.

54. WHT Diary, cited in Russell, "Thomas," 169, 244-45, 249, 251, 255-56; bills to WHT from Lusby and Duvall, 1843-44, WHT Papers, DU; bills to WHT from E. Owen and Son, 2 March 1850 and 1857-58, WHT Papers micro., DU; WHT to B. E. Green, 22 Sept. 1854, Green Papers.

CHAPTER 5
The Chief in Love

1. WHT to Sarah Love, 4 Jan. 1857, WHT Papers, DU.

2. WHT Genealogy, Stringfield Papers, WCU. WHT to Sarah Love, 4 Jan. 1857; WHT to James R. Love, 15 Nov. 1839, in WHT Letterbook 1839-40, both in WHT Papers, DU.

3. WHT to Sarah, 4 Jan. 1857, WHT Papers, DU.

4. Clingman to WHT, 23 Feb. 1857, WHT Papers micro., DU.

5. WHT to Sarah, 4 Jan. 1857, WHT Papers, DU.

6. Allen, *Annals of Haywood*, 305-6; Arthur, *Western North Carolina*, 171; Seventh Census of the U.S., 1850, N.C. (Haywood and Henderson counties), 14:121; WHT Genealogy, Stringfield Papers, WCU; interview by Russell with Gladys Avery Tillett, n.d., cited in Russell, "Thomas," 267.

7. James E. Wooley and Vivian Wooley, compilers, *Marriage Bonds of Haywood and Jackson Counties, North Carolina* (Easley, S.C.: Southern Historical Press, 1978), 78.

8. Gourdin to WHT, 6 May 1858, WHT Papers, DU.
9. Sarah to WHT, 17 and 26 Nov., 1858, WHT Papers micro., DU.
10. J. Coman to Sarah Jane Burney Love, 1 Jan. 1834, WHT Papers, DU; Contract between Caroline Thomas and WHT, Register's Office, Jackson Co., N.C., Book D, pp. 863-64, copy in WHT Papers micro., DU; Last Will and Testament of James Robert Love, 21 Aug. 1858, Stringfield Papers, WCU.
11. Sarah to WHT, 26 Nov. and 3 Dec. 1858, WHT Papers micro., DU.
12. WHT to Sarah, 13 Dec. 1857, 3 and 10 Jan. 1858, 13 Feb. 1858, 25 Nov. 1857, WHT Papers micro., DU.
13. WHT to Sarah, 13 Dec. 1857 and 13 Feb. 1858, WHT Papers micro., DU.
14. WHT Diary, 4-14 March 1858, cited in Russell, "Thomas," 139-40.
15. Sallie to WHT, 3 Dec. 1858, WHT Papers, DU.
16. WHT to Sarah, 2 Jan. 1859, WHT Papers micro., DU.
17. WHT to Sarah, 13 Dec. 1857; Sarah to WHT, 17 Nov. 1858; WHT to Sarah, 27 Nov. 1859, all in WHT Papers, DU. Thomas Family Genealogy, WHT III Papers, WCU.

William Holland Thomas, Jr., grew up to be a farmer at Stekoa Fields. He married Elvina J. Bryson, and they became the parents to five children. He died in 1897 at the age of thirty-eight.

James Robert Thomas spent much of his adult life looking after the affairs of his father, his father's estate, and the minor children of his deceased brother. He married Mary Josephine Smith of Raleigh, fathered two sons and a daughter, and died in 1936.

Sarah Love Thomas became the second wife of Alphonso C. Avery in 1888, and she was the mother of two sons and one daughter. She died in 1954 at the age of ninety-three. See Russell, "Thomas," 276-78.

18. WHT to Sarah, n.d., WHT Papers, WCU; WHT to Sarah, 8 Aug. 1859, WHT Papers micro., DU.
19. Sarah to WHT, 2 Nov. 1859, WHT Papers, WCU.
20. Indian claims paid by Terrell, 1857-61; WHT's report on the meeting of the Cherokee council at Quallatown, 20 May 1859, both in WHT Papers, DU. Taylor to Secretary of Interior Jacob Thompson, 17 April and 18 Aug. 1857; WHT to Clingman, 18 Oct. 1857; WHT to Thompson, 11 Feb. and 1 March, 1858, all in RG 75, NA. Taylor to WHT, 25 Nov. 1859, WHT Papers, WCU. Contract between WHT and Nacheuh, 1 Jan. 1857, Martha Hyde Collection, WCU. WHT to Terrell, 2 May 1860, Terrell Papers, WCU.
21. George E. Frizzell, "Remarks of Mr. Thomas, of Jackson," *Journal of Cherokee Studies* 7 (Fall 1982): 64-68.
22. Turnpike Book 1859, WHT Papers, DU; WHT to Jacob Siler, 18 May 1859, and Jacob Siler to WHT, 22 Dec. 1859, both in Siler Papers, UNC.
23. WHT to John C. Bryson, 5 May 1858, WHT Papers, DU; Promissory note from WHT to Johnston, 21 Sept. 1858, Terrell Papers, WCU; Deed of

Trust from WHT to Love, 6 Sept. 1858, WHT Papers micro., DU; WHT Diary, 17 Aug. 1858, cited in Russell, "Thomas," 218.

24. Terrell to WHT, 17 May 1859, WHT Papers, DU; Deeds from WHT to Francis F. Oram, 4 Nov. 1859, WHT Papers micro., DU; Eighth Census of the U.S., 1860, N.C. (Jackson and Johnston counties) 23:1-155; Wheeler, *Sketches*, 218.

25. WHT to Sarah, 2 Jan. 1858, WHT Papers micro., DU; *Private Laws of N.C.*, sess. of 1856-57, p. 33; *Senate Journal*, sess. of 1856-57, pp. 70-71, and sess. of 1858-59, p. 4; *Raleigh (N.C.) Standard*, 8, 22, 29 Dec. 1858; Lefler and Newsome, *North Carolina*, 359, 368; WHT to W. W. Holden, 29 June 1860, WHT Papers, DU.

26. The Thomas quotations are in a pamphlet dated 1 Jan. 1857, "Report on the Extension of the North Carolina Railroad . . . ," WHT Papers, DU, cited by Inscoe, *Mountain Masters*, 170-71.

27. Robert B. Vance to Zebulon B. Vance, 18 April 1860, cited in Inscoe, *Mountain Masters*, 147. See also Inscoe, 144-49.

28. *Raleigh (N.C.) Standard*, 27 Nov. and 26 Dec. 1860, 16 Jan. 1861; *Raleigh (N.C.) State Journal*, 22 Dec. 1860; *Senate Journal*, sess. of 1860-61, pp. 44-126, 129, 137-43.

29. WHT to Sarah, 1 Jan. 1861, WHT Papers micro., DU.

CHAPTER 6
Secession and War

1. WHT to Terrell, 24 Dec. 1864, WHT Papers, DU.
2. WHT, *Resolutions on Federal Affairs* (Raleigh: n.p., 1861), 1-7. A Copy of this pamphlet is in WHT Papers micro., DU.
3. Ibid.
4. *Raleigh (N.C.) Standard*, 16 Jan. 1861.
5. Ibid. See also *Senate Journal*, sess. of 1860-61, p. 4.
6. *Raleigh (N.C.) State Journal*, 30 Jan. 1861.
7. *Raleigh (N.C.) Standard*, 30 Jan. 1861.
8. William K. Boyd, "North Carolina on the Eve of Secession," *Annual Report of the American Historical Association . . . 1910* (Washington, D.C.: American Historical Association), 1912:165-77; Kruman, *Parties and Politics*, 180-221; John G. Barrett, *The Civil War in North Carolina* (Chapel Hill: University of North Carolina Press, 1963), 4-16.
9. WHT to Sarah, 24 Jan. 1861, WHT Papers micro., DU.
10. Robert P. Ambrose, "A 'Critical Year' (April 1860-1861): A Study of Unionist Sentiment in Western North Carolina during the Culminating Year of the Secession Movement" (M.A. thesis, University of North Carolina at Greensboro, 1975), 33-36; *Raleigh (N.C.) Standard*, 30 Jan. and 27 Feb. 1861; John W. Ellis Letterbook 1859-61, 14 March 1861, Ellis Papers, NCDAH.

11. WHT, "To My Immediate Constituents of Jackson County," 22 Feb. 1861, printed in *Winston-Salem (N.C.) The Peoples Press*, 1 March 1861, p. 2. See also J. Carlyle Sitterson, *The Secession Movement in North Carolina* (Chapel Hill: University of North Carolina Press, 1939), 278-82, 210-12.

12. Love to WHT, 20 April 1861, WHT Papers micro., DU. Although he often signed his letters "James R. Love, Jr.," he was named for his uncle, not his father. See also Sitterson, *Secession Movement*, 240-42; Eighth Census of the U.S., N.C., Jackson and Johnston counties, 23:103; *Senate Journal*, sess. of 1860-61, pp. 3-5; and Ambrose, "The 'Critical Year,'" 38-46.

13. Barrett, *Civil War in North Carolina*, 14-15; *Senate Journal*, 1st extra sess. 1861, pp. 15-20, 53-56; *Raleigh (N.C.) Standard*, 15 May 1861.

14. *Raleigh (N.C.) Register*, 22 May 1861; *Charleston (S.C.) Mercury*, 11 May 1861. See also *Greensboro (N.C.) Times*, 22 May 1861, and Arthur, *Western North Carolina*, 609.

15. J. M. Bryson and Peter King to WHT, 14 May 1861, Secretary of State Papers, Convention of 1861-62, NCDAH; John G. McCormick, *Personnel of the Convention of 1861* (Chapel Hill: University of North Carolina Press, 1900), 12-91; Kemp P. Battle, *Legislation of the Convention of 1861* (Chapel Hill: University of North Carolina Press, 1900), 100-101; *Journal of the Convention of the People of North Carolina*, 1st sess., pp. 5, 6, 35, 46, 82, 85, and 2d sess., p. 21; *Raleigh (N.C.) Standard*, 5 June 1861.

16. *Journal of the Convention*, 1st sess., pp. 15-16; William K. Boyd, ed., *Memoirs of W. W. Holden* (Durham, N.C.: Seeman Printery, 1911), 2:17. See also Kruman, *Parties and Politics*, 181, 220-21, and Stringfield Memoirs, Stringfield Papers, DU.

17. Battle, *Legislation of the Convention of 1861*, 130, 99.

18. *Public Laws of N.C.*, sess. of 1860-61, pp. 53, 86-98; Ellis Papers, Jan.-May 1861.

19. George W. Hayes to Governor Ellis, 31 May 1861; J. Ramsay Dills and W. K. Enloe to Ellis, 28 June 1861; J. M. Dobson, et. al., to Ellis, 11 June 1861; B. M. Edney to Ellis, 20 May 1861, all in Ellis Papers. *Greensboro (N.C.) Times*, 22 June 1861. *Raleigh (N.C.) Standard*, 27 April 1861. Matthew R. Love to Sister, 20 June 1861, WHT Papers micro, DU.

20. WHT to Sarah, 17 June 1861, WHT Papers, DU.

21. Ibid.

22. *Journal of the Convention*, 1st sess., pp. 1-5, 44, 80, 104-5; *Raleigh (N.C.) Standard*, 19 June 1861; *Public Laws of N.C.*, 2d extra sess., 1861, pp. 52-53.

23. Neely, "North Carolina's Eastern Band of Cherokees," in Williams, ed., *Southeastern Indians*, 161-62; Mooney, "Myths," 169.

24. Jarrett to WHT, 25 July 1861, WHT Papers, DU.

25. *Senate Journal*, 2d extra sess., 1861, pp. 215, 217; *Raleigh (N.C.) Standard*, 18 Sept. 1861; Assistant Adjutant-General R. H. Chilton to WHT, 19 Sept. 1861,

in *OR*, 2:pt. 2, p. 304. Unless otherwise noted, all citations of *OR* herein are from series 1.

26. WHT to Mercer Fain, 17 Oct. 1861; Testimony of Robert P. Dick re WHT, 28 April 1894, both in WHT Papers, WCU. James H. Boykin, *North Carolina in 1861* (New York: Bookman Associates, 1961), 195. *House Journal*, 2d extra sess., 1861, p. 262. Finger, *Eastern Band*, 83.

27. Terrell to John H. Dillard, 22 Sept. 1874, in Records of *Cherokees vs. Thomas*.

28. WHT to Clark, 8 Oct. 1861, Henry T. Clark Papers, NCDAH.

29. Vernon H. Crow, *Storm in the Mountains: Thomas' Confederate Legion of Cherokee Indians and Mountaineers* (Cherokee, N.C.: Press of the Museum of the Cherokee Indian, 1982), 2; Finger, *Eastern Band*, 6. See also "The Indians of Western N.C.," in *Winston-Salem (N.C.) The Peoples Press*, 8 Feb. 1861, p. 1; D. Brewer Snipes, "Cherokees in Gray," in *Raleigh (N.C.) The State* 47, no. 9 (Feb. 1980): 9–10; *Memphis (Tenn.) Daily Appeal*, 17 May 1861; and Colby, "Routes to Rainey Mountain," 153.

30. Welch and Taylor to Clark, 17 Oct. 1861, and WHT to Clark, 17 Oct. 1861, both in Clark Papers; *Journal of the Convention*, 1st sess., p. 4; Arthur, *Western North Carolina*, 401.

31. *Raleigh (N.C.) Standard*, 26 Oct. 1861, quoting the *Hendersonville (N.C.) Henderson Times*, n.d.

32. WHT, "To the Freemen of the Tenth Congressional District," 26 Oct. 1861, Broadside Collection, DU. See also *Raleigh (N.C.) Standard*, 26 Oct., 6 and 16 Nov., 1861.

33. WHT Notebook 1862–65, pp. 5–6, NCDAH; Leonard Bloom, "The Acculturation of the Eastern Cherokee: Historical Aspects," *NCHR* 19 (Oct. 1942): 356.

34. WHT Papers, WCU.

35. WHT to Clark, 14 March 1862, Clark Papers.

36. Finger, *Eastern Band*, 83–84; Jefferson Davis, *Messages and Papers of Jefferson Davis and the Confederacy, Including Diplomatic Correspondence, 1861–1865*, comp. James D. Richardson (New York: Chelsea House-Robert Hector Publishers, 1966), 1:151.

37. Crow, *Storm in the Mountains*, 4; John W. Moore, *Roster of North Carolina Troops in the War Between the States* (Raleigh: Ashe, 1882), 4:152; WHT to Clark, 13 and 17 April, 1862, Clark Papers.

38. William W. Stringfield, "Sixty-Ninth Regiment," in *Histories of the Several Regiments and Battalions from North Carolina, in the Great War 1861–65*, ed. Walter Clark (Goldsboro, N.C.: Nash Brothers, 1901), 5:736; Moore, *Roster*, 4:152; William W. Stringfield, "North Carolina Cherokee Indians," *North Carolina Booklet* 3, no. 2 (June 1903): 20; Crow, *Storm in the Mountains*, 4; Finger, *Eastern Band*, 84–85.

39. Smith to Carrie S. Smith, 13 March 1862, cited in Charles Faulkner Bryan, Jr., "The Civil War in East Tennessee: A Social, Political and Economic Study"

(Ph.D. diss., University of Tennessee, 1978), 98. See also Bryan, 97, 344-48, and Oliver P. Temple, *East Tennessee and the Civil War* (1899; reprint, Freeport, N.Y.: Books for Libraries Press, 1971), 399, 425.

40. Terrell Reminiscences, Terrell Papers, WCU. See also WHT to Governor, 13 April 1862, Clark Papers; *Atlanta (Ga.) Daily Intelligencer*, 10 May 1862; Crow, *Storm in the Mountains*, 4-5; and Finger, *Eastern Band*, 85.

41. WHT to Clark, 17 April 1862, Clark Papers. See also Clark to Augustus S. Merrimon, 5 March 1862, Clark Letterbook 1861-62, Clark Papers; and Stringfield, "Sixty-Ninth Regiment," 729.

42. *Knoxville (Tenn.) Daily Register*, 2 May 1862; *OR*, 2:130, 10:pt. 1, p. 50, 16: pt. 2, p. 972; Terrell Reminiscences, Terrell Papers, WCU; Mooney, "Myths," 93-94, 162.

43. Bryan, "Civil War in East Tennessee," 100; Richard M. McMurry, *Two Great Rebel Armies* (Chapel Hill: University of North Carolina Press, 1989), 59-62.

44. Crow, *Storm in the Mountains*, 7-9; Finger, *Eastern Band*, 86.

45. WHT to Clark, 25 May 1862, Clark Papers; *Asheville (N.C.) News*, 5 June 1862.

46. WHT to Sarah, 25 June 1862, WHT Papers, DU.

47. Stringfield Memoirs, Stringfield Papers, DU.

48. Ibid. See also Crow, *Storm in the Mountains*, 10-12.

49. Terrell to Zebulon B. Vance, 22 Feb. 1864, in Zebulon Baird Vance, *The Papers of Zebulon Vance*, ed. Gordon B. McKinney and Richard M. McMurry (Frederick, Md.: University Publications of America, 1987), reel 22; Terrell Reminiscences, Terrell Papers, WCU; Moore, *Roster*, 4:154-55; *OR*, 16:pt. 2, p. 879; Stringfield, "Sixty-Ninth Regiment," 729-30.

50. WHT Notebook 1862-65, WHT Papers, NCDAH; *OR*, 16:pt. 2, pp. 790, 797-98, 841, 851; "Historical Sketch of Walker's Battalion of Thomas's NC Legion," *Haywood Co. (N.C.) Courier*, 2 September 1898, clipping in Stephen Whitaker Papers, NCDAH; Terrell Reminiscences, Terrell Papers, WCU; Bryan, "Civil War in East Tennessee," 107-10; Crow, *Storm in the Mountains*, 14-15, 198.

51. Crow, *Storm in the Mountains*, 1, 15-16; Finger, *Eastern Band*, 91.

52. *Greeneville (Tenn.) Banner*, 15 Sept. 1862, quoted in *(Atlanta) Southern Confederacy*, 20 Sept. 1862.

53. The best account of alleged savagery by the Cherokees in the Civil War is Finger, *Eastern Band*, 90-93. For an interpretation, which largely follows Terrell, that the Indians took many scalps, see Crow, *Storm in the Mountains*, 16. The essential primary accounts include Stringfield to Mooney, 19 April 1915, Stringfield Papers, WCU; Terrell Reminiscences, Terrell Papers, WCU; and Stringfield, "Sixty-Ninth Regiment," 736.

54. Compiled Confederate Service Records, North Carolina, Thomas Legion, NA, MC270-573; Moore, *Roster*, 4:151-75, 196-216; Stringfield, "Sixty-Ninth Regiment," 729-33; Mooney, "Myths," 169; Crow, *Storm in the Mountains*,

13, 145-47, 150. For a complete roster of all companies in Thomas's legion, see Crow, 149-235.

CHAPTER 7
Colonel Thomas

1. *OR*, 16:pt. 2, p. 985. See also McMurry, *Two Great Rebel Armies*, 114-15, 132.
2. *OR*, 18:811, 10:pt. 2, p. 395. See also Crow, *Storm in the Mountains*, 21-22.
3. WHT to Vance, 22 Nov. 1862, in *The Papers of Zebulon Baird Vance*, ed. Frontis W. Johnston, Vol. 1, *1843-1862* (Raleigh: State Department of Archives and History, 1963), 1:385-86. See also Stringfield, "Sixty-Ninth Regiment," 733-35.
4. WHT to Sarah, 28 Jan. 1863, WHT Papers, DU.
5. *OR*, 16:pt. 2, pp. 811, 853; Davis to Vance, Jan. 1863, and Heth to Vance, 17 Jan. 1863, both in McKinney and McMurry, eds., *Vance Papers*, reel 13.
6. Jefferson Davis, *Jefferson Davis Papers, Constitutionalist: His Letters, Papers, and Speeches*, ed. Dunbar Rowland (New York: J. J. Little & Ives Co., 1923), 5:414.
7. S. S. Scott to James H. Seddon, 18 Feb. 1863; WHT to Scott, 3 April 1862; Scott to R. W. Johnson, 1 May 1864, all in Terrell Papers, NAA. See also Mooney, "Myths," 170-71, and Ina W. and John J. Van Noppen, *Western North Carolina since the Civil War* (Boone, N.C.: Appalachian Consortium Press, 1973), 7.
8. *OR*, 23:pt. 2, pp. 644, 711; Stephen Whitaker to Father and Mother, 25 March 1863, Whitaker Papers; WHT to John C. Breckinridge, 27 April 1864, WHT Papers, DU. See also Crow, *Storm in the Mountains*, 29.
9. Arthur, *Western North Carolina*, 609; Terrell to Vance, 22 Feb. 1864, in McKinney and McMurry, eds., *Vance Papers*, reel 22.
10. Joseph Keener to Vance, 3 April 1863, in McKinney and McMurry, eds., *Vance Papers*, reel 18.
11. WHT to Sarah, 4 June 1863, WHT Papers, DU.
12. *OR*, 23:pt. 2, pp. 792, 945; Bryan, "Civil War in East Tennessee," 112-14.
13. WHT power of attorney to Fain, 19 June 1863, Terrell Papers, WCU; Deed from WHT to Thomas S. Arthur, George F. Towns, and Thomas N. Cox, 7 July 1863, Deed Book G-7, pp. 78-81, Jackson County Courthouse; WHT to Fain, 9 June and 1 Dec. 1863, WHT Papers, WCU; WHT to Sarah, 4 June 1863, WHT Papers, DU.
14. Compiled Confederate Service Records, N.C., Thomas Legion, NA, MC270-573; Terrell to Vance, 22 Feb. 1864, in McKinney and McMurry, eds., *Vance Papers*, reel 22; Stephen Whitaker to James Whitaker, Sr., 25 Aug. 1863, Whitaker Papers; Crow, *Storm in the Mountains*, 34-35, 150.
15. Maria Stringfield to William W. Stringfield, 3 Sept. 1863, Stringfield Papers, NCDAH; Stringfield, "Sixty-Ninth Regiment," 738-40; Crow, *Storm in the Mountains*, 35-37; Thomas Lawrence Connelly, *Autumn of Glory: The Army of Tennessee, 1862-1865* (Baton Rouge: Louisiana State University Press, 1967), 149.

16. Crow, *Storm in the Mountains*, 35–37; Van Noppen and Van Noppen, *Western North Carolina*, 7.
17. WHT to A. T. Davidson, 22 Jan. 1864, WHT Papers, DU; Stringfield, "Sixty-Ninth Regiment," 738–40; *OR*, 30:pt. 3, pp. 473–74, 501–04.
18. Crow, *Storm in the Mountains*, 50–51.
19. M. L. Brittain to Vance, 1 Nov. 1863, and Fain to Governor Vance, 18 July 1863, both in McKinney and McMurry, eds., *Vance Papers*, reels 18 and 20.
20. "Col. Thomas' Cherokee Indians," unidentified newspaper clipping, 11 Nov. 1863, WHT Papers, DU.
21. R. B. Vance to WHT, 4 Nov. 1863, WHT Papers, DU.
22. WHT to Col. William C. Walker, 8 and 14 Nov. 1863, both in Whitaker Papers. See also Crow, *Storm in the Mountains*, 52.
23. Longstreet to WHT, 29 Nov. 1863, WHT Papers, DU; Crow, *Storm in the Mountains*, 52–53; Bryan, "Civil War in East Tennessee," 130; WHT to Mercer Fain, 1 Dec. 1863, Fain Papers, WCU.
24. *OR*, 31:pt. 1, pp. 438–39; Crow, *Storm in the Mountains*, 53–54.
25. WHT to James Taylor, 24 Dec. 1863, Taylor Papers, DU.
26. Crow, *Storm in the Mountains*, 55–56; Stringfield Memoirs, Stringfield Papers, DU.
27. *OR*, 32:pt. 1, pp. 75–76; WHT to A. T. Davidson, 22 Jan. 1864, WHT Papers, DU; Crow, *Storm in the Mountains*, 56–57.
28. *OR*, 32:pt. 1, p. 76. Joseph E. Johnston to Zebulon Vance, 3 Feb. 1864; E. W. Herndon to Zebulon Vance, 22 Feb. 1864, both in McKinney and McMurry, eds., *Vance Papers*, reel 22.
29. W. Murdoch to Vance, 18 Jan. 1864, and WHT to Vance, 24 Jan. 1864, both in McKinney and McMurry, eds. *Vance Papers*, reel 21.
30. *OR*, 32:pt. 1, p. 137–38, 159; pt. 2, p. 749.
31. *Raleigh (N.C.) Daily Confederate*, 17 May 1864.
32. Neely, "North Carolina's Eastern Band of Cherokees," 162.
33. *OR*, 32:pt. 1, p. 159; pt. 2, p. 749. Crow, *Storm in the Mountains*, 58–59.
34. Petition to Vance from Walker's Battalion and Love's Regiment, 25 Feb. 1864; Terrell to Vance, 22 Feb. 1864; D. Snider and W. A. Pressnett to Vance, 24 Feb. 1864, all in McKinney and McMurry, eds., *Vance Papers*, reel 22. Love to WHT, 28 March 1864, WHT Papers micro., DU. Vance's response is written on backs of the Petition and Terrell's letter. See also Stringfield, "Sixty-Ninth Regiment," 742–43.
35. WHT to Governor and Council of S.C., 28 Feb. 1864, *OR*, 53:313–14; K. L. Simons to WHT, 9 March 1864, and WHT to Love, 27 April 1864, both in WHT Papers, DU; Margaret E. Love to Vance, 10 May 1864, *Vance Papers*, reel 23; Affidavit by William Hicks, 1 Dec. 1866, and Receipt from J. Keener to William A. Coleman, 17 April 1865, both in WHT Papers micro., DU.

36. Allen, *Annals of Haywood*, 307; Testimony of Hilliard, cited in Russell, "Thomas," 402; Love to parents, 4 March 1864, WHT Papers, DU.
37. Charges against WHT, 11 May 1864, a fragment, WHT Papers micro., DU; Crow, *Storm in the Mountains*, 60-61, 66.
38. Hicks to Vance, 25 June 1864, *Vance Papers*, reel 24.
39. WHT to Cooper, 8 July 1864, WHT Papers, DU.
40. WHT to Cooper, 2 Aug. 1864, WHT Papers, DU.
41. WHT to Sgt. Aaron Brown, 26 Aug. 1864, WHT Papers, DU.
42. Crow, *Storm in the Mountains*, 99-100; W. W. Stringfield to Andrew Patton, 4 Oct. 1915, and Stringfield to W. S. Terrell, 10 April 1913, both in Stringfield Papers, WCU; James Taylor to WHT, 10 Aug. 1864, Terrell Papers, WCU. On deserters and Union sentiment in North Carolina, see Mary Shannon Smith, "Union Sentiment in North Carolina during the Civil War," *Proceedings of Sixteenth Annual Session of the State Literary and Historical Association of North Carolina* (Raleigh: Edwards and Broughton), 1916: 50-64, and Richard Bardolph, "Inconstant Rebels: Desertion of North Carolina Troops in the Civil War," *NCHR* 41 (April 1964): 163-89.
43. Campbell's endorsement of a letter of Zebulon Vance, July 1863, *OR*, ser. 4, 2:674, cited in Crow, *Storm in the Mountains*, 101; Stringfield Memoirs, Stringfield Papers, DU; WHT to Sarah, 13 Nov. 1864, WHT Papers micro., DU.
44. WHT to Sarah, 13 Nov. 1863, WHT Papers micro., DU; *OR*, 43:pt. 2, p. 919, 42:pt. 3, pp. 1196, 1279; Stringfield Memoirs, Stringfield Papers, DU; Crow, *Storm in the Mountains*, 101.
45. Vance to Seddon, 13 Dec. 1864, *Vance Papers*, reel 13.
46. *OR*, 42:pt. 3, p. 1254.
47. Martin to Lee, 11 March 1865, cited in Crow, *Storm in the Mountains*, 116.
48. *OR*, 46:pt. 2, pp. 1005-6, 1013; Crow, *Storm in the Mountains*, 118.
49. Stringfield to WHT, 21 Feb. 1865, WHT Papers, DU.
50. *OR*, 49:pt. 1, pp. 31, 1048; Crow, *Storm in the Mountains*, 121-23; Stringfield Memoirs, Stringfield Papers, DU.
51. *OR*, 49:pt. 2, p. 309; Ina W. Van Noppen, "The Significance of Stoneman's Last Raid," *NCHR* 38 (January 1961): 32.
52. Crow, *Storm in the Mountains*, 126.
53. Ibid., 130-38.
54. Ibid., 138-40; *OR*, 49:pt. 2, pp. 669, 754-55; R. T. Underwood, Reminiscences, 6 May 1865, R. T. Underwood Papers, DU; Stringfield, "Sixty-Ninth Regiment," 758-61 (mistakenly gives the date as May 10); Stringfield Memoirs, Stringfield Papers, DU.
55. Stringfield to Mooney, 17 Sept. 1900, Stringfield Papers, WCU.

CHAPTER 8
In a Mad Man's Cell

1. WHT Loyalty Oath, 1865, and extract of Burgess Fitzgerald to unknown addressee, 25 Aug. 1865, WHT Papers, DU; Allen, *Annals of Haywood*, 305

2. WHT to citizens of Sevier County, Tenn., 4 Oct. 1865, WHT Papers micro., DU; John H. Wheeler to WHT, 13 Aug. 1866, and Wheeler to W. T. Dortch, 15 Aug. 1866, both in WHT Papers, DU.

3. Wheeler to WHT, 13 Aug. 1866, WHT Papers micro., DU.

4. WHT to Sarah, 4 Nov. 1865, WHT Papers micro., DU.

5. Interview by Russell with J. Scroop Styles, Asheville, N.C., n.d.

6. Contract between Caroline Thomas and W. H. and Sarah L. Thomas, 22 April 1871, Deed Book D-4, p. 863, Jackson County Courthouse.

7. WHT to Citizens of Sevier County, 4 Oct. 1865, WHT Papers micro., DU.

8. Contract between WHT and Terrell, 25 Dec. 1865, WHT Papers, DU; Contract between WHT and Mingus, 6 March 1866, WHT Papers micro., DU; Melius, Currier, and Sherood to WHT, 12 April 1866, WHT Papers, WCU; Russell, "Thomas," 408.

9. WHT to Mingus, 20 Nov. 1865, cited in Russell, "Thomas," 242; Mooney, "Myths," 171-72; Mooney, Notes on 1890 interview, File 2497, Mooney Papers, NAA; Cherokee Census in Thomas Ledger 1839-45, pp. 69-193, WHT Papers, DU; Finger, *Eastern Band*, 101.

10. Copy of an act of 24 Feb. 1866 authorizing certain Cherokee Indians to remain permanently in N.C.; J. B. Jones to Commissioner of Indian Affairs D.N. Cooley, 16 March 1866; WHT to Commissioner of Indian Affairs, 17 Aug. 1866; Cherokee Indians to Commissioner of Indian Affairs, 7 Aug. 1866, all in RG 75, NA. Stringfield Memoirs, Stringfield Papers, DU. Finger, *Eastern Band*, 101-3. Frizzell, "The Legal Status of the Eastern Band," 10, 27, 42. Bridgers, "A Legal Digest of the North Carolina Cherokees," 25.

11. Interview by Russell with Margaret Stringfield, Waynesville, N.C., n.d. Margaret Stringfield was the niece of Sarah and William Thomas. In this interview, she was remembering something that had happened eighty years earlier and probably had been told to her by her mother, who was Sarah's sister, Maria Stringfield. The credibility of her story is enhanced by testimonies from contemporary witnesses that on other occasions Thomas was subject to outbursts of violent behavior.

12. E. A. Fisher to Sarah Thomas, 26 and 30 March 1867; J. T. Adams and J. E. Nichols statement, 8 April 1867; W. E. Anderson's receipt for $25 from WHT, all in WHT Papers, DU.

13. Love to Marcus Erwin, 7 Feb. 1874, Taylor Papers, DU.

14. Mooney, "Myths," 161, 172.

15. Terrell to R. J. Powell, 13 May 1867, WHT Papers, DU.

16. Jack Frederick Kilpatrick, "Two Notices by Will Thomas," *Southern Indian Studies* 14 (Oct. 1962): 27-28. Deed Books J-10, p. 930; H-8, p. 960; E-5, p. 963, Jackson County Courthouse. Account Book for N.C. Cherokees, WHT Papers, WCU. R. B. Johnston to WHT, 22 April 1867, Taylor Papers, DU.

17. Facts in relation to the suits with J. W. Cooper, 7 Dec. 1875; A. S. Merrimon to WHT, 1 April 1868; William Johnston to WHT, 8 April 1868, all in Terrell Papers, WCU. Receipt from F. R. Ammons to WHT, 20 March 1868, and Terrell to J. R. Thomas, Sr., 27 Mar. 1896, both in WHT Papers micro., DU.

18. Terrell to T. D. Johnston, 1 Dec. 1873, Thomas D. Johnston Papers, UNC. Sarah Thomas to Stringfield, 30 May 1874; Terrell to J. R. Thomas, Sr., 27 March 1896, both in WHT Papers micro., DU. Terrell to G. F. Ivey, 29 Jan. 1906, Terrell Papers, WCU. Terrell to Robert P. Dick, n.d., in *Records of Cherokees vs. Thomas*.

19. Answer of William Johnston to a bill of complaint, 28 June 1873, in Records of *Cherokees vs. Thomas*; Terrell to Ivey, 29 Jan. 1906, and *venditioni exponas* from State of N.C. to Sheriff of Cherokee County, 29 June 1869, both in Terrell Papers, WCU; T. D. Johnston to Terrell, 15 Feb. 1897, WHT Papers, DU; Terrell to WHT, 29 Nov. 1875, and Terrell to E. S. Parker, 9 June 1869, both in WHT Papers micro., DU.

20. Finger, *Eastern Band*, 102-10. George E. Frizzell, "The Politics of Cherokee Citizenship, 1898-1930," *NCHR* 61 (April 1984): 208-9. Wardell, *A Political History of the Cherokee Nation*, 241. James Taylor to WHT, 27 July 1868, Terrell Papers, WCU. D. W. Siler to Commissioner of Indian Affairs N. G. Taylor, 1 May 1868; Preston Surret to N. G. Taylor, 13 June 1868; R. G. Powell to N. G. Taylor, 24 Aug. 1868; James Taylor to N. G. Taylor, 31 Aug. 1868; S. W. Swetland to N. G. Taylor, 1 Feb. 1869; S. W. Swetland to Commissioner of Indian Affairs E. S. Parker, 9 Aug. and 20 Nov. 1869; Terrell to E. S. Parker, 9 June 1869, all in RG 75, NA.

21. Terrell to Ivey, 19 Jan. 1906, Terrell Papers, WCU; Statement by Terrell and Thomas D. Johnston, 15 Nov. 1883, Final Record Book K, 42, Jackson County Courthouse; Bill of Sale between William Johnston and Enola, and other Cherokees, for $6,500, 29 Sept. 1869, and receipt dated 10 Jan. 1870, James Taylor Papers, DU.

22. U.S. Rep. Alexander H. Jones to Terrell, 19 Jan. 1870, Terrell Papers, WCU. *U.S. Statutes*, 16:362-63. John Ross, et al., to Board of Indian Commissioners, 26 Oct. 1871; Taylor to Board of Indian Commissioners, 15 Sept. 1871, both in Taylor Papers, DU. John Ross to President of United States, 11 Nov. 1870; Ross to Secretary of the Interior C. Delano, 11 Dec. 1871, both in RG 75, NA. Wardell, *Political History*, 246. WHT to William Johnston, 17 June 1871, WHT Papers, DU.

23. Terrell's account of his and Johnston's work, n.d., Terrell Papers, WCU; Terrell to Robert P. Dick, n.d., in Records of *Eastern Band vs. Thomas*; Court

Order for an Inquiry into the state of the mind of WHT, 11 Aug. 1874, Indian Collection-Cherokees, NCDAH; Finger, *Eastern Band*, 119.

24. WHT to Chiefs . . . of . . . . Cherokee Indians, 20 Feb. 1871, WHT Papers, DU.

25. Terrell to T. D. Johnston, 7 July 1873, Johnston Papers, UNC.

26. *House Ex. Doc.* 196 (47 Cong., 1 sess.), 3. Testimony of Terrell, 31 Aug. 1874, and Answer of Thomas to bill of complaint, 28 June 1873, both in Records of *Cherokees vs. Thomas*. WHT Memorandum, n.d.; James Terrell to Second Auditor of the Treasury, 28 April 1873; *Cherokee Indian Claims, Petitioner Docket 282*, all in WHT Papers, DU. Taylor to Acting Commissioner of Indian Affairs H. R. Clum, 8 March 1873, and copies of both suits, in RG 75, NA. WHT answer to complaint, 28 June 1873, Taylor Papers, DU. [Nicholas Woodfin] to Terrell, 12 July 1873, Terrell Papers, WCU.

27. *House Ex. Doc.* 196, pp. 35-36.

28. Dony to Commissioner of the General Land Office, 1-9 Sept. 1874, in Selected Letters Received by the Office of Indian Affairs Relating to Cherokees of North Carolina, 1851-1905, NA, M-1059, 2/215, 257-63.

29. Terrell to C. M. McLoud, 4 Jan. 1878, Terrell Papers, WCU.

30. *House Ex. Doc.* 196, pp. 37-40. Taylor to Terrell, 20 Nov. 1874, and Terrell to E. S. Smith, 20 April and 21 July 1875, all in Terrell Papers, WCU. Deposition of George T. Mason, 17 Oct. 1874, WHT Papers, DU. N.C. Cherokees to President of the United States, 7 Oct. 1874; Flying Squirrel to Commissioner of Indian Affairs, 12 Oct. 1874; Report of Dony, 29 Oct. 1874; Robert P. Vance to Commissioner of Indian Affairs, 26 Oct. 1875; James Stevenson and Paul Brodie to Commissioner of Indian Affairs, 12 Nov. 1875, all in RG 75, NA. See also Finger, *Eastern Band*, 120-21, and Irvin M. Peithmann, *Red Men of Fire: A History of the Cherokee Indian* (Springfield, Ill.: Charles C. Thomas, Publisher, 1964), 120-25.

31. Terrell to WHT, 22 Dec. 1874, Taylor and Terrell to E. S. Smith, 24 Dec. 1874, both in Terrell Papers, WCU.

32. Resolutions of General Council of Eastern Band of Cherokee Indians, 16 Nov. 1874, RG 75, NA.

33. Frizzell, "Legal Status," 45, 47-48; Bridgers, "Legal Digest," 25 28; Finger, *Eastern Band*, 122-25; Peithmann, *Red Men of Fire*, 124; Paul Stuart, *The Indian Office: Growth and Development of an American Institution*, 1865-1900 (Ann Arbor: University of Michigan Press, 1978), 40; Edward E. Hill, *The Office of Indian Affairs*, 1824-1880 (New York: Clearwater Publishing Co., 1974), 32-35.

34. Stringfield to Maria, 9, 15, 29 March 1868, 27 Jan., 2 Feb., 16, 24 April, 19 May 1869, and Sarah Thomas to Stringfield, 12 April 1869, all in Stringfield Papers, WCU; Stringfield Memoirs, Stringfield Papers, DU.

35. Hilliard to Sister, n.d., WHT Papers, DU.

36. Sarah Thomas to Stringfield, 22 Jan. 1871, Stringfield Papers, WCU.

37. Sarah Thomas to Maria Stringfield, 13 July 1873, and Sarah Thomas to Stringfield, 4 Oct. 1873, both in Stringfield Papers, WCU.
38. Sarah Thomas to Maria Stringfield, 8 Dec. 1875, and Maria to Stringfield, 13 Jan. 1876, both in Stringfield Papers, WCU.
39. Sallie Love Thomas to "Ma," 2 Jan. 1875, WHT Papers, DU.
40. Sallie to "Ma," 24 March 1877, WHT Papers, DU.
41. Sarah Thomas to Maria Stringfield, 8 Dec. 1875, Stringfield Papers, WCU.
42. Sarah Thomas to Stringfield, 22 Jan. 1871, 4 Oct. 1873; Sarah to Maria Stringfield, 8 Dec. 1875, all in Stringfield Papers, WCU. Sarah Thomas to Maria, 19 Feb. 1872; WHT to Lyman C. Draper, 4 June 1874; WHT to Maria, 5 July 1876, all in WHT Papers, DU.

There is no evidence, other than in letters Thomas wrote when he was not rational, that he was at Malvern Hill. That battle took place on July 1, 1862, outside Richmond. Thomas wrote a letter from Strawberry Plains on June 25. Conceivably, he could have traveled from Strawberry Plains to the Richmond area in that amount of time, but since there is no mention of it in his contemporary letters or the *Official Records*, one must conclude that his statement was either fantasy or a deliberate fabrication to disguise the nature of his illness.

43. Terrell to T. D. Johnston, 6 Feb. 1877, Terrell Papers, WCU.
44. Rebecca Harding Davis, "Qualla," *Lippincott's Magazine of Popular Literature and Science* 41 (Nov. 1875): 578. For families to keep mentally disturbed relatives locked in a basement or special room at home was not unusual during the eighteenth and nineteenth centuries.
45. Interview by Godbold with Gordon McKinney, Cullowhee, N.C., 29 Nov. 1985. The modern house on the site of the Thomas house perhaps contains part of the original dwelling. On one side of it is a stone room, but the date 1901 is carved over the entrance. Whether the room was constructed or remodeled then, or the date is incorrect, is unknown. Stone rooms, or even stone houses, were common in western North Carolina. The legend that the stone room was built to house Thomas, for which there is no written proof, has sometimes been repeated by twentieth-century residents of the house.
46. Maria to Stringfield, 22 and 30 Dec., 1876, Stringfield Papers, WCU.
47. Sarah Thomas to Willie, 8 Aug. 1876, WHT Papers, DU.
48. Maria to Stringfield, 12 and 19 Feb. 1877, Stringfield Papers, WCU.
49. 16 May 1877, WHT Papers, DU.
50. Terrell to T. D. Johnston, 19 June 1877, Johnston Papers, UNC.
51. WHT to Vance, 30 May 1877, in *Vance Papers*, reel 26.
52. WHT to Vance, 30 July 1877, in *Vance Papers*, reel 26.
53. Stringfield to Vance, 22 July 1877, in *Vance Papers*, reel 29.
54. Vance to WHT, 11 Aug. 1877; WHT to Vance, 21 Sept. 1877, both in *Vance Papers*, reel 26.

55. For characteristics of syphilis and its cause of mental illness in the nineteenth century, see Allan M. Brandt, *No Magic Bullet: A Social History of Venereal Disease in the United States since 1880* (New York: Oxford University Press, 1985), 129; Gerald N. Grob, *Mental Illness and American Society, 1875-1940* (Princeton: Princeton University Press, 1983), 188-89; Fredrick C. Redlich and Daniel X. Freedman, *The Theory and Practice of Psychiatry* (New York: Basic Books, 1966), 606; and James H. Jones, *Bad Blood: The Tuskegee Syphilis Experiment* (New York: Free Press, 1981), 3, 4, 93, 122, 185.

For Indian treatments of syphilis and sores, see Virgil J. Vogel, *American Indian Medicine* (Norman: University of Oklahoma Press, 1970), 139-40, 211; John P. Brown, *Old Frontiers: The Story of the Cherokee Indians from Earliest Times to the Date of Their Removal to the West, 1838* (Kingsport, Tenn.: Southern Publishers, 1938), 31; and Paul B. Hamel and Mary U. Chiltoskey, *Cherokee Plants and Their Uses: A 400-Year History* (Sylva, N.C.: Herald Publishing Co., 1975), 24-27.

56. For general accounts of asylum life, see "Moral Treatment in America's Lunatic Asylums," *Hospital and Community Psychiatry* 27 (July 1976): 468-70; J. W. Ashby, "The First North Carolina State Hospital," *Southern Medicine and Surgery* 104 (June 1942): 326-27; K. W. Stevenson, "A Brief History of Mental Health Care in North Carolina," *North Carolina Medical Journal* 26 (Nov. 1965): 509-15; Russell Hollander, "Life at the Washington Asylum for the Insane," *Historian* 44 (Feb. 1982): 229-41; Clark R. Cahow, *People, Patients, and Politics: The History of the North Carolina Mental Hospitals, 1848-1960* (New York: Arno Press, 1980), 23-39, 166-70; Gerald N. Grob, *Edward Jarvis and the Medical World of Nineteenth-Century America* (Knoxville: University of Tennessee Press, 1978), 40-42; Gerald N. Grob, *Mental Institutions in America: Social Policy to 1875* (New York: Free Press, 1973), 153-59, 165-70, 209, 223-29, 359-60, 387; Henry M. Hurd, ed., *The Institutional Care of the Insane in the United States and Canada* (Baltimore: John Hopkins Press, 1916), 1:75-76, 240, 3:280-89, 4:397-98, 418, 460; and David J. Rothman, *Conscience and Convenience: The Asylum and Its Alternatives in Progressive America* (Boston: Little, Brown, and Co. 1980), 17-37, 307, 320, 349.

57. WHT, Sr., to WHT, Jr., 29 Aug. 1881, WHT Papers, DU; Hope Summerell Chamberlain, *History of Wake County, North Carolina, with Sketches of Those Who Have Most Influenced Its Development* (Raleigh: Edwards and Broughton, 1922), 232-34.

58. Interview by Russell with Margaret Stringfield, Waynesville, N.C.; two rent contracts, both dated 1 May 1877, in WHT Invoice Book 1838 and Daybook 1840-1842, p. 76, WHT Papers, DU.

59. Judge R. F. McKee to Hilliard, 5 April 1878, Terrell Papers, WCU; Hilliard to Judge G. C. L. Gukdger, 27 Feb. 1879, WHT Papers micro., DU.

60. Terrell to Hilliard, 24 Jan. 1878, and Terrell's record of land sales, 1875-1881, both in Terrell Papers, WCU; Terrell to James R. Thomas, Sr., 27 March 1896, WHT Papers micro., DU.

61. G. Henry, Attorney, to Terrell, 20 May 1881; James R. Thomas to Terrell, 10 Oct. 1884, 19 Nov. 1887, numerous letters in 1889; William H. Thomas, Jr., to Terrell, 9 March 1885; Sallie Love Thomas to Terrell, 4 March and 2 April 1885; Terrell to James R. Thomas, 27 March 1896; James R. Thomas to Terrell, 6 March 1897, all in Terrell Papers, WCU. Report of James R. Thomas, Sr., to the Superior Court of Jackson County, n.d., WHT Papers micro., DU. WHT, Sr., to WHT, Jr., 29 Aug. 1881, WHT Papers, DU.

62. Hurd, ed., *Institutional Care of the Insane*, 3:284, 4:460-61; William B. Bushong, "A. G. Bauer, North Carolina's New South Architect," *NCHR* 60 (July 1983): 307-8; Mooney, Notes on 1890 interview, File 2497, Mooney Papers, NAA.

63. Mooney, Notes of 1890 interview, File 2497, Mooney Papers, NAA. See also Colby, "Routes to Rainey Mountain," 3, 63, 109-10, 151, 171, 173-74; Duane H. King, "James Mooney, Ethnologist," *Journal of Cherokee Studies* 7 (Spring 1982): 4-9; L. G. Moses, *Indian Man: A Biography of James Mooney* (Champaign: University of Illinois Press, 1984), 22, 32, 51; Finger, *Eastern Band*, 153, 155, 176, 178.

64. Murphy to Stringfield, 10 May 1893, and Hilliard to Maria, May 1893, both in Stringfield Papers, WCU; interview by Russell with WHT III, Asheville, N.C., n.d.

Selected Bibliography

Manuscripts

Chapel Hill, N.C. Southern Historical Collection, Louis Round Wilson Library, University of North Carolina
    Duff Green Papers
    Thomas D. Johnston Papers
    Jacob Siler Papers
    William Holland Thomas Letterbook, 1844-46
    Gladys Avery Tillett Papers
    Zebulon Baird Vance Papers
Cullowhee, N.C. Hunter Memorial Library, Western Carolina University
    Charles E. Bird Papers
    Mercer Fain Papers
    Martha Hyde Papers
    James R. Love Papers, and addition
    Robert Love Papers
    William W. Stringfield Papers
    James Terrell Papers
    William Holland Thomas Papers, and additions
    William Holland Thomas III Papers
Durham, N.C. William R. Perkins Library, Duke University
    Alfred W. Bell Papers
    Broadside Collection (Rare Book Room)
    Robert Newman Gourdin Papers
    Edward Harden Papers
    Thomas Lenoir, Sr., Papers
    Albert Siler Papers
    William Williams Stringfield Papers
    James Taylor Papers
    William Holland Thomas Papers
    R. T. Underwood Papers

East Point, Ga. Federal Records Center
  Records of the *Eastern Band of Cherokees vs. William Holland Thomas, et. al.*
Madison, Wis. State Historical Society of Wisconsin
  Lyman Copeland Draper Collection
Raleigh, N.C. North Carolina Division of Archives and History
  Thomas Bragg Papers
  Henry Toole Clark Papers
  Calvin J. Cowles Papers
  Allen Turner Davidson and Theodore F. Davidson Papers
  Edward Bishop Dudley Papers
  John Willis Ellis Papers
  William Alexander Graham Papers
  Legislative Papers
  List of Warrants Issued to the Officers and Soldiers in the Continental Line Raised in and Belonging to the State of North Carolina
  John Motley Morehead Papers
  North Carolina Indian Collection — Cherokees
  David Settle Reid Papers
  Secretary of State Papers, Convention of 1861-62
  State Treasurer, Cherokee Land Sale Book, 1820-29
  Montford Stokes Papers
  William Williams Stringfield Papers
  David Lowery Swain Papers
  William Holland Thomas Notebook, 1862-65
  Zebulon Baird Vance Papers
  Stephen Whitaker Papers
Sylva, N.C. Jackson County Courthouse
  Dockets of the Superior Court 1852-59, 1853-59, 1854-69, 1853-72
  Jackson County Deed Books D-4, E-5, G-7
  Jackson County Miscellaneous Records I
Washington, D.C. National Anthropological Archives, the Smithsonian Institution
  James Mooney Papers
  James W. Terrell Papers
Washington, D.C. National Archives and Records Administration
  Record Group 75: Records of the Bureau of Indian Affairs, Letters Received, 1824-81
  Record Group 93: Revolutionary War, Compiled Military Records
Waynesville, N.C. Haywood County Courthouse
  Haywood County Deed Books B and F

Manuscript Collections on Microfilm

Compiled Confederate Service Records. Thomas Legion. Washington: National Archives Microfilm Publication MC270-573.
Record Group 123: United States Court of Claims. Reels 6 and 131. Washington: National Archives Microfilm Publication M1104.
Selected Letters Received by the Office of Indian Affairs Relating to the Cherokees of North Carolina, 1851-1905. Reel 2. Washington: National Archives Microfilm Publication M1059.
Vance, Zebulon Baird. *The Papers of Zebulon Vance*. Edited by Gordon B. McKinney and Richard M. McMurry. Frederick, Md.: University Publications of America, 1987. 38 reels with printed index.

Public Documents and Printed Collections

American State Papers. Edited by Walter Lowrie, et al. 38 vols. Washington, D.C.: Gales and Seaton, 1832-61.
Carrington, Henry Beebee. "The Eastern Band of Cherokees of North Carolina." *Eleventh Census* (1890), 7: 502-8. Washington, D.C.: GPO, 1894.
Cheney, John L., Jr., ed. *North Carolina Government, 1585-1974: A Narrative and Statistical History*. Raleigh: North Carolina Department of the Secretary of State, 1975.
Clarke, Walter P., ed. *The State Records of North Carolina*. 30 vols. Raleigh: E. M. Uzzell and Company, 1914.
Cohen, Felix S., ed. *Handbook of Federal Indian Law*. Washington, D.C.: GPO, 1945.
Confederate States of America. Laws, Statutes, etc. *Public Laws of the Confederate States of America*. Richmond, Va.: R. M. Smith, Printer to Congress, 1862-64.
———. *The Statutes at Large of the Provisional Government of the Confederate States of America*. Richmond, Va.: R. M. Smith, Printer to Congress, 1864.
Davis, Jefferson. *Jefferson Davis, Constitutionalist: His Letters, Papers, and Speeches*. Edited by Dunbar Rowland. 10 vols. New York: J. J. Little & Ives Co. 1923.
———. *The Messages and Papers of Jefferson Davis and the Confederacy, Including Diplomatic Correspondence, 1861-1865*. Edited and compiled by James D. Richardson. 2 vols. New York: Chelsea House-Robert Hector Publishers, 1966.
Gilbert, William Harlen, Jr. "The Eastern Cherokees." *Bureau of American Ethnology Bulletin 133: Anthropological Papers No. 23*. Washington, D.C.: GPO, 1943.
Graham, William Alexander. *The Papers of William Alexander Graham*. Vols. 1-5 ed. James G. de Roulhac Hamilton. Vol. 6 ed. Max R. Williams. Raleigh: State Department of Archives and History, 1957-76.
Kilpatrick, Anna Critts, and Kilpatrick, Jack Frederick, eds. "Chronicles of

Wolftown: Social Documents of the North Carolina Cherokees, 1850–1862." *Bureau of American Ethnology Bulletin 196*. Washington, D.C.: GPO, 1966.

Mangum, Willie Person. *The Papers of Willie Person Mangum*. 5 vols. Edited by Henry Thomas Shanks. Raleigh: State Department of Archives and History, 1950–56.

Mooney, James. "Myths of the Cherokee." *Nineteenth Annual Report of the Bureau of American Ethnology to the Secretary of the Smithsonian Institution, 1897–98*. Part 1. Washington, D.C.: GPO, 1900.

Nitze, Henry B. C., and Wilkens, Henry A. J. "Gold Mining in North Carolina and Adjacent South Appalachian Regions." *North Carolina Geological Survey Bulletin*, no. 10. Raleigh: Guy V. Barnes, 1897.

North Carolina. General Assembly. *Directory of the General Assembly of the State of North Carolina*, sess. of 1860–61. Raleigh: Press of North Carolina Institution for the Deaf and Dumb.

―――. *Executive and Legislative Documents*, sess. of 1860–61. Raleigh: State Printer.

―――. House. *Journal*, sessions of 1860–63, 1881, 1895. Raleigh: State Printers.

―――. Senate. *Journal*, sessions of 1848–62, 1865–66. Raleigh: State Printers.

―――. Laws, Statutes, etc. *Acts Passed by the General Assembly of the State of North Carolina*, sessions of 1831–32, 1835. Raleigh: State Printers.

―――. *Private Laws of North Carolina*, sessions of 1848–61. Raleigh: State Printers.

―――. *Public Laws of North Carolina*, sessions of 1848–61. Raleigh: State Printers.

―――. *Revised Code of North Carolina, Enacted by the General Assembly at the Session of 1854*. Compiled by Bartholomew F. Moore and Asa Biggs. Boston: Little, Brown, and Co., 1855.

Peters, Richard, ed. *The Public Statutes at Large of the United States of America: Treaties between the U.S. and Indian Tribes*. Vol. 7. Boston: Little and Brown, 1846.

Prucha, Francis Paul, ed. *Documents of United States Indian Policy*. Lincoln: University of Nebraska Press, 1975.

Ross, John. *The Papers of Chief John Ross*. 2 vols. Edited by Gary E. Moulton. Norman: University of Oklahoma Press, 1985.

Royce, Charles C. "The Cherokee Nation of Indians: A Narrative of Their Official Relations with the Colonial and Federal Governments." *Bureau of American Ethnology, Fifth Annual Report to the Smithsonian Institution, 1883–84*. Washington, D.C.: GPO, 1887. Pages 121–378.

―――. "Indian Land Cessions in the United States." *Bureau of American Ethnology, Eighteenth Annual Report, Part II, to the Smithsonian Institution, 1896–97*. Washington, D.C.: GPO, 1899. Pages 523–997.

South Carolina. Laws, Statutes, etc. *Acts of the General Assembly of the State of South Carolina*, sessions of 1852, 1854. Columbia: State Printers.

United States Bureau of Indian Affairs. *Report of the Commissioner of Indian Affairs*. 22 vols. Washington, D.C.: GPO, 1872–91.

United States Census. 5th, 1830, N.C., vol. 5 (Gates-Hyde counties). 6th, 1840,

N.C., vol. 5 (Halifax-Jones counties). 7th, 1850, N.C., vol. 14 (Haywood and Henderson counties). 8th, 1860, N.C., vol. 4 (Brunswick and Buncombe counties). 9th, 1870, N.C., vols. 5 (Buncombe and Burke counties) and 22 (Jackson and Johnston counties). 10th, 1880, N.C., vol. 23 (Wake County).

United States Congress.

19 Cong., 1 sess., *House Doc.* 21. *Presidential message with documents on treaty with Cherokee Indians, ratified in 1819.* Serial 133.

20 Cong., 1 sess., *House Doc.* 92. *Memorial of John Culbertson.* Serial 171.

20 Cong., 2 sess., *House Doc.* 95. *Presidential message on Articles of Cession, U.S. and Georgia, and Cherokee treaty.* Serial 186.

22 Cong., 1 sess., *House Doc.* 45. *Memorial of Cherokee Indian delegation.* Serial 217.

24 Cong., 1 sess., *Senate Doc.* 340. *Memorial of Cherokee delegation east of Mississippi river for interposition of Congress to secure justice to them from the United States.* Serial 283.

25 Cong., 2 sess., *Senate Doc.* 120. *On Cherokee treaty of 1835, with accompanying documents.* Serial 315.

25 Cong., 2 sess., *House Doc.* 99. *Remonstrance of delegation of Cherokee Indians against treaty of 1835.* Serial 325.

25 Cong., 2 sess., *House Doc.* 316. *Protest of delegation of Cherokee Indians against treaty of 1835.* Serial 329.

25 Cong., 3 sess., *House Doc.* 224. *Cherokee Indians Residing in North Carolina.* Serial 348.

25 Cong., 3 sess., *Senate Doc.* 1. *Annual Report of Office of Indian Affairs.* Serial 338.

26 Cong., 1 sess., *Senate Doc.* 1. *Annual Report of Office of Indian Affairs.* Serial 354.

28 Cong., 1 sess., *House Doc.* 234. *Memorial of treaty party, on expenditures under Cherokee treaty of 1835-36.* Serial 443.

29 Cong., 1 sess., *Senate Doc.* 298. *Presidential message on internal feuds among Cherokees.* Vol. 5. Serial 474.

29 Cong., 1 sess., *Senate Doc.* 408. *Cherokee Indians residing in North Carolina, praying payment of claims, agreeably to 8th and 12th articles of treaty of 1835.* Vol. 8. Serial 477.

29 Cong., 2 sess., *Senate Report* 157. *Memorial of Representatives of Benjamin T. Hart.* Serial 512.

30 Cong., 1 sess., *House Ex. Doc.* 63. *Claims under Cherokee treaty of 1835-36.* Serial 521.

30 Cong., 1 sess., *House Ex. Doc.* 65. *Presidential message transmitting report on Cherokee Indians.* Vol. 8. Serial 521.

30 Cong., 1 sess., *House Report* 632, pt. 2. *Cherokee Indians in North Carolina.* Serial 526.

30 Cong., 2 sess., *Senate Ex. Doc.* 28. *Claims against Cherokees, under treaty of August 6, 1848.* Serial 531.

32 Cong., 1 sess., *House Misc. Doc.* 64. *Amount of money paid to agent for Cherokee Indians of North Carolina.* Serial 652.

33 Cong., 1 sess., *House Report* 133. *Terms and treaties hereafter to be made with certain tribes of Indians.* Serial 743.
41 Cong., 2 sess., *House Ex. Doc.*1, pt. 3. *Annual Report of the Secretary of the Interior 1869.* Serial 1414.
43 Cong., 2 sess., *House Ex. Doc.* 1, pt. 5. *Annual Report of Commissioner of Indian Affairs, 1874.* Vol. 6. Serial 1639.
43 Cong., 2 sess., *House Ex. Doc.* 169. *Letter from Attorney-General, transmitting facts on agents of eastern band of Cherokee Indians.* Vol. 15. Serial 1648.
46 Cong., 2 sess., *Senate Misc. Doc.* 76. *Proposed amendment to Indian appropriation bill advancing $500,000 to Cherokee Nation.* Serial 1891.
47 Cong., 1 sess., *House Ex. Doc.* 196. *Lands and funds of Eastern Cherokee Indians of North Carolina.* Vol. 23. Serial 2031.
57 Cong., 1 sess., *Senate Doc.* 452. 2 vols. *Treaties, laws, etc., relating to Indian affairs.* Vol. 34. Serial 4253.
United States Laws. *The Statutes at Large of the United States of America, 1789-1873.* 17 vols. Boston: Little, Brown and Co., 1845-73.
Vance, Zebulon Baird. *The Papers of Zebulon Baird Vance.* Edited by Frontis W. Johnston. Vol. 1. *1843-1862.* Raleigh: State Department of Archives and History, 1963.
The War of the Rebellion: A Compilation of the Official Records of the Union and Confederate Armies. 128 vols. Washington, D.C.: GPO, 1880-1901.
Wooley, James E., and Wooley, Vivian, compilers. *Marriage Bonds of Haywood and Jackson Counties, North Carolina.* Easley, S.C.: Southern Historical Press, 1978.

Books and Pamphlets

Allen, William Cicero. *The Annals of Haywood County, North Carolina.* N.p. 1935.
Annual Report of the President and Chief Engineer to the Stockholders of the Blue Ridge Rail Road Company, at the Annual Meeting Held in Charleston, Nov. 6, 1855. Charleston: Walker and Evans, 1855.
Arthur, John Preston. *Western North Carolina: A History from 1730 to 1913.* Raleigh: Edwards and Broughton, 1914.
Barrett, John G. *The Civil War in North Carolina.* Chapel Hill: University of North Carolina Press, 1963.
Battle, Kemp Plummer. *Legislation of the Convention of 1861.* Chapel Hill: University of North Carolina Press, 1900.
Boorstin, Daniel J. *The Americans: The National Experience.* New York: Alfred A. Knopf, 1965.
Boykin, James H. *North Carolina in 1861.* New York: Bookman Associates, 1961.
Brandt, Allan M. *No Magic Bullet: A Social History of Venereal Disease in the United States since 1880.* New York: Oxford University Press, 1985.

Browder, Nathaniel C. *The Cherokee Indians and Those Who Came After: Notes for a History of Cherokee County, North Carolina, 1835-1860.* Hayesville, N.C.: the author, 1973.

Brown, John P. *Old Frontiers: The Story of the Cherokee Indians from Earliest Times to the Date of Their Removal to the West, 1838.* Kingsport, Tenn.: Southern Publishers, 1938.

Cahow, Clark R. *People, Patients, and Politics: The History of the North Carolina Mental Hospitals, 1848-1960.* New York: Arno Press, 1980.

Carlisle, Homer E. *The Removal of the Eastern Cherokees.* Muskogee, Okla.: Hoffman Printing Co., 1983.

Carter, Samuel, III. *Cherokee Sunset, A Nation Betrayed: A Narrative of Travail and Triumph, Persecution and Exile.* Garden City, N.Y.: Doubleday and Co. 1976.

Cashion, Jerry Clyde. *Fort Butler and the Cherokee Indian Removal from North Carolina.* Raleigh: State Department of Archives and History, 1970.

Chamberlain, Hope Summerell. *History of Wake County, North Carolina, with Sketches of Those Who Have Most Influenced Its Development.* Raleigh: Edwards and Broughton, 1922.

Clark, Walter, ed. *Histories of the Several Regiments and Battalions from North Carolina, in the Great War 1861-'65.* 5 vols. Goldsboro, N.C.: Nash Brothers, 1901.

Connelly, Thomas Lawrence. *Army of the Heartland: The Army of Tennessee, 1861-1862.* Baton Rouge: Louisiana State University Press, 1967.

———. *Autumn of Glory: The Army of Tennessee, 1862-1865.* Baton Rouge: Louisiana State University Press, 1971.

Cooper, William J., Jr. *The South and the Politics of Slavery, 1828-1856.* Baton Rouge: Louisiana State University Press, 1978.

Crow, Vernon H. *Storm in the Mountains: Thomas' Confederate Legion of Cherokee Indians and Mountaineers.* Cherokee, N.C.: Press of the Museum of the Cherokee Indian, 1982.

Dain, Norman. *Concepts of Insanity in the United States, 1789-1865.* New Brunswick, N.J.: Rutgers University Press, 1964.

Davidson, Theodore F. *Reminiscences and Traditions of Western North Carolina.* Asheville: Service Printing Co., 1928.

Dippie, Brian W. *The Vanishing American: White Attitudes and U.S. Indian Policy.* Middletown, Conn.: Wesleyan University Press, 1982.

Dix, Dorothea Lynde. *Memorial Soliciting a State Hospital for the Protection and Cure of the Insane.* Raleigh: Seaton Gales, 1848.

Ellis, Daniel. *Thrilling Adventures of Daniel Ellis.* New York: Harper and Brothers, 1867.

Featherstonhaugh, George William. *A Canoe Voyage Up the Minnay Sotor; With an Account of the Lead and Copper Deposits in Wisconsin; of the Gold Region in the Cherokee Country; and Sketches of Popular Manners.* 2 vols. London: R. Bentley, 1847.

Finger, John R. *The Eastern Band of Cherokees, 1819-1900.* Knoxville: University of Tennessee Press, 1984.
Fogelson, Raymond D. *The Cherokees: A Critical Bibliography.* Bloomington: Indiana University Press, 1978.
Foreman, Grant. *Indian Removal: The Emigration of the Five Civilized Tribes.* Norman: University of Oklahoma Press, 1953.
Franks, Kenny A. *Stand Watie and the Agony of the Cherokee Nation.* Memphis: Memphis State University Press, 1979.
Fraser, Walter J.; Saunders, R. Frank, Jr.; and Wakelyn, Jon L., eds. *The Web of Southern Social Relations: Women, Family, and Education.* Athens: University of Georgia Press, 1985.
Frome, Michael. *Strangers in High Places: The Story of the Great Smoky Mountains.* Garden City, N.Y.: Doubleday and Co. 1966.
Grob, Gerald N. *Edward Jarvis and the Medical World of Nineteenth-Century America.* Knoxville: University of Tennessee Press, 1978.
―――. *Mental Illness and American Society, 1875-1940.* Princeton: Princeton University Press, 1983.
―――. *Mental Institutions in America: Social Policy to 1875.* New York: Free Press, 1973.
Gwathmey, John Hastings, comp. *Historical Register of Virginians in the Revolution.* Richmond: Dietz Press, 1938.
Halliburton, R., Jr. *Red over Black: Black Slavery among the Cherokee Indians.* Westport, Conn.: Greenwood Press, 1977.
Hammel, Paul B., and Chiltoskey, Mary U. *Cherokee Plants and Their Uses: A 400-Year History.* Sylva, N.C.: Herald Publishing Co., 1975.
Harmon, George Dewey. *Sixty Years of Indian Affairs: Political, Economic, and Diplomatic, 1789-1850.* Chapel Hill: University of North Carolina Press, 1941.
Hill, Edward E. *The Office of Indian Affairs, 1824-1880: Historical Sketches.* New York: Clearwater Publishing Company, 1974.
Holden, W. W. *Memoirs of W. W. Holden.* Edited by William Kenneth Boyd. Durham, N.C.: Seeman Printery, 1911.
Hoskins, Shirley. *Cherokee Blood.* 3 vols. Chattanooga, Tenn.: the author, 1982.
Hudson, Charles M. *The Southeastern Indians.* Knoxville: University of Tennessee Press, 1976.
Hull, Augustus Longstreet. *Annals of Athens, Georgia, 1801-1901.* Athens: Banner Job Office, 1906.
Hurd, Henry M., ed. *The Institutional Care of the Insane in the United States and Canada.* 4 vols. Baltimore: Johns Hopkins Press, 1916.
Inscoe, John C. *Mountain Masters, Slavery, and the Sectional Crisis in Western North Carolina.* Knoxville: University of Tennessee Press, 1989.
Jones, James H. *Bad Blood: The Tuskegee Syphilis Experiment.* New York: Free Press, 1981.

Kephart, Horace. *The Cherokees of the Smoky Mountains*. 1936. Revised and edited by John R. Finger. Gatlinburg, Tenn.: Great Smoky Mountains Natural History Association, 1983.

———. *Our Southern Highlanders: A Narrative of Adventure in the Southern Appalachians and a Study of Life among the Mountaineers*. 1913. Reprint. Knoxville: University of Tennessee Press, 1976.

King, Duane H., editor. *The Cherokee Indian Nation: A Troubled History*. Knoxville: University of Tennessee Press, 1979.

Kruman, Marc W. *Parties and Politics in North Carolina, 1836-1865*. Baton Rouge: Louisiana State University Press, 1983.

Kvasnicka, Robert M., and Viola, Herman J., eds. *The Commissioners of Indian Affairs, 1824-1977*. Lincoln: University of Nebraska Press, 1979.

Lanman, Charles. *Letters from the Alleghany Mountains*. New York: G. P. Putnam, 1849.

Lefler, Hugh Talmadge, and Newsome, Albert Ray. *North Carolina: The History of a Southern State*. Revised edition. Chapel Hill: University of North Carolina Press, 1963.

Lefler, Hugh Talmadge, ed. *North Carolina History, Told by Contemporaries*. Chapel Hill: University of North Carolina Press, 1948.

McCormick, John Gilchrist. *Personnel of the Convention of 1861*. Chapel Hill: University of North Carolina Press, 1900.

McLoughlin, William G. *The Cherokee Ghost Dance: Essays on the Southeastern Indians, 1789-1861*. Macon, Ga.: Mercer University Press, 1984.

———. *Cherokee Renascence in the New Republic*. Princeton: Princeton University Press, 1986.

———. *Cherokees and Missionaries, 1789-1839*. New Haven: Yale University Press, 1984.

McMurry, Richard M. *Two Great Rebel Armies: An Essay in Confederate Military History*. Chapel Hill: University of North Carolina Press, 1989.

Medford, W. Clark. *Great Smoky Mountain Stories and Sun Over Ol' Starlin*. Waynesville, N.C.: the author, 1966.

———. *Mountain People, Mountain Times*. Waynesville, N.C.: the author, 1963.

Moore, John W. *Roster of North Carolina Troops in the War Between the States*. 4 vols. Raleigh: Ashe, 1882.

Moses, L. G. *Indian Man: A Biography of James Mooney*. Champaign: University of Illinois Press, 1984.

Pegg, Herbert Dale. *The Whig Party in North Carolina, 1835-1860*. Chapel Hill: The Colonial Press, Inc., 1969.

Peithmann, Irvin M. *Red Men of Fire: A History of the Cherokee Indian*. Springfield, Ill.: Charles C. Thomas, Publisher, 1964.

Phillips, Ulrich Bonnell. *A History of Transportation in the Eastern Cotton Belt to 1860*. New York: Columbia University Press, 1908.

Powers, Elizabeth D., with Hannah, Mark E. *Cataloochee, Lost Settlement of the Smokies.* Charleston, S.C.: the authors, 1982.

Ramsey, James G. McGregor. *The Annals of Tennessee.* Charleston, S.C.: Walker and James, 1853.

Redlich, Fredrick C., and Freedman, Daniel X. *The Theory and Practice of Psychiatry.* New York: Basic Books, 1966.

Reid, John Phillip. *A Law of Blood: The Primitive Law of the Cherokee Nation during the Early Years of European Contact.* New York: New York University Press, 1970.

Report of the President and Directors to the Annual Meeting of the Stockholders of the Blue Ridge Rail Road Company, in South Carolina, Held in Charleston, the 22d November, 1856. Charleston: Walker and Evans, 1856.

Report of Walter Gwynn, Chief Engineer of the Blue Ridge Rail Road Company, in South Carolina, to a Meeting of the Stockholders, Held in Charleston, the 22d November 1856. Charleston: Walker and Evans, 1856.

Rights, Douglas LeTell. *The American Indian in North Carolina.* Durham: Duke University Press, 1947.

Rothman, David J. *Conscience and Convenience: The Asylum and Its Alternatives in Progressive America.* Boston: Little, Brown, and Company, 1980.

———. *The Discovery of the Asylum: Social Order and Disorder in the New Republic.* Boston: Little, Brown, and Company, 1971.

Satz, Ronald N. *American Indian Policy in the Jacksonian Era.* Lincoln: University of Nebraska Press, 1975.

Scott, Winfield. *Memoirs of Lieut.-General Scott.* 2 vols. New York: Sheldon and Co., 1864.

Sherrill, William L. *Annals of Lincoln County, North Carolina.* Charlotte, N.C.: Observer Printing House, 1937.

Sitterson, J. Carlyle. *The Secession Movement in North Carolina.* Chapel Hill: University of North Carolina Press, 1939.

Smathers, George Henry. *The History of Land Titles in Western North Carolina.* Asheville: Miller Printing Co., 1938.

Starkey, Marion L. *The Cherokee Nation.* New York: Alfred A. Knopf, 1946.

Starr, Emmet. *History of the Cherokee Indians and Their Legends and Folk Lore.* Oklahoma City: Warden Co., 1921.

Stuart, Paul. *The Indian Office: Growth and Development of an American Institution, 1865-1900.* Ann Arbor: University of Michigan Press, 1978.

Sydnor, Charles S. *The Development of Southern Sectionalism, 1819-1848.* Baton Rouge: Louisiana State University Press, 1948.

Temple, Oliver P. *East Tennessee and the Civil War.* 1899. Reprint. Freeport, N.Y.: Books for Libraries Press, 1971.

Thomas, William Holland. *Argument in Support of the Claims of Cherokee Indians Remaining East of the Mississippi River.* Washington, D.C.: n.p., 1839.

———. *Explanation of the Rights of the North Carolina Cherokee Indians.* Washington, D.C.: n.p., 1851.
———. *A Letter to the Commissioner of Indian Affairs, upon the Claims of the Indians Remaining in the States East.* Washington, D.C.: Buell and Blanchard, 1853.
———. *Resolutions on Federal Affairs.* Raleigh: n.p., 1861.
Thomas, William Holland, and Baxter, S. S. *Argument of Thomas and Baxter in Favor of Paying the Suspended Interest under the Act of July 29, 1848.* Washington, D.C.: n.p., n.d.
Trout, Ed, and Watson, Olin. *A Piece of the Smokies: A Pictorial History of Life in the Smoky Mountains.* Maryville, Tenn.: the authors, n.d.
Tucker, Glenn. *Zeb Vance, Champion of Personal Freedom.* Indianapolis: Bobbs-Merrill Co., 1966.
Van Noppen, Ina W., and Van Noppen, John J. *Western North Carolina since the Civil War.* Boone, N.C.: Appalachian Consortium Press, 1973.
Viola, Herman J. *Diplomats in Buckskins: A History of Indian Delegations in Washington City.* Washington, D.C.: Smithsonian Press, 1981.
Vogel, Virgil J. *American Indian Medicine.* Norman: University of Oklahoma Press, 1970.
Wager, Paul W. *County Government and Administration in North Carolina.* Chapel Hill: University of North Carolina Press, 1928.
Wardell, Morris L. *A Political History of the Cherokee Nation, 1838–1907.* 1938. Reprint. Norman: University of Oklahoma Press, 1977.
Wetmore, Ruth Y. *First in the Land: The North Carolina Indians.* Winston-Salem, N.C.: John F. Blair, 1975.
Wheeler, John H. *Historical Sketches of North Carolina, from 1584 to 1851.* Philadelphia: Lippincott, Grambo, and Co., 1851.
Williams, Max R., ed. *The History of Jackson County.* Sylva, N.C.: Jackson County Historical Association, 1987.
Williams, Walter L., ed. *Southeastern Indians: Since the Removal Era.* Athens: University of Georgia Press, 1979.
Wiltse, Charles M. *John C. Calhoun.* 3 vols. Indianapolis: Bobbs-Merrill Company, 1944–51.
Woodward, Grace Steele. *The Cherokees.* Norman: University of Oklahoma Press, 1963.
Wright, James Leitch, Jr. *The Only Land They Knew: The Tragic Story of the American Indians in the Old South.* New York: Free Press, 1981.
Zeigler, Wilbur Gleason, and Grosscup, Ben S. *The Heart of the Alleghanies; or, Western North Carolina.* Raleigh: A. Williams and Co., 1883.

Articles

Ashby, J. W. "The First North Carolina State Hospital." *Southern Medicine and Surgery* 104 (June 1942): 326–27.

Avery, Mrs. Alphonso Calhoun [Sarah Love Thomas]. "Col. William Holland Thomas." *North Carolina University Magazine* 29, no. 5 (May 1899): 291-95.
Bardolph, Richard. "Inconstant Rebels: Desertion of North Carolina Troops in the Civil War." *North Carolina Historical Review* 41 (April 1964): 163-89.
Bloom, Leonard. "The Acculturation of the Eastern Cherokee: Historical Aspects." *North Carolina Historical Review* 19 (Oct. 1942): 322-57.
Boyd, William K. "North Carolina on the Eve of Secession." *Annual Report of the American Historical Association for the Year* 1910 (Washington, D.C.: American Historical Association), 1912: 165-77.
Bridgers, Ben Oshel. "A Legal Digest of the North Carolina Cherokees." *Journal of Cherokee Studies* 4 (Winter 1979): 21-43.
Bushong, William B. "A. G. Bauer, North Carolina's New South Architect." *North Carolina Historical Review* 60 (July 1983): 304-32.
Conser, Walter H., Jr. "John Ross and the Cherokee Resistance Campaigns, 1833-1838." *Journal of Southern History* 44 (May 1978): 191-212.
Davidson, Allen Turner. "Reminiscences of Western North Carolina." *Lyceum* 1 (June 1890-May 1891).
Davis, Kenneth Penn. "The Cherokee Removal, 1835-1838." *Tennessee Historical Quarterly* 32 (Winter 1973): 311-31.
Davis, Rebecca Harding. "Qualla." *Lippincott's Magazine of Popular Literature and Science* 41 (Nov. 1875): 576-86.
Finger, John R. "The Abortive Second Cherokee Removal, 1841-1844." *Journal of Southern History* 42 (May 1981): 207-26.
———. "The North Carolina Cherokees, 1838-1866: Traditionalism, Progressivism, and the Affirmation of State Citizenship." *Journal of Cherokee Studies* 5 (Spring 1980): 17-29.
———. "The Saga of Tsali: Legend versus Reality." *North Carolina Historical Review* 56 (Winter 1979): 1-18.
Frizzell, George E. "The Politics of Cherokee Citizenship, 1898-1930." *North Carolina Historical Review* 61, no. 2 (April 1984): 205-30.
———. "Remarks of Mr. Thomas, of Jackson." *Journal of Cherokee Studies* 7 (Fall 1982): 64-68.
Grob, Gerald N. "The State Mental Hospital in Mid-Nineteenth Century America: A Social Analysis." *American Psychologist* 21 (June 1966): 510-23.
Harmon, George Dewey. "The Indian Trust Funds, 1797-1865." *Mississippi Valley Historical Review* 21 (June 1934): 23-30.
———. "The North Carolina Cherokees and the New Echota Treaty of 1835." *North Carolina Historical Review* 6 (July 1929): 237-53.
Hollander, Russell. "Life at the Washington Asylum for the Insane, 1871-1880." *Historian* 44 (Feb. 1982): 229-41.
Inscoe, John C. "Mountain Masters: Slaveholding in Western North Carolina." *North Carolina Historical Review* 61 (April 1984): 143-73.

Kilpatrick, Jack Frederick. "Two Notices by Will Thomas." *Southern Indian Studies* 14 (Oct. 1962): 27-28.
King, Duane H. "James Mooney, Ethnologist." *Journal of Cherokee Studies* 7 (Spring 1982): 4-9.
King, Duane H., and Evans, E. Raymond. "Tsali: The Man Behind the Legend." *Journal of Cherokee Studies* 4 (Fall 1979): 194-201.
King, I. F. "The Coming and Going of Ohio Droving." *Ohio Archaeological and Historical Quarterly* 17 (July 1908): 247-53.
Kutsche, Paul. "The Tsali Legend: Culture Heroes and Historigraphy." *Ethnohistory* 10 (Fall 1963): 329-57.
Lawson, John. "Wil-Usdi: The White Man Who Was Made a Cherokee Chief." *Tar Heel* 8 (Dec. 1980): 27-30.
Litton, Gaston. "Enrollment Records of the Eastern Band of Cherokee Indians." *North Carolina Historical Review* 17 (July 1940): 199-231.
McLoughlin, William G. "Cherokee Nationalism and the Right of Internal Taxation." *Prologue: Journal of the National Archives* 14 (Summer 1982): 69-80.
McLoughlin, William G., and Conser, Walter H., Jr. "The Cherokees in Transition: A Statistical Analysis of the Federal Cherokee Census of 1835." *Journal of American History* 64 (Dec. 1977): 678-703.
"Moral Treatment in America's Lunatic Asylums." *Hospital and Community Psychiatry* 27 (July 1976): 468-70.
Newsome, Albert Ray, ed. "The A. S. Merrimon Journal, 1853-1854." *North Carolina Historical Review* 8 (July 1931): 300-330.
Robertson, H. G. "The Eastern Band of Cherokee Indians, from 1835 to 1893." *North Carolina University Magazine* 31 (1901): 173-80.
Russell, Mattie U. "Devil in the Smokies: The White Man's Nature and the Indian's Fate." *South Atlantic Quarterly* 73 (Winter 1974): 53-69.
Smith, Mary Shannon. "Union Sentiment in North Carolina during the Civil War." *Proceedings of the Sixteenth Annual Session of the State Literary and Historical Association of North Carolina* (Raleigh: Edwards and Broughton), 1916.
Stevenson, K. W. "A Brief History of Mental Health Care in North Carolina." *North Carolina Medical Journal* 26 (Nov. 1965): 509-15.
Stringfield, William Williams. "North Carolina Cherokee Indians." *North Carolina Booklet* 3, no. 2 (June 1903): 5-24.
Van Noppen, Ina W. "The Significance of Stoneman's Last Raid." *North Carolina Historical Review* 38 (Jan., April, July, Oct. 1961): 19-44, 149-72, 341-61, 500-526.
Walker, Felix. "Memoirs of a Southern Congressman." *Journal of American History* 1 (Jan.-March 1907): 49-60.
Wetmore, Ruth Y. "The Green Corn Ceremony of the Eastern Cherokees." *Journal of Cherokee Studies* 8 (Spring 1983): 46-56.
Young, Mary. "Cherokee Nation: Mirror of the Republic." *American Quarterly* 33 (Winter 1981): 502-24.

Newspapers

Asheville News, 1855-63
Charleston [S.C.] *Mercury*, 1861
Daily Appeal (Memphis), 1861
Daily Confederate (Raleigh), 1864
Daily Intelligencer (Atlanta), 1862
Daily Register (Knoxville), 1862
Greensboro Times, 1861
Henderson Times, 1861
Highland Messenger (Asheville), 1842-48
North Carolina Standard (Raleigh), 1848-61
Peoples Press (Winston Salem), 1861
Pickens [S.C.] *Courier*, 1853
Raleigh Register, 1861
Southern Confederacy (Atlanta), 1862
State Journal (Raleigh), 1860-61

Unpublished Materials

Ambrose, Robert P. "A 'Critical Year' (April 1860-April 1861): A Study of Unionist Sentiment in Western North Carolina during the Culminating Year of the Secession Movement." M.A. thesis, University of North Carolina at Greensboro, 1975.

Bryan, Charles Faulkner, Jr. "The Civil War in East Tennessee: A Social, Political and Economic Study." Ph.D. diss., University of Tennessee, 1978.

Colby, William Munn. "Routes to Rainey Mountain: A Biography of James Mooney, Ethnologist." Ph.D. diss., University of Wisconsin, 1978.

Frizzell, George E. "The Legal Status of the Eastern Band of Cherokee Indians." M.A. thesis, Western Carolina University, 1981.

Holland, Cullen Joe. "The Cherokee Indian Newspapers, 1828-1906: The Tribal Voice of a People in Transition." Ph.D. diss., University of Minnesota, 1956.

Russell, Mattie. "William Holland Thomas, White Chief of the North Carolina Cherokees." Ph.D. diss., Duke University, 1956.

Index

Abingdon, Va., 116
Acquone, N.C., 32
Alabama, 24, 36, 44
Alarka, N.C., 32
Allegheny Mountains, 1
American Revolution, 2, 8, 9, 13, 91
Anderson, S.C., 74
Andrews, N.C., 28
Antietam Creek, 107, 109
Appomattox Courthouse, Va., 127
Armstead, Walker K., 21
Asheville, N.C., 12, 49, 54, 71, 75, 83, 96, 98, 118, 119, 127, 133, 136, 138, 141, 147
Astoogatogeh, 101, 105, 107
asylum, 181n56. *See* North Carolina Hospital for the Insane, Western Insane Asylum, *and* William Holland Thomas, health
Athens, Ga., 31, 50, 83
Athens, Tenn., 38
Atlanta, Ga., 97, 102
Augusta, Ga., 29, 31, 42, 50, 52
Axley, Felix, 45, 57

ballplay, 62–64, 68, 103. *See also* Cherokee culture
Balsam Mountains, 7, 8
Baltimore, Md., 31, 83

Bangs, Anson and Eli T., 74, 75
Baptist Gap, 105, 107
Barringer, Rufus, 138
Bartlett, William C., 127, 128
Baxter, Thomas, 50
Beauregard, P. G. T., 93
Benton, Thomas Hart, 75
Big Buck, 18
Big Cove, 22
Big George, 39
Bird Town, N.C., 22
Blackstone, William, 31
Blue Ridge Mountains, 27, 32, 75, 96, 111, 123
Blue Ridge Railroad, 74, 75, 84, 87
Board of Cherokee Commissioners, 41, 43, 45, 47, 56, 135
Booth, Junius Bruus, 54
Boston Guide to Health, 52
Boudinot, Elias, 23, 42, 44
Bragg, Braxton, 103, 116
Bragg, Thomas, 59, 83
Branner, Jo, 83
Bristol, Tenn., 111
Brittain, M. L., 76
Broughton Hospital, 147. *See also* Western Insane Asylum
Bryson, Goldman, 116, 117
Buckner, Simon, 114, 115

Buffalo Town, 26, 46, 56, 58, 59
Buncombe County, N.C., 8, 54, 88
Burnside, Ambrose E., 115-16
bushwackers, 107, 118, 123. *See also* deserters *and* Unionists
Bushyhead, George, 131, 135, 136
Byrd II, William, 9

Calhoun, John C., 31, 32, 67, 72, 73
Calhoun, Tenn., 28, 38, 48
California, 72, 76
Calvert family, 2, 3, 11
Campbell, James A., 124
Campbell, William, 2
Candler, George W., 97-98
Cass, Lewis, 21, 71
Cathcart, William, 47
characteristics of mountain people, 3
Charleston, S.C., 29, 31, 42, 48, 49, 50, 67, 74, 80, 87
Charleston, Tenn., 127
Charlotte, N.C., 83, 138
Chattanooga, Tenn., 102, 103, 110, 116, 127
Cheoah, 26, 28, 32, 46, 65, 135
Cherokee, N.C., 150, 154n32
Cherokee Cession, 8, 67
Cherokee Company, 65
Cherokee County, N.C., 6, 28, 32, 45, 49, 67, 76, 93, 95, 96, 104, 111, 116, 117, 118, 120, 135
Cherokee Indians: adopt Thomas family, 140; in Civil War, 94, 96-109, 116, 117-19, 120, 126, 127, 128, 149 (*see also* William Holland Thomas in Civil War); claims, 46, 57-60, 63, 82, 85; culture, 22, 47, 63-67, 145, 149 (*see also* ballplay *and* Green Corn Ceremony); legal status, 26, 28, 36, 59, 65, 85-86, 96, 97, 131-32, 133, 135, 140, 149; mythology, 5, 7; in North Carolina, 1, 3, 5, 8-11, 13, 18, 23-27, 32-33, 36-47, 56-67, 82, 85, 129, 131, 136-39, 149; removal, 1, 20, 23, 26, 28, 32, 33, 36-45, 48, 60, 136; scalping, 105, 107; treaties of, 5, 11, 26, 57, 63, 93, 97, 100 (*see also* Treaty of New Echota); in west, 41-42, 44, 47, 56, 67
Cherokee Nation, 5, 8, 18, 19, 21, 22, 23, 25, 26, 28, 32, 33, 34, 36, 37, 43, 57, 100, 140
Cincinnati, Ohio, 87
Civil War, 1, 18, 22, 47, 48, 49, 53, 59, 71, 87, 93, 99-105, 110-28, 145. *See also* Cherokee Indians in Civil War *and* William Holland Thomas in Civil War
Clark, Henry T., 97, 98, 100, 102, 103
Clay, Henry, 67, 72
Clay County, Ga., 111
Clay County, N.C., 135
Cleveland, Tenn., 117
Clingman, Thomas L., 79, 92
Coleman, David, 75
Collins, D. K., 108
Columbia, S.C., 74, 99
Colvard, Andrew, 51, 101
Colvard, Mark, 51
Colvard family. *See* Calvert family
Coman, James, 79
Compromise of 1850, 72, 73
Confederacy (Congress), 88, 91, 92, 94, 95, 96, 97, 98, 99, 100, 101, 110-11, 113-15, 118-19, 122, 123-25, 126
Conley, James, 108
Conley, R. T., 108
Conner, H. W., 74
Cooper, James W., 108

Cooper, Samuel, 122
Coosawhatchie, S.C., 29
Corinth, Miss., 103
Crawford, T. Hartley, 40, 41, 42, 43, 44, 45, 46
Cudjo, 49, 53, 162n42
Cumberland Mountains (Gap), 96, 102, 103, 105, 107, 111
Cunningham, Moses, 33-34

Davidson, Allen T., 98, 99, 104
Davidson, Francis M., 120
Davis, Jefferson, 96, 97, 100, 101-2, 110, 111, 113, 119, 120, 124, 125
Davis, William G. M., 111
Deep Creek, 120, 150
deserters, 111, 114-15, 116, 117, 121, 122, 123, 124, 125, 176n42. *See also* bushwackers *and* Unionists
Dick, Robert P., 136, 138
Dickagiskah, 76
Dillard, John Henry, 138
Dillard, Mary Ann, 79
Dillsboro, N.C., 17
Dix, Dorothea Lynde, 72, 132, 145
Dix Hill, 132, 146, 147. *See also* North Carolina Hospital for the Insane
Donelson, Daniel S., 113
Dony, Francis N., 138
Douglas, Stephen A., 130
Ducktown, Tenn., 86, 87, 116, 117
Dudley, Edward B., 27, 28, 32, 33, 34, 36-37, 55

Early, Jubal A., 123
Eastern Band. *See* Cherokee Indians in North Carolina
Eastern Band of Cherokee Indians vs. William H. Thomas, et al., 136-39
Eaton, John H., 46

Edwards, Weldon N., 94
Ellis, John W., 88, 92, 93, 94-95, 97
Emancipation Proclamation, 107
England, 1, 2, 50, 95
Enloe, Abraham, 13
Enloe, Scroop, 13
Enloe, Wesley, 13
Euchella, 5, 37, 39
Euchella vs. Welsh, 5, 27-28, 37
Eyetoogah, 18

Fain, Mercer, 76, 114, 117
Fifteenth Pennsylvania Cavalry, 117
First Wisconsin Cavalry, 120
Fisher, Allen, 30, 49
Flying Squirrel, 39, 40, 133
Forsyth, Ga., 45
Fort Butler, 28, 30, 33, 34, 36
Fort Cass, 28, 38, 48
Fort Delaney, 28
Fort Montgomery, 28
Fort Sumter, 93, 94
Foster, William S., 38, 39
Fourteenth Illinois Cavalry, 120
Francis, Michael, 32, 71
Franklin, N.C., 45, 87, 101
French Broad River, 8, 75, 87

Garfield, James, 146
Gatlinburg, Tenn., 117, 119
Georgia, 2, 18, 21, 23, 24, 27, 29, 36, 47, 51, 67, 73, 74, 76, 92, 103, 121, 123
Gettysburg, Pa., 115
Gibbon, Edward, 31
ginseng, 9, 18, 19, 29, 48, 49
gold, 18-19, 21
Gourdin, Henry, 74, 80
Graham, James, 45
Graham, William A., 65
Grant, Ulysses S., 115, 116, 127, 128

Great Smoky Mountain National Park, 150
Great Smoky Mountains, 3, 13, 37, 38, 99, 100, 102, 111, 115, 117, 118, 123
Green, Benjamin, 46, 54, 55, 57, 58
Green, Duff, 46, 55, 57, 58
Gren Corn Ceremony, 47, 64. *See also* Cherokee Indians, culture
Greensboro, N.C., 138
Greenville, S.C., 74
Greybeard, Peter, 101

Hanging Dog Creek, 101
Harris, C. A., 42
Hayes, George W., 30, 76, 96, 98
Haywood County, N.C., 8, 9, 24, 25, 28, 32, 34, 40, 67, 69, 71, 77, 80, 92, 95, 109, 111, 129
Haywood Rangers, 95
Helper, Hinton Rowan, 90-91
Henry, James L., 119
Heth, Henry, 110, 111
Hicks, William, 122, 123
Hilliard, W. L., 83, 121, 132, 141, 144, 146, 147, 149
Hillsboro, N.C., 138
Hindman, Thomas C., 44-45
Hinds County, Miss., 12
Hitchcock, Charles M., 76
Hiwassee River, 33
Hoke, John, 30
Holden, William W., 94, 129
Holston River, 102, 103
Hubley, Edward B., 46
Hunter, Archibald R. S., 34
Hunter, Kermit, 150
Hyatt, Ute, 32
Hyde, William P., 53

Indian Appropriations Act of 1848, 57, 58, 63

Indian Gap, 118, 130
Indian Office, 42, 43, 44, 45, 57, 58
Indiantown, 12. *See also* Quallatown

Jackson, Alfred E., 113, 114, 116, 118, 121, 122
Jackson, Andrew, 21, 23
Jackson County, N.C., 47, 67, 76, 80, 86, 88, 91, 92, 94, 95, 100, 111, 114, 125, 129, 132, 133, 135, 146, 154n32
Jamesville, N.C., 28
Jarrett, G. T., 96
Jarrett, Nimrod S., 18, 49
Jefferson, Thomas, 71
Johnson, Andrew, 129
Johnston, Joseph E., 119
Johnston, Robert, 131, 133, 135, 136
Johnston, Thomas D., 133, 135, 136, 139, 147
Johnston, William, 86, 131, 133, 135, 137
Jonathan's Creek, 2, 9
Jones, Evan, 11, 22, 36
Jones, William E., 123
Junaluska, Chief, 19, 86, 101, 105
Junaluska Zouaves, 94, 97

Kansas-Nebraska Act, 75
Keener, Joseph, 30, 113-14
Kentucky, 76, 96, 110
Killion, M., 36
King, H. P., 29, 30, 49
King, Johnson W., 30, 48, 49, 54, 77, 133
Kirby, Isaac M., 127
Kirk, George, 127
Knoxville, Tenn., 74, 101, 102, 103, 104, 114, 115, 116, 120
Knoxville and Charleston Railroad, 74
Knoxville and Chattanooga Railroad, 127

Lanman, Charles, 27, 156n32
Larned, C. H., 38
Lea, Albert M., 44
Lee, Robert E., 115, 125, 128
Lincoln, Abraham, 88, 90, 91, 92, 93, 94, 95, 102, 107, 114, 129
Lincolnton, N.C., 30
Lindsay, William, 34, 36
Little Tennessee River, 5, 38, 73
Little Will. *See* William Holland Thomas
Long Blanket, 21
Longstreet, James, 117, 118-19
Loudon, Tenn., 127
Louisiana, 49
Louisville, Ky., 87
Love, James R. I, 17, 76, 78, 80, 82
Love, James R. II, 93, 95, 108, 109, 115, 117, 120, 121, 123, 124, 127, 132
Love, John, 95
Love, Maria Williamson Coman, 78
Love, Matthew H., 95, 101, 141, 142
Love, Robert, 8, 79
Lover, Robert II, 95, 132, 142, 144
Love, Samuel L., 129, 132, 144
Love, Thomas, 8

McCalla, R. C., 101
McCowan, John P., 105, 107
Macon County, N.C., 24, 25, 32, 58, 67, 69, 72, 74, 76, 93, 95, 135
Madison County, N.C., 111, 116
Malvern Hill, Va., 142
Manly, Charles, 71
Manning, John L., 74
Martin, James G., 125, 127
Maryland, 2, 123
Mason, George T., 76
Mason, John Y., 56
Massachusetts, 72
Mexican War, 57, 69, 72, 125

Mingus, Abraham, 130
Mingus, John, 131
Mississippi, 12
Mississippi River, 23, 26, 27, 43, 87, 115
Montgomery, Ala., 91
Mooney, James, 4, 6, 20, 62, 66, 68, 147, 149
Morgan, George Washington, 100, 101
Morganton, N.C., 75, 147, 148
Mount, Mrs., 55
Mount, Samuel R., 48, 55
Mount Prospect, N.C., 2, 3, 8. *See also* Waynesville, N.C.
Mullay, John C. (roll), 57, 59, 100
Murphy, N.C., 28, 30, 33, 44, 48, 77, 98, 116, 117, 133
Murphy, Patrick Livingston, 147, 149

Nanlahaly, Dick, 18
Nantahala, N.C., 32
Nantayalee Jake, 39
Nelson, David, 2
New Echota, Ga., 18, 19, 23, 24, 33, 34
New Orleans, La., 49
New York, 24, 31
North Carolina: Cherokee Battalion, 103, 104; General Assembly, 8, 9, 28, 30, 75, 87, 94, 99, 131; Hospital for the Insane, 72, 132, 134, 142, 144, 145-47 (*see also* Dix Hill); politics, 44, 45, 51, 67, 69, 71, 72, 73, 75, 87-88, 90-92; secession, 73, 88, 91-95, 98, 99; mentioned, 1, 2, 5, 9, 12, 18, 22, 23, 26, 27, 33, 36, 39, 43, 47, 48, 53, 54, 123, 131, *and* passim
Nottely, N.C., 28
Nunnehi, 7

Oconaluftee Indians. *See* Cherokee Indians
Oconaluftee River, 4, 5, 12, 18, 100, 150
Ogonstoka, 102
Oklahoma, 37
Oram, Francis F., 86

Pacific Railroad, 76
Palmer, John B., 119, 120, 121, 125
Palmer, William J., 117–18, 119
Patton, Andrew, 53
Paulding County, Ga., 51
Payne, N. N., 33, 34
Pemberton, John, 115
Philadelphia, 31, 86
Pierce, Franklin, 71
Poinsett, Joel, 40, 41
Polk, James K., 46, 47, 48, 56, 69
Pretty Woman Town, N.C., 22

Qualla Boundary, 41, 47, 67, 139
Qualla Indians. *See* Cherokee Indians in N.C.
Quallatown, N.C., 8, 12, 13, 16, 17, 18, 26, 27, 28, 30, 31, 32, 37, 39, 40, 45, 46, 47, 49, 56, 58, 59, 60, 65, 79, 93, 97, 99, 100, 101, 118, 119, 120, 122, 127, 130, 131, 133, 138, 142. *See also* Indiantown

Racoon Creek, 2, 8
railroads, 31, 32, 49, 50, 67, 69, 73–76, 80, 86. *See also* Blue Ridge Railroad, Knoxville and Charleston Railroad, Knoxville and Chattanooga Railroad, Pacific Railroad, South Carolina Railroad, Tennessee River Railroad Co., Tennessee and Virginia Railroad, *and* Western North Carolina Railroad

Raleigh, N.C., 67, 71, 76, 82, 83, 84, 88, 90, 91, 98, 132, 134, 147
Ramsay, J. G., 91
Reid, David S., 69, 71
Richard III, 54
Richmond, Va., 97, 100, 121, 123, 124
Ridge, John, 23, 41, 44
Ridge, Major, 23, 25, 26, 41, 44
Roanoke Island, 99
Robbinsville, N.C., 28
Robinson, James, 45
Rogers, Johnson K., 57, 58, 59
Rogers, William, 45
Rogersville, Tenn., 105
Rose, Robert, 49, 133
Ross, John, 23, 41, 44, 47
Ruffin, Thomas, Jr., 138
Rutherford County, N.C., 9

Salisbury, N.C., 75, 127
San Diego, Calif., 76
Savannah, Ga., 31, 87
Schermerhorn, John F., 24, 32, 49
Scott, S. S., 113
Scott, Winfield, 36, 37, 38
Scott's Creek, 17, 28, 30, 48, 49, 76
secession. *See* North Carolina, secession
Second North Carolina Mounted Regiment, 127
Seddon, James A., 124, 125
Seven Pines, 108
Sevier County, Tenn., 100, 131
Sevierville, Tenn., 12, 49, 116, 117, 119
Seward, William H., 91
Shakespeare, William, 54
Sharpsburg, Md., 107
Shepherd, William B., 73
Sheridan, Philip, 123
Sherrill, Angelina, 53, 140
Sherrill, Samuel, 51
Shiloh, Tenn., 101, 103

Shultz's Mill, 119
Siler, David W., 58
Sixteenth N.C. Regiment, 109
Sixth N.C. Infantry Regiment, 95, 97
Sixty-ninth N.C. Regiment, 107-9, 121-22, 124
slaves (slavery), 18, 49, 51, 72-73, 75, 77, 82, 84, 86, 90, 91, 107, 122, 130
Smith, Andrew Jackson, 38
Smith, Edmund Kirby, 100, 101, 103, 105, 113
Smithsonian Institution, 4, 6, 20, 62, 66, 68, 147
Soco Creek, 1, 3, 5, 9, 12, 32, 37, 40, 127, 150
South Carolina, 18, 29, 31, 51, 67, 74, 75, 88, 90, 98, 121, 123
South Carolina Railroad, 74
Standing Wolf, 18
Stanly, Edward, 92
Starrett, Preston, 57
Stekoa, N.C., 32
Stekoa Fields, 13, 14, 48, 51, 52, 53, 76, 80, 82, 86, 104, 117, 118, 129, 132, 139, 140, 144, 146, 149, 154n32
Stokes, Montford, 21
Stoneman, George, 127
Strawberry Plains, Tenn., 102, 103, 110, 111, 112, 114, 115, 140
Stringfield, Maria Love, 104, 140, 141, 142, 144, 146, 177n11
Stringfield, William W., 103-4, 105, 107, 108, 109, 119, 120, 123, 124, 127, 128, 140, 141, 145, 146, 149
Strother, George, 2, 9
Strother, John, 2
Swain County, N.C., 154n32
syphilis, 145, 181n55. *See also* William Holland Thomas, health

Taylor, Campbell H., 116
Taylor, F. M., 98

Taylor, James, 59, 60, 63, 131, 133
Taylor, Zachary, 2, 67, 71
temperance (society), 19, 20, 40, 48, 64
Tennessee, 8, 9, 24, 32, 36, 39, 47, 49, 73, 74, 75, 76, 87, 92, 94, 96, 101, 105, 109, 110, 113, 116, 117, 121, 122, *and* passim
Tennessee River, 76, 103
Tennessee River Railroad, 73, 74
Tennessee and Virginia Railroad, 102
Terrell, James W., 20, 59-60, 61, 63, 76, 86, 90, 97, 101, 105, 107, 108, 109, 113, 120, 121, 130-35, 137-39, 142, 144, 146, 147
Terrell, William S., 101, 105
Texas, 72
Third Tennessee Regiment, 102
Thomas, James Robert (son), 84, 89, 140, 144, 147, 169n17
Thomas, Jr., William Holland (son), 83, 84, 88-89, 141, 142, 147, 169n17
Thomas, Richard (father), 1, 2
Thomas, Sallie Love (daughter), 84, 140, 143, 146-47, 169n17
Thomas, Sarah Love (wife), 78-85, 88-89, 93, 95, 99, 104, 109, 114, 129, 130, 131, 132, 133, 135, 140-42, 144, 149
Thomas, Temperance (mother), 1, 2, 3, 8, 9, 11, 12, 13, 28, 31, 48, 49, 51, 52, 53, 80, 82, 108, 144, 149
Thomas, William Holland: agent for Indians, 21-22, 24-26, 28, 32-35, 36, 40, 149; busines activities, 27-35, 42, 47-52, 76, 86, 130, 133; as chief, 40-47, 57-58, 65, 67, 79, 120, 129, 132, 137, 147, 149; childhood and youth, 1-3, 7-9, 11, 12-13; children, 83, 84,

Thomas, William Holland (*continued*)
88–89, 104, 109, 129, 131, 132; in Civil War, 99–109, 110–28, 142 (*see also* Thomas's legion); court-martial, 115, 119, 121–22, 123–24; debts, 17, 29, 77, 82, 85, 86, 114, 129, 139, 146; health, 52, 77, 121, 129, 132, 136, 138, 140–42, 144–47, 149; lands of, 18, 47, 67, 69, 76, 135; loyalty oath, 129; marriage, 53, 54, 78–80; as orphan, 53, 56, 71, 79, 85, 91, 132; in politics, 51, 58, 67, 69, 71–77, 86–88, 90–95, 98–100; religion of, 9, 31, 43, 50, 52–53, 65, 77, 85, 141; and slaves, 49, 51, 77, 84, 86, 130 (*see also* slaves, slavery); sued, 135–39; and women, 29, 54–55, 77

Thomas's legion, 104, 107–9, 110, 111, 113–28. *See also* Civil War *and* William Holland Thomas in Civil War

Timson, John, 44, 45

Trail of Tears, 1. *See also* Cherokee Indians, removal

Treaty of New Echota, 23, 24, 26, 32, 33, 36, 40, 42, 43, 56

Tsali, 37–40, 55, 149

Tuckasegee and Keowee Turnpike Co., 86

Tuckasegee River, 5, 13, 14, 18, 38, 120, 154n32

Turner, Banister, 80

turnpikes, 31, 49, 77, 86, 100, 118, 130, 144

Tyler, John, 45

Uktena, 7

Unionists, 111, 117, 118, 123. *See also* bushwackers *and* deserters

United States Congress, 9, 23, 42

Unto These Hills, 150

Valleytown, N.C., 11, 24, 28, 32, 101, 104

Van Buren, Martin, 40, 47

Vance, Robert, 88, 116, 117–19

Vance, Zebulon B., 75, 87, 88, 110, 111, 114, 118, 119–20, 121, 122, 125, 144–45

Vaughn, John C., 102, 117

Vicksburg, Miss., 115

Virginia, 2, 7, 8, 71, 83, 92, 93, 94, 97, 101, 102, 103, 105, 109, 117, 123

Virginia Railroad, 110

Walker, Columbus, 118

Walker, Felix, 9, 153n16

Walker, Felix Hampton, 9, 10, 12

Walker, William C., 104, 114, 116, 117, 118

Washington, George, 71, 91

Washington, D.C., 21, 22, 24, 25, 26, 31, 40, 41, 44, 45, 46, 48, 49, 52, 54, 55, 72, 74, 76, 77, 82, 96, 123, 132, 135

Watie, Stand, 23

Wayne, Anthony, 8

Waynesville, N.C., 2, 8, 12, 76, 78, 83, 87, 127, 128, 130, 131, 138, 145, 149. *See also* Mount Prospect, N.C.

Webster, Daniel, 72

Webster, N.C., 49, 101, 118, 122

Welch, Jonathan, 98

Welch, William T., 17, 108

Wells, Bartlett, 130

West Point, 125

Western Insane Asylum, 147–48

Western North Carolina Railroad, 73, 75, 87, 110

Whitaker, David L., 101

White Sulphur Springs, N.C., 78, 83, 136

Whittier, N.C., 13

Wilkins, William, 55
Willnotah, 19, 20, 21
Wil-Usdi. *See* William Holland Thomas
Wolf Town, N.C., 22, 62
Woodfin, Nicholas, 133
Wool, John Ellis, 33, 34, 37, 40, 42

Yellow Hill, N.C., 22
Yonaguska, 1, 5, 7, 10-11, 12, 13, 16, 18, 19, 21, 22, 24, 27, 37, 39, 40, 49, 53, 55, 64, 137, 149, 150, 153n24, 156n32
Yonaguska vs. Coleman, 5

www.ingramcontent.com/pod-product-compliance
Lightning Source LLC
Chambersburg PA
CBHW030317080526
44584CB00012B/601